THE SIMPLE LIFE

D0173043

THE SIMPLE LIFE

edited by

LARRY ROTH

BERKLEY BOOKS, NEW YORK

This book is an original publication of The Berkley Publishing Group.

THE SIMPLE LIFE

A Berkley Book / published by arrangement with the editor

PRINTING HISTORY
Berkley trade paperback edition / April 1998

The Penguin Putnam Inc. World Wide Web site address is
http://www.penguinputnam.com

ISBN: 0-425-16168-4

BERKLEY®
Berkley Books are published by The Berkley Publishing Group,
a member of Penguin Putnam Inc.,
200 Madison Avenue, New York, New York 10016.
BERKLEY and the "B" design are trademarks
belonging to Berkley Publishing Corporation.

PRINTED IN THE UNITED STATES OF AMERICA
10 9 8 7 6 5 4 3 2 1

CONTENTS

INTRODUCTION

For me, one of the really enjoyable aspects of being part of the New Frugality movement has been meeting, either in person or through their work, others in the movement. Our backgrounds are diverse. Some of us grew up in abject poverty, in at least a couple of cases without indoor plumbing. Others come from America's middle and even upper middle classes. Some of us remain, by society's standards, poor; others are financially well off. But, whatever routes we took, all of us have come to the conclusion that there must be more to life than trading our life energy for things we can live without. And many of us have made the conscious decision to remain frugal no matter how many things we can now "afford."

You may be asking yourself, "Does America really need yet another book on frugality?" In a word, yes. Americans do not understand frugality. A few years ago I appeared on a television talk show, and, while it was clear the audience was interested in learning how to save money, the host and a part-time psychologist and media groupie who appeared on the show with me were clearly interested in caricaturing those of us who are less than profligate with our money. The mainstream media's view of frugality was recently stated bluntly, succinctly, and probably accidentally by ABC TV correspondent John Stossel, who gave as his reason for moving away from consumer reporting, "I got sick of it. I also now make so much money I just lost interest in saving a buck on a can of peas." Mr. Stossel and his media ilk make so much money that the financial status of the "little people" who watch them on television and read their views in print is irrelevant to them, just as it was for Marie Antoinette. Let those who are struggling to buy bread eat cake. In the view we see presented by the media, if one is not spending all of his or her money, there is something psychologically "wrong" with that person. This view is so prevalent in our time that to be frugal is to run the risk of being labeled deviant or even unpatriotic. The psychologist/groupie I encountered during my talk show experience was there to speculate about the possible reasons for my unnatural frugal condition. In fact, there seems to be a cadre of simpletons who, evidently believing overspending has somehow become altruistic, try to guilt-trip the fiscally responsible by saying, "If everyone saved money like you do, the economy would be in trouble." Don't look now, folks, but the economy *is* in trouble. Downsizing, rightsizing, and dumbsizing are costing millions of Americans their jobs. And no matter how well you have supported your local department stores, I doubt that they will reciprocate when you need help. Spending is not a patriotic duty. In fact, Benjamin Franklin, one of our founding fathers, advised, "A penny saved is a penny earned." And overspending is not altruistic. Actually, it seems to me that just the opposite is true. Improving your financial health is likely to keep you from becoming a burden both to society and to your family. And what could be more patriotic or altruistic than being self-sufficient and self-reliant?

So why this book? This book presents to you, in one volume, the views and rationales of a variety of frugal people, from Amy Dacyczyn, perhaps the most well known, to some whose names you may never have heard before. You will discover that the various frugality writers have a wide range of reasons for deciding to live as they do.

In reading through these contributions, you will note that in many cases the writers encountered a crisis or decided on a goal that was seemingly beyond their financial reach. Frugality was seen as a solution—as a *means* to overcome their crises or reach their goals. It is important that you understand these contributors did not wake up one morning and say to themselves, "Gee! I think I'm going to spend the rest of my life seeing just how cheap I can be." Frugality, in other words, is not an end for us. It is a means to an end.

In some cases the authors initially decided to work a second job, have their spouses find employment, or somehow bring more income into their lives. In most cases this just doesn't work. Every job brings with it expenses (clothing and transportation, for starters). Nearly every dollar earned from a job is automatically reduced first to a little more than ninety-two cents by Social Security and Medicare taxes. Then it's reduced further by federal, state, and in some cases local income taxes. These days you can easily earn a dollar and wind up taking home fifty cents (this is especially true when a spouse goes to work). But if you find a way to cut a dollar out of your budget, you keep everything. In short, a dollar earned from a job is fifty cents in your pocket. A dollar in reduced expenses equals two dollars earned at a job.

Some contributors came to their lifestyle as a result of environmental concerns. Others, after having visited or lived in Third World countries, found overconsumption morally repugnant. Others yearned to be free of corporate jobs, so they saved their money and learned to live on less. Others simply like to "beat the system" by having a middle-class lifestyle at a fraction of the retail price, so to speak, which brings me to my next point. In this book you will learn frugality has no fixed definition. What one person believes is frugal others will find not so frugal. Some in the movement, for example, believe eating in restaurants is profligate. Others believe it is valid entertainment, but they will tell you how to save money while dining out. Some might wonder whether having pets may be both less expensive and less stressful than having children. Still others may opt for having neither. All of these viewpoints are valid. And, if you think about it, frugality itself is a moving target. It is a function of the era in which we live as well as a function of our income. If we go back one hundred years, we'll find no discussion of whether cable TV is necessary or merely desirable. We'll also find no discussion of frugal air fares, of how to cut car costs, save on air conditioning costs, and so on. Similarly, if a person is homeless, his or her perception of how to cut costs will be different from, say, that of the Jane Fonda character in the 1977 movie, *Fun with Dick and Jane*, who, faced with her husband's job loss, says, "We'll cancel our membership in the Book-of-the-Month Club!"

Think of this book as a cafeteria. Read the stories of the contributors and their recommendations. Pick and choose what makes sense to you. As you discover being frugal does not have to mean a steady diet of rice and beans, wearing clothing salvaged from Dumpsters, and fixing everything in your life with duct tape, perhaps this book will help you find your own frugality, which ultimately is what the movement is all about.

At the end of each of these selections, if the author has a product for sale, he or she will tell you how to obtain a copy. In the case of newsletters, the editors will tell you how to get a sample. Please be kind to the editors and follow their instructions. Most of the newsletters are one-person or one-family operations. They cannot afford to send you a sample and pay the postage. And addressing envelopes takes time, so, if they ask for a self-addressed, stamped envelope (SASE), please send them one. The bottom line here is this: If you don't comply with their requirements, they don't owe you a response. On the other hand, none of us objects to your saving money by sharing our products with your friends. If you subscribe to one newsletter and a friend subscribes to another, and you swap newsletters when each of you has finished reading, not only is that fine with us, but it shows you may already be part of the New Frugality movement and you just didn't realize it!

The contributors to this book hold a wide range of political and societal viewpoints. One contributor, for example, expresses concerns about immigration. As the grandson of immigrants, I do not share these concerns. Another contributor is a close relative of one of the Republican presidential candidates who ran against Franklin Roosevelt. Really! And yet another contributor is an unapologetic revolutionary whose approach to frugality is a part of his political philosophy. Whether you agree with, or, for that matter, pay attention to the philosophies espoused by the individual contributors to this book is up to you. There will be no quiz.

Finally, you may have noted that at least a couple of New Frugality writers you may have heard about are not included in this anthology. Some, because of busy schedules or conflicting commitments, opted out. Some, unfortunately, were not invited to participate because of questionable recommendations and business practices. And there are still others out there I am not yet aware of.

I hope you enjoy this anthology by the best and brightest frugal folks of the 1990s. Happy reading and keep cheap.

My (Untold) Story

Amy Dacyczyn

Amy Dacyczyn needs no introduction. Her newsletter, the Tightwad Gazette, *which had 100,000 subscribers before she decided to retire in 1996, has probably had as much to do with getting people to give some thought to where their money goes as anything else has. Her books, which have made the* New York Times *list of best-sellers, have reached even more people. In her final issue, published in December 1996, she reprinted for the first time just a few of the letters she's received from people whose lives she changed. Only someone with a heart of stone would be unmoved by some of those stories. And now here's a part of Amy's story we've never read before.*

Perhaps more than any contributor to this anthology, my story has been told over and over (and over, yawn) in countless magazine, newspaper, radio, and television stories over the past eight years. It goes like this: When my husband, Jim, and I married in 1982 we decided we wanted a large family, a large pre-1900 house in the country, and we didn't want to put our children into day care. Despite having a combined gross income of under $30,000, we saved $49,000 in seven years. We also spent another $38,000 on "investment purchases" such as furniture, appliances, and cars, and we were debt free. In 1989 we moved to Maine, shopped intensively for a house, and then put most of our savings down on our dream house. In 1990 I launched a successful newsletter called the *Tightwad Gazette*, which later became spin-off books of the same title—which explains all the media attention.

Yeah, yeah. You've heard it all before.

When my friend Larry Roth asked me to participate in this project I immediately understood that my challenge would be to add something different to what the audience is likely to have previously read or heard through the media or through my newsletter. So my contribution, in part, will explore some aspects of my story which have never been discussed before, and which clearly show how I learned that frugality works. It's the "prequel" version.

All humans are shaped by past experiences. People decide how to live by incorporating the good of their pasts while rejecting the experiences that they felt were bad. When I contemplate the factors that led to my decision to adopt a frugal lifestyle I see that I too engaged in this sifting process.

In terms of frugality, I was the child of a mixed marriage. Like many men of his generation, my father measured his self-worth by his professional accomplishments rather than by the quality of his personal relationships. This was particularly true as I approached adulthood, when he became a follower not only of Napoleon Hill, author of *Think and Grow Rich*, but of many of the motivational-speaker gurus of the eighties. As taught by those thinkers, he adopted the "Don't save more, earn more" philosophy of money management. He felt that thrift was small-minded thinking.

My mother, on the other hand, was the thrifty one. Our family always had a garden, always ate oatmeal five days a week, and always ate bread from a bakery thrift shop. My three sisters and I always wore secondhand clothing, which, in the pre-yard-sale sixties, meant that the quality of our wardrobes wasn't spectacular.

My parents reached their own peculiar compromise; my father could spend as long as he didn't go into debt. His earning ability combined with my mother's saving ability, along with the luck of never encountering an unavoidable financial crisis, meant that we had a solidly middle-class life. Our family was rarely short on cash, but I suspect that there was little rainy-day money.

Although I remember my mother speaking of not wasting money, my sisters and I were not taught overarching philosophies about frugality. We were not taught how to practice thrift—how to get good deals or how to judge value. I grew up not knowing how to prepare a meal, much less how to buy food inexpensively. Neither was my mother exceedingly creative, precise, or resourceful in her approach. Thrift, to us, was what our mother did to make ends meet. The way in which she applied frugality is the way most thrifty people did it, and still do.

My parents were willing to spend on us to a point, after which all other wants had to be purchased with our baby-sitting money. I learned to supplement the secondhand clothes with new items I bought with my own money. That was the sole financial concept I carried with me into adulthood; I could have whatever I wanted as long as I was willing to earn the money to buy it.

After I graduated from high school in 1973 my parents moved from Massachusetts to North Carolina. I stayed behind and went to art school in Boston. The art-school years were a bit lean, but by the early eighties, I earned as much as $20 per hour working as a graphic artist. During those years, my spending style mirrored that of both of my parents. I always chose inexpensive places to live and always spent little on clothes. By keeping basic expenses low I found I had a surplus to spend on restaurant meals, movies, theater tickets, cab rides, expensive Christmas presents, and other temporary pleasures. Like my father, I never went into debt, but neither did I think about a long-term savings plan. The $1,000 I kept in a checking account was a point of reference—when my account rose above that point I spent more, and when it fell below the mark I spent less.

In my midtwenties I had an on-again/mostly-off-again relationship with a late-thirties businessman. The first year we dated Robert earned $140,000, which, back then, seemed like wealth. His spending style was like my father's, except that Robert had a fatter wallet. I dined at the most expensive restaurants in the city, went on sailing and ski trips, and received expensive gifts. Typically, Robert thought nothing of spending thousands to rent a ski lodge for a season and then using it just once, or having four season's tickets to the ballet and then missing almost every performance. Robert's money-is-like-water approach to finances disturbed me, and I questioned it from the start. Despite his assurances, I strongly suspected that his income, although generous, was not enough to guarantee his happiness or buy everything he wanted. Toward the end of our three years Robert asked me to accompany him to look at real estate. Robert was disappointed to discover he didn't have enough money to buy any of the minimansions or luxury condominiums. I silently reflected on the tens of thousands of dollars I'd watched him squander over the previous three years. When that relationship ended I was twenty-seven, and came away having learned some powerful lessons.

* "Earning more" doesn't guarantee financial security. Despite his income, Robert's financial future was risky because he wasn't content to live on less than he earned. I recall thinking I would have more security if I married "a happy plumber."
* More is not better. Before Robert, I never thought hard about how I spent money. Movie-escapism felt good, as did being waited on in a restaurant. As a result of Robert's spending, as well as a fair amount of my own, I had sampled many luxuries. These things cost significantly more than cheaper alternatives, but they were not significantly more satisfying. But more, I had been overexposed to extreme wastefulness. I developed an aversion to waste and was forced to examine my own spending.
* I would never again let anyone or anything derail my personal vision for my life. Before I went to live in Boston, I knew I wanted to live in a rural area, own a large pre-1900 house as my parents and grandparents did, and raise a large family. I liked the city, but I was not cut out to live an upscale urban life.

Well, I didn't find a plumber. I met and married a Navy recruiter. Like me, Jim was no stranger to frugality. His parents, the children of Ukrainian immigrants, grew up on farms during the Depression. Jim's family gardened, did home canning, and built their own home partially from recycled materials. Jim's mother could reupholster a chair and sew her own suits. His father could build a lathe using an old washing-machine motor. Yet, as in my case, what frugal lessons Jim was taught in his childhood didn't stick.

Jim and I were thirty-three and twenty-seven when we married. Between the two of us we had over twenty years in the work force, yet our total net worth consisted of my $1,000, his old Suburban, and his sporting equipment. Nevertheless, Jim was agreeable to my vision, earned enough so that we could be a one-income family, and was content to live within his means. It was clear to us that if we wanted to buy a home on his income we would have to change our spending habits. And while neither of us grew up being taught the philosophy of frugality, much of the method was shown to us by example. It was familiar and thus easy for us to fall back on.

We financed our own frugal wedding (he wore his uniform and I wore a forty-dollar dress from Filene's Basement). We opted to live in my four-room apartment in a run-down triple decker—the rent was *very* cheap. We began to track our spending and make adjustments. We watched for sales and eliminated low-value expenditures. That first year was the last time Jim and I went out on a dinner date together (that is, that we paid for). It was a lobster dinner at a floating-boat restaurant. After we paid the bill, I looked at Jim and said, "This wasn't that good. Let's not do this again." Shortly thereafter, we went to our last theater movie—*The Cotton Club* with Richard Gere—and had a similar conversation. For the first time for either of us, our savings account grew and we were hooked.

Our first child was born about nine months after the wedding and I stopped working full-time. Eighteen months after the wedding Jim was transferred to Norfolk, Virginia. By then we had saved $20,000. As our family (and expenses) grew, saving became more difficult. We joined a wholesale club and used coupons. Having never lived in the suburbs before, yard sales were new to us. Once we discovered how to mine that wealth, the majority of our clothing, tools, toys, gifts, and household goods would come from that source.

At one point, we made a scouting trip to New England to look at real estate, and realized we still did not have enough money. When we returned to Virginia, I stepped up my efforts. I began frequenting the "finance" and "how-to" aisles at the library looking for new ideas. I revamped our food bill, developed my price-book system for tracking grocery prices, and began calculating the costs of everything.

Four years, two children, and an additional $20,000 in savings later, Jim was transferred to Maine. Although Maine was more affordable than most of New England, we found nothing in our price range that came close to meeting our expectations. We moved into government housing for fifteen months. During that time we had our fourth child, saved another $9,000 and looked at 176 houses. And our persistence paid off. In 1989 we put most of our savings down on a spectacular $125,000 fixer-upper.

Throughout the years, we had been criticized for being "too extreme." We didn't allow the criticism to derail our pursuit of the dream. Had we not saved as we did, we would have needed about $55,000 in annual income to buy the same house—we would have needed to be a two-income family for thirty years. We knew we had accomplished what most people thought to be impossible, and sharing what we learned inspired us to start the newsletter.

Of course, there's an apparent bit of irony to our circumstances. Our newsletter was financially successful and so we "earned more." Yet this doesn't undermine my basic message. The financial success of our newsletter was a fluke few could duplicate. I know I couldn't. Yet the basics of frugality can be practiced by anyone. Through the years thousands of readers wrote to tell me how the strategies I taught dramatically improved the quality of their lives, and often their standard of living.

Some people think there is something "wrong" about my choice to continue being frugal even though I no longer "need" to be. But when our newsletter rocketed to success in 1991, Jim and I understood that if we continued to be frugal we could afford to retire early. We retired our newsletter in December 1996. Our invested savings, Jim's military retirement check, and our continued frugality will allow us to continue to have a middle-class lifestyle.

Beyond the desire to retire early, there are other reasons we still live a frugal lifestyle. It's a wonderful game that I have no desire to give up—paying retail just isn't as much fun! In addition to saving money, most of the strategies are also good for the environment. Finally, frugality enables me to give to others—the same surplus with which I could buy myself a low-value luxury could also buy a high-value necessity for someone else.

But mostly, I remain frugal for my six children, now aged six to fourteen. Even before I married, scoffers doubted my frugal plan, saying, "It will never work when you have kids." After I had kids they said, "It will never work when your kids go to school." After my kids went to school they said, "It will never work when your kids get to be teenagers." Now that I have a teenager, and it's still going well, they still scoff. One recent magazine story said our frugal child-rearing would not work once our children go off to college. I suppose the scoffers would say frugality won't work once my kids have kids.

The truth is that you can raise children frugally, offer them a great quality of life, and get few complaints in return. Because we are extremely resourceful and creative in acquiring their needs, our children have few wants. As just one recent example, our fourteen-year-old son, Alec, saved up $42 to buy an air rifle. But we bought it for him as a Christmas gift (it was a $30 display model, the same one he wanted). Upon discovering his $42 was freed up for another purchase, he immediately began to cruise through the Service Merchandise catalog. He found his electronics set for $15—the one I had bought for $1 at a yard sale. He found his walkie-talkie headsets for $79—the exact same ones he had bought for $2 at a yard sale months earlier. He laughed as he realized there was nothing he wanted, that he didn't already have, that was worth the retail price. So he decided to save his money.

When kids learn lessons with their own money, it's easier for them to understand the financial choices their parents make. This doesn't mean my kids *never* complain. It means they rarely complain and we successfully manage the occasional areas of disagreement.

So while I might be able to afford to shower my children with a steady stream of new goods, I don't feel that would prepare them for life. It's unlikely they will enjoy the same financial success that Jim and I have.

Today, the average wage for a single worker is less than $30,000 annually. This means that most people who choose to raise a family on one income must practice some frugality. I want my children to understand that not only is this choice realistic, but when frugality is practiced with creativity, precision and resourcefulness, the resulting standard of living can be abundant.

AMY'S FIFTEEN TIPS

Amy sent fifteen tips and told me to pick the best ten. After reading them, I'm sure you will agree that they are all excellent and original. And, well, why waste anything? I would no more cut Amy's list to fit the "ten best" format than I would trim the Mona Lisa *to fit a ready-made frame.*

1. Think small. Most people think small expenses don't count. They do—especially the small things you do every day. If you change a habit and save $1 a day, that adds up to $365 a year. A change that saves $10 a day adds up to $3,650 a year.
2. Economize first on "disposable" purchases. Food, clothing (especially for children), entertainment, and gift giving are part of your life for a short time. It also happens that these are the areas where most people can make the most dramatic changes. In a week it won't matter what you ate for dinner tonight, so food is a good area to economize (keeping in mind proper nutrition). Many of my readers report that they cut their food bills in half, saving thousands annually—and that their diets became healthier at the same time.
3. When it comes to "investment purchases"—the items that will be part of your life for years—buy the quality level that will satisfy you in the long run. I held out for over ten years trying to find ten used dining room chairs that I liked and that matched. I finally mail-ordered new ones for $55 each. I chose them because they are durable and have a simple style that will look good for decades. Although seemingly expensive, the annual cost of owning them will be small.

4. Figure your "hourly wage" for money-saving tasks. If hanging a load of laundry saves fifty cents and requires fifteen minutes, that's like earning two dollars per hour tax free. Tasks that require seconds or days can be computed the same way. This exercise is surprising. The oft pooh-poohed practice of reusing aluminum foil might save a theoretical eighteen dollars per hour (really). However, driving slower to save gasoline—say, 45 mph on a deserted 65 mph highway—might save you less than one dollar per hour. Use this hourly wage concept to guide you in choosing which activities are the best use of your time. Also consider what activities you enjoy, and what activities satisfy other values in your life. You might decide to drive slower anyway because it conserves resources.

5. Measure value on the "one-to-ten wow" scale. Doing this, or asking family members to do this, allows me to judge if we got sufficient value for the money. My child might rate a fifty-cent yard-sale treasure a wow of a seven, whereas the same toy purchased new for fifteen dollars might rate an eight. The new toy might be slightly preferred, but the yard sale purchase is the better value because the "cost per wow" is significantly lower, thereby leaving a surplus with which to buy other toys.

6. Learn new skills. To save money Jim and I have learned many skills, and over time this has evolved into a remarkable compounding of skills, which enables us to do most anything we set out to do. For example, a sewing basket given to my daughter needed a repair. Jim figured out a way to steam-bend the needed piece of wood using common kitchen items. The wood was sanded, stained, and finished to match. This experience added to his repertoire of knowledge and will enable him to repair something more valuable in the future.

7. Stay behind the times. Many things—books, magazines, fashions, music, electronics, and so on—become cheaper if you wait. Fashions turn up at yard sales next season. Movies are eventually shown on television. Electronics become cheaper, and of better quality, if you wait.

8. Be creative. Someone once said to me, "I solve a problem by throwing money at it." But when you eliminate the big-money so-

lution, you force yourself to find a creative/frugal one. And when you find it, it's so utterly simple you wonder why you ever considered the expensive way. Two hours before a Halloween party our son Neal told us he didn't want the planned costume. So we shredded and blow-torched an old raincoat and baseball cap, added scorchlike spots of spray paint, streaked his face with black and fake blood, and added a hat tag that said, "BOMBS R US, Neal Dacyczyn, Demolitions Expert." He made it to the party and had one of the best costumes.

9. Get your "rush" from saving money. Most people buy new things they don't need because it gives them a short-term "high." They must spend again to repeat the feeling. Frugal people replace the spendthrift high with one that comes from *saving* money. I like antiques and collectibles and can afford to pay retail for what I like. But it's just more fun to find a signed, framed 1930 photograph for fifty cents at a yard sale than to buy the same item for fifteen dollars in an antiques shop. Yard sale finds rank just behind trash picking for the ultimate rush.

10. Put out the word. Network with friends and relatives to find bargains. By casually mentioning your needs to others, you'll find that surprisingly often someone will have the very thing you need, taking up space in their attic. Or someone might tell you where they saw the thing you need on sale. This strategy is a two-way street. Reciprocation is crucial.

11. Negotiate. The price of many items—including some retail merchandise—is negotiable. A yard sale vendor will almost always take a lower price, especially late in the day. If approached discreetly, the owner of a smaller retail store might also negotiate. Much of negotiating is a learned art, but the first step is simply to ask. You learn from practice.

12. Dare to be different. Following social custom can be expensive, and many customs are illogical. For instance, business-world culture dictates that women need a minimum of five to ten outfits, yet no one notices how often a man wears the same suit in a given

week. By being brave enough to ignore this silly double standard, a woman can cut her wardrobe costs in half.

13. Don't fall for the "theoretical savings" ploy. Advertisers convince us to spend money under the pretenses of saving money. For example, coupon use can be effective, but often you end up spending more to save more. Cold cereal usually costs $4 a pound, but I routinely buy store-brand cereal, on sale, for $1 a pound. Even if I doubled a one-dollar-off coupon to "save" $2 off the usual $4 price, I would have to spend 200 percent to "save" fifty percent. Focus on what you actually spend, not on what you theoretically save.

14. Free entertainment is good, but entertainment that actually saves money is better. For example, sewing can be an expensive hobby but I like to sew using scavenged materials. I made a hood to go on my five-year-old's black winter coat using the fabric and filler from raggedy black snow pants. I challenged myself to make it look like a manufacturer-made one, and I did. To me this was more fun than making a frilly quilted pillow from new materials.

15. Experiment. A woman wrote to ask me if homemade bread dough could be frozen like the store-bought type. While I didn't know the answer, I did know that this woman spent more in postage than she might have spent by experimenting with a small quantity of dough. In contrast, I'm currently engaged in a long-term experiment to improve my popovers. Every couple of weeks I try a different popover recipe with a soup meal. The recipes call for various methods, temperatures, and quantities of ingredients. I'm recording the results of using different combinations of variables, and I feel confident I'll eventually crack the code.

Amy's books, The Tightwad Gazette, The Tightwad Gazette II, *and* The Tightwad Gazette III *are compilations of most of the articles that appeared in the first six years of the newsletter. The books are available in major bookstores and libraries. She will also sell the books by mail-order for $12 each, which includes shipping and handling and which may save you some sales tax. To purchase books from her, send a check to: The Tightwad Gazette, P.O. Box 201, Leeds, ME 04263.*

How Do You Define the Simple Life?

◩

Edith Flowers Kilgo

I first became acquainted with Edith Flowers Kilgo's work when I read an article she wrote on why she could not afford her job. I liked that article so much I reprinted it (with Edith's permission, of course) in Beating the System. *Her story is unusual in that she grew up in enforced simplicity (i.e., poverty), did very well financially, and then chose to return to her simple roots.*

Have you ever lived in a four-room, tar-papered house with no plumbing? Walked barefoot to school? Sat down to a meal of only corn bread and milk?

Ever worn clothes made from the sacks chicken feed or flour came in? I have.

At age eight I entered the workforce with a burlap bag on my shoulder, picking beans in the blistering South Georgia heat.

Yet, forty years later, before I fled the corporate world to seek the simple life, my husband, Randal, and I had what passes for the American dream: a fourteen-room brick house on a suburban acre; a private-school education for our daughter; late-model cars; and salaries that encouraged us to buy the latest toys and fashions without scrutinizing price tags. Upscale catalogs clogged our mailbox, as did daily offers of credit lines and gold cards.

Not too bad for a sharecroppers' daughter, most would think.

We subscribed to decorating magazines. Unaware of the irony, we scoured attics and antique fairs for sturdy, honest reminders of our childhoods: wooden dough bowls, pottery, folk art. These objects spoke to our unexpressed longings, but we rarely had time to dust our acquisitions, much less enjoy them.

If everything was so dandy, why were we always so stressed, exhausted, sick, and irritable? In addition, Randal and I were collecting nagging little reminders of our mortality. An ache here. A pain there. We could no longer run full-tilt all week and have anything left for ourselves on weekends.

We paid others to do things for us—that lovely lawn was not of our doing, and we were desperately seeking a cleaning person. We had no time for friends, relatives, or even ourselves. If we were so "successful," why were we so miserable?

When Randal and I first made our decision to downscale, I honestly believed I would willingly live in a one-room shack, wear thrift-store clothes, and eat beans the rest of my life before I would sell my soul again for a weekly paycheck—of course I, of all people, should have known better. But the desperation that kicked me in the gut is a common symptom among those of us eager to escape the rat race.

But thankfully, we didn't need to live in a refrigerator box. After working the figures, I decided I could quit my job. Randal took a demotion and pay cut to work fewer hours with less stress. We still had enough funds to live on, provided we paid attention to our money. I wasn't worried. After all, I'd learned simplicity and frugality from world-class experts: my parents.

But when we downscaled, the one thing we knew we did not want was the joyless stinginess that permeates some simplified lifestyles. It seemed to us that many of the things regarded as mandatory for simple living are depressing and unnecessary. While we admitted that, yes, it is fun to eat in nice restaurants occasionally, and to wear decent clothes, and to drive a dependable car, we also understand that those things should be earned privileges, not rights. Dessert comes after the main course: paying bills and setting aside funds for the future.

Frugality and simplicity are not, we believe, about forgoing all pleasures, but about making wise choices. It isn't wrong to spend money, but it is foolish to spend money senselessly.

Downscaling is not living in a cave with a hoarded fortune, either. It's about making the best use of funds—and each practitioner of downscaling has to decide his or her own "best" individually tailored path to simplicity and frugality.

These are concepts Randal and I considered three years ago when we established our *Creative Downscaling* newsletter. We determined then that we'd never advocate anything that undermined our readers' self-respect. We already knew from another experience twenty-five years earlier that it is possible to downscale with dignity and live frugally with style.

This is the second time we have downscaled. The first was in 1968 when our daughter was born and I wanted to stay home with her. Randal, just twenty-six at the time, was not then at the peak of his earning years. Times were tough, but we learned to stretch a dollar until it squealed. I even wrote two books based on our experiences: *Money in the Cookie Jar*—a how-to for running a home business—and *Money Management*. I also had more than four hundred articles published in magazines such as *Good Housekeeping, The Mother Earth News, Woman's Day,* and *Prevention;* wrote columns for several national magazines; ran a number of home businesses; and lectured. When Karen reached college age, I wanted a change and reentered the workforce as an editor for Georgia State University in Atlanta. It was there I learned the skills that would lead us to publish the newsletter.

Our goal is to show others how to live on less without succumbing to soul-shriveling practices that cause resentment and feelings of deprivation. Our goal is "upscale, simplified living."

Like us, many reach middle age with an impressive list of belongings. Our lifestyles are more affluent than any previous generation's. Today's small families live in three to four times the floor space great-grandparents required for large broods. But bigger houses mean more maintenance, more insurance, more mortgage, more worries.

We work longer hours with less time to enjoy expensive belongings. The daily commute—thirty minutes or more on average—adds more stress.

Drive through any suburban neighborhood in midmorning. Is anybody home enjoying the manicured lawn, the decorator window treatments, the designer furniture, the backyard swimming pool, or the gas-fired grill on the redwood deck?

Cruise through at dinnertime. No lights beckon from kitchens and dining rooms. Want to see some people? Try McDonald's or the mall.

Although "poor but happy" has become a Hollywood cliché, my childhood taught me that happiness is not about buying things. By almost any definition, my family's situation during my childhood would be called simple: no television, e-mail, telephone, beeper, or fax; no mortgage; no credit card bills.

As for frugality—my goodness, every nickel we had was counted twelve times. We had no choice but to be fiscally conservative—it was either that or give up eating.

My parents, Henry Flowers and Winnie Rouse, married in 1931. She was fifteen years old. He was twenty. They shared a bedroom in his parents' house with a brother and his bride. Clothesline draped with quilts divided the room, offering the only privacy the two sets of newlyweds had. Times were hard. Nobody complained. It was just the way life was.

There were no jobs, but my father always found work. Nothing was too hard, too tiring, too physical, or too demeaning for him. While other men could not find one job, my father always had two or three jobs at any given time. He tried sharecropping, commercial fishing, collecting garbage, working in a sawmill, and even gathering moss to sell to mattress companies. My mother worked alongside him in the fields. Later, she was a cook, then a seamstress, and even for a time ran a boardinghouse.

I was born in 1946, their fifth child—and the only one who survived. That was before health insurance, and medical bills helped keep my parents at the poverty line, no matter how hard they worked.

When I was ten, my father rented, for twenty dollars a month, a 600-square-foot tar-papered house with no plumbing, in the middle of the woods. It was the first time we'd had our own place. I loved that little cabin. At night, wind soughing through the Georgia pines lulled me to sleep. Strange as it may sound, I collected rocks for fun, an activity that entertained me far more than any store-bought doll could have.

Through hard work, my parents eventually achieved the American dream: two cars in the garage; a neat brick house in the suburbs; pension plans; and a daughter in college. And when my father died in 1992 he left me an inheritance eight times his annual salary. Not a fortune, to be sure, but quite an accomplishment for a 105-pound man with one year of schooling.

How did my parents do it? Determination and hard work, those ubiquitous components of success, were obviously a part of it. But frugality was the prime ingredient.

The lesson I learned by my parents' example was that all work is honorable and even though the paycheck may be small, it is important to save something. A buried mayonnaise jar held their gleanings. Sometimes it was only a dollar or two—but hard won when a day's pay for manual labor during the Depression was only fifty cents.

My parents were never stingy. After his death, I learned that my father worked so hard during the Depression years because he was supporting four other families as well as his own. And he managed to do it while somehow finding time to put his family and friends first.

But that kind of balance is missing in most people's lives today. Baby boomers learned the principle of hard work from Depression-surviving parents, but somehow many missed the important lesson: Living well is a worthwhile goal, but sacrificing your life, health, and family in pursuit of money—or simplicity—is not living well at all.

Unfortunately, many hard-driving corporate types who walk away from high-pressure careers to seek the simple life often approach frugality and simplicity with the same overachieving intensity. Instead of simplicity, many find themselves whipped, defeated, and bitter, and back in the big city groveling for the old job a year later. Why?

Possibly because the simple life is not, as many are convinced, about buying anything (food dehydration systems, log cabins, jeans, four-wheel-drive vehicles, generators, and the like), or about tossing out all of one's worldly goods. The simple life cannot be achieved by flailing about, but by simply relaxing and letting life happen in a sensible and logical fashion.

Money is something simplifiers don't like to admit is necessary, although it is. I realize that the reason I am now able to live the simple life is because I first acquired some money to manage. The secret to simple living is not poverty or deprivation, but minimalism: learning what is important and necessary—and then doing without the rest.

The best way to finance the simple life is by spending less right now. Simplicity is less about buying and more about conserving and making the most of what you have, whether it's time, talent, or money.

The old Depression-era admonition to "use it up, wear it out, make it do, do without" fits into the equation. Creative downscaling is really about having the initiative to ask yourself, "What, other than cash, would fix this problem?" The answer to many money dilemmas is simple: The less you spend on things that don't matter, the more you have to spend on things that do.

But most of all, creative downscaling is about making people a priority over things. Would you rather your children learn from you to hang out at the mall or to serve in a soup kitchen?

These days my goal is to teach others who have lost their way how to find happiness with the principles—better spending habits, debt control, healthful living, job autonomy, and a philosophy that places people and relationships first—that ultimately lifted my sharecropper parents to a comfortable middle-class life.

The lesson I learned from my "deprived" childhood and my "successful" adult life is that life is always going to be a challenge, no matter what your financial status, but joys are there as well. Hard work pays off. Frugality is nothing more complicated than good stewardship. Even in the hard times there's enough to share when you have a "loaves and fishes" mentality. Hard work counts, but time for those you love is the real business of life.

Authors Joe Dominguez and Vicki Robin point out in *Your Money or Your Life* that material goods are what we get in exchange for our very lives. Every gadget, gizmo, and gewgaw that comes into anybody's house is purchased with a piece of life that was exchanged for a salary. Would most of us still want that gizmo if we truly comprehended what it cost? I, for one, am not willing to exchange a portion of my life for frivolous goods. If I inherited a million dollars tomorrow, I can't imagine that I would live my live any differently.

Sometimes people, especially reporters, want to know exactly what the simple life is. I tell them I don't know. I can't define the simple life for anyone other than myself.

For you, the simple life is what you believe it to be. You'll know you are there when contentment takes the place of stress, when you can sleep soundly through the night, when you can spend as much time as you need to with people you care about, and when the term *short fuse* applies to an electrical problem and not to your problem-solving approach.

Simple living is not about location either. You can live a simple life in a high-rise if that's your mindset.

It isn't necessarily about escaping to the country to raise goats or subsisting on beans and rice. It's about making decisions that make you healthier and happier and then having the courage to do what you need to do.

Or, as a newsletter subscriber wrote to me, "It isn't about what you do without. It's about what you do instead."

EDITH'S TEN GIANT STEPS TO CREATIVE DOWNSCALING

1. Define your needs, wants, and goals. Only you can say what is important or trivial. The simple life is not solely about frugality, but about making wise decisions that allow you to have the things you care about while cutting loose from things that stress you.

2. Put people first. If you're ready to give more of yourself and less of purchased goods, you're ready for the simple life. Time is the greatest gift of all.

3. Be realistic about material goods. People differ in emotional makeup. Assess your feelings about buying. One reader wrote to tell me that "the more you have, the more you have broken."

   Learn to see each purchase not in dollars and cents, but in terms of how it impacts your life. Each dollar spent represents a dollar earned in exchange for a portion of your life. What is an item's true worth when measured as a piece of your life span?

4. Decide how much money you need and what it costs you to work. When I worked as university editor, it cost me $15,000 a year just for transportation, parking fees, gasoline, taxes, clothes, lunches, Social Security, disability insurance, and missed opportunities (such as shopping for appliances on sale, growing a garden, and cooking dinners at home instead of going out when I was too tired to cook). Too much of what I earned we spent just to support my job.

5. Consider self-employment. Working for yourself is the wave of the future. Home businesses offer the best chance for good income with low stress.

6. Do a trial run. Although we plunged in, caution is better. Three months before making the switch, practice living frugally and doing more things for yourself. Many people lack the skills or temperament for do-it-yourself; be honest about limitations before placing yourself in a situation that allows no choice. Try to downscale gradually.

7. Look for big-ticket cuts. In a two-career family, time is always short. If you have only a few minutes a day in which to practice frugality, pass on washing foil and reusing tea bags. Instead, read your insurance policy and possibly find a few hundred extra dollars; ask the doctor's office for itemized bills so you can compare insurance payments; pay attention to the grocery scanner. These more down-to-earth habits are the big money savers and should logically come before the minor save-a-cent activities.

8. Give up things that don't enrich. Can it be that your morning coffee purchased on the way to work is costing you $500 a year? Do the math. Then invest in a twenty-dollar coffeemaker and brew your own. Go through spending habits one by one; you'll find dozens of painless "do-withouts."

9. Try to make it a team effort. It's hard to downscale when other family members don't care. Arithmetic is your ally. When a reluctant spouse sees that a sausage and biscuit a day equals, at year's end, a nice vacation, that is attention getting.

10. Say no. The biggest obstacle to downscaled living is an obligation-cluttered life. Maybe a bridge club or golf dates enriched your life at one point, but if time now means more, reassess. Consider your volunteer activities, too. Are you committed to causes that are no longer fulfilling? It's better to give up half a dozen things you don't enjoy and give your full attention to one or two causes you really believe in.

Creative Downscaling *is published six times a year. U.S. subscription rate is $15. A sample is $1 plus a self-addressed, stamped envelope. Creative Downscaling, Dept. LR, P.O. Box 1884, Jonesboro, GA 30237-1884.*

THE PLEASURES OF FRUGALITY

Joe Dominguez and Vicki Robin

Joe Dominguez's cassette course, "Transforming Your Relationship with Money and Achieving Financial Independence," was a turning point for many people. Through that course, they became aware of how much of their life's energy they were giving up in exchange for often meaningless material possessions. The lives of many more people were changed when the principles of this course were condensed into the best-selling book, Your Money or Your Life, *which Joe Dominguez and Vicki Robin cowrote in 1992. Shortly after Joe and Vicki agreed to contribute to this anthology, Joe became ill. He died in January 1997 (see "Remembering Joe Dominguez" in this volume). The following is excerpted, with permission, from* Your Money or Your Life *(Viking Penguin, 1992).*

It is both sad and telling that there is no word in the English language for living at the peak of fulfillment, always having plenty but never being burdened with excess. The word would need to evoke the careful stewarding of tangible resources (time, money, stuff) coupled with the joyful expansion of spiritual resources (creativity, intelligence, love).

The word *frugality* used to serve that function, but frugality has gotten a bad reputation in the latter half of the twentieth century.

How did frugality lose favor among Americans? It is, after all, a perennial ideal and a cornerstone of the American character. Both Socrates and Plato praised the "golden mean." Both the Old Testament ("Give me neither poverty nor wealth, but only enough") and the teachings of Jesus ("Ye cannot serve both God and Mammon") extol the value of material simplicity in enriching the life of the spirit. In American history well-known individuals (Benjamin Franklin, Henry David Thoreau, Ralph Waldo Emerson, Robert Frost) as well as groups (Amish, Quakers, Hutterites, Mennonites) have carried forward the virtue of thrift—both out of respect for the earth and out of a thirst for a touch of heaven. And the challenges of building our nation required frugality for most of our citizens. Indeed, the wealth we enjoy today is the result of centuries of frugality. The "more is better" consumer culture is a Johnny-come-lately on the American scene. Our bedrock is frugality, and it's high time we made friends with the word—and the practice!

Let's explore this word *frugality* to see if we can't redeem it as the key to fulfillment in the nineties. We looked up *frugal* in a 1986 Merriam-Webster dictionary and found "characterized by or reflecting economy in the expenditure of resources." That sounds about right—a serviceable, practical, and fairly colorless word. Yet digging deeper, Webster tells us that *frugal* shares a Latin root with *frug* (meaning virtue), *frux* (meaning fruit or value) and *frui* (meaning to enjoy or have the use of). Now we're talking. Frugality is enjoying the virtue of getting good value for every minute of your life energy and from everything you have the use of.

That's very interesting. In fact, it's more than interesting. It's transformative. Frugality means we are to enjoy what we have. If you have ten dresses but still feel you have nothing to wear, you are probably a spendthrift. But if you have ten dresses and have enjoyed wearing all of them for years, you are frugal. Waste lies not in the number of possessions but in the failure to enjoy them. Your success at being frugal is measured not by your penny-pinching but by your degree of enjoyment of the material world.

Enjoyment of the material world? Isn't that hedonism? While both have to do with enjoying what you have, frugality and hedonism are opposite responses to the material world. Hedonism revels in the pleasures of the senses and implies excessive consumption of the material world and the continual search for more. Frugal people, however, get value from everything—a dandelion or a bouquet of roses, a single strawberry or a gourmet meal. A hedonist might consume the juice of five oranges as a prelude to a pancake breakfast. A frugal person, on the other hand, might relish eating a single orange, enjoying the color and texture of the whole fruit, the smell and light spray that comes as you begin to peel it, the translucence of each section, the flood of flavor that comes as a section bursts its juices over the tongue . . . and the thrift of saving the peels for baking.

To be frugal means to have a high joy-to-stuff ratio. If you get one unit of joy for each item you have, that's frugal. But if you need ten items to even begin registering on the joy meter, you're missing the point of being alive.

There's a word in Spanish that encompasses all this: *aprovechar*. It means to use something wisely—be it old zippers from worn-out clothing or a sunny day at the beach. It's getting full value from life, enjoying all the good that each moment and each thing has to offer. You can "aprovechar" a simple meal, a flat of overripe strawberries, or a cruise in the Bahamas. There's nothing miserly about aprovechar; it's a succulent word, full of sunlight and flavor. If only "frugal" were so sweet . . .

The "more is better and it's never enough" mentality in North America fails the frugality test not solely because of the excess, but because of the lack of enjoyment of what we already have. Indeed, North Americans have been called materialists, but that's a misnomer. All too often it's not material things we enjoy as much as what these things symbolize: conquest, status, success, achievement, a sense of worth, and even favor in the eyes of the Creator. Once we've acquired the dream house, the status car, or the perfect mate, we rarely stop to thoroughly enjoy them. Instead, we're off and running after the next coveted acquisition.

Another lesson we can derive from the dictionary definition of *frugal* is the recognition that we don't need to possess a thing to enjoy it—

we merely need to use it. If we are enjoying an item, whether or not we own it, we're being frugal. For many of life's pleasures it may be far better to "use" something than to "possess" it (and pay in time and energy for the upkeep). So often we have been like feudal lords, gathering as many possessions as possible from far and wide and bringing them inside the walls of our castle. If we want something (or wanted it in the past, or imagine we might want it in the future), we think we must bring it inside the boundaries of the world called "mine." What such a consumer fails to recognize is that what is outside the walls of "mine" doesn't belong to the enemy; it belongs to the "rest of us." And if what lies outside our walls is not "them" but "us," we can afford to loosen our grip a bit on our possessions. We can gingerly open the doors of our fortress and allow goods (material and spiritual) to flow into and out of our boundaries.

Frugality, then, is also learning to share, to see the world as "ours" rather than as "theirs" and "mine." And, while not explicit in the word, being frugal and being happy with having enough means that there will be more available for others. Learning to equitably share the resources of the earth is at the top of the global agenda, and some creative frugality in North America could go a long way toward promoting that balance.

Frugality is balance. Frugality is the Greek notion of the golden mean. Frugality is being efficient in harvesting happiness from the world you live in. Frugality is right-use (righteous)—the wise stewarding of money, time, energy, space, and possessions. Goldilocks expressed the frugality ideal when she declared the porridge "not too hot, not too cold, but just right." Frugality is just like that—not too much, not too little, but just right. Nothing is wasted. Or left unused. It's a clean machine. Sleek. Perfect. Simple, yet elegant. It's that magic word—*enough.* The jumping-off point for a life of fulfillment, learning, and contributing to the welfare of the planet.

"Frugal, man." That's the cool, groovy way to say "far out" in the nineties. Surfers will talk about frugal waves. Teenage girls will talk about frugal dudes. Designers will talk about frugal fashions. Mark our words!

When we talk about saving money, we aren't talking about being cheap, making do, or being a skinflint or a tightwad. We're talking about creative frugality, a way of life where you get the maximum fulfillment for each dollar spent. And considering that you buy money with your time (the hours you spend on the job), it seems foolish to consider wasting it on stuff you don't enjoy and never use. If you are forty years old, actuarial tables indicate that you have just 329,601 hours of life energy left in your bank. That may seem like a lot now, but those hours will feel very precious at the end of your life. Spend them well now and you won't have regrets later.

In the end, this creative frugality is an expression of self-esteem. It honors the life energy you invest in your material possessions. Saving those minutes and hours of life energy through careful consuming is the ultimate in self-respect.

The following is excerpted from Your Money or Your Life. *A similar excerpt appeared in the Sept./Oct. 1992 issue of* Utne Reader.

10 SURE WAYS TO SAVE MONEY

1. Don't go shopping. If you don't "go shopping," you won't spend money. Ignore advertising that whets your appetite for stuff you don't need. More than the simple act of acquiring needed goods and services, shopping is an attempt to fill myriad needs: for socializing, for a reward, for an antidote to depression, for esteem boosting, self-assertion, and status. It obviously fails, since we have to shop so often.

2. Live within your means. Buy only what you can prudently afford, avoid debt unless you are sure you can pay it off promptly, and always have something put away. Buying on credit often results in paying three times the purchase price. This doesn't mean you have to cut up all your credit cards—just use them judiciously.

    Living within your means suggests that you wait until you have the money before you buy something. You avoid interest charges that way, and you also have a cooling-off period during which you may well discover that you don't want some of those things after all. Those who hesitate save money.

3. Take care of what you have. There is one thing we all have that we want to last a long time—our bodies. Simple attention to the proven preventive health practices will save you lots of money. Extend this principle to the upkeep of all your possessions.

4. Wear it out. What's the last item you actually wore out? Americans discard 1,455 pounds of garbage every year. Much of it is probably still usable. If it weren't for the fashion industry (and boredom), we could all enjoy the same basic wardrobe for many years. Survey your possessions. Are you simply upgrading or duplicating last year's electronic equipment, furniture, kitchenware, carpeting, and linens or are you truly in need of new ones? Think how much money you would save if you simply decided to use things even twenty percent longer.

5. Do it yourself. Can you tune your car? Fix a plumbing leak? Do your taxes? Cut your family's hair? Form your own nonprofit corporation? Basic living and survival skills can be learned through adult education classes, extension agents, workshops, and books. What you can't do, you can hire others to do, and ask them to show you how they do it.

6. Anticipate your needs. With enough planning you will not need to buy many items until they go on sale—at 20 to 50 percent off. Keep current on catalogs and flyers of national and local catalog merchandisers. Anticipating your needs also eliminates one of the biggest threats to your frugality: impulse buying.

7. Research value, quality, durability, and multiple use. *Consumer Reports* and other publications give excellent evaluations and comparisons of almost everything you might buy. Don't just be a bargain junkie and automatically buy the cheapest item available. Durability is critical for something you plan to use for the next twenty years. Multiple use is also a factor: One heavy-duty kitchen pot can (and should) replace half a dozen specialty appliances like a rice cooker, a popcorn popper, a Crockpot, a deep-fat fryer, a paella pan, and a spaghetti cooker.

8. Get it for less. There are numerous ways to hunt bargains: use mail-order discounters; comparison shop by phone; bargain with merchants.
9. Buy it used. Clothing, kitchenware, furniture—all can be found used, and you may be surprised at the high quality of much "pre-owned" merchandise. As a matter of fact, donating brand-new items to thrift stores is one way that shopaholics justify excess purchases. On the other hand, if you are a thrift-store or garage-sale addict, look at whether you are really saving money or whether you are buying items just because they're "such a bargain."
10. Stop trying to impress other people. They are probably so busy trying to impress you that they will, at best, not notice your efforts.

The ultimate way to save money: Beyond watching your pennies and watching for sales, watch your thoughts. The Buddha said that desire is the source of all suffering. It is also the source of all shopping.

Advertising doesn't make you buy stuff. Other people's expectations don't make you buy stuff. Television doesn't make you buy stuff. Your thoughts make you buy stuff.

Remember, frugality isn't deprivation. It's valuing your most precious resource—your life energy (the hours you work to earn the money you spend). It is also about loving the planet and future generations so much that you want to leave this earth in better shape than you found it.

Group study guides for use with Your Money or Your Life *are available: "Study Guide for Groups" is for use in the workplace or community and "Study Guide for Contemporary Christians" is for church groups. Each is available for $5 postpaid from New Road Map Foundation, P.O. Box 15981, Seattle, WA 98115.*

A Cheapskate Meets His Match
(and Marries Her)

🎔

Roy and Lorraine Maxson

One of the most common questions I get is "How can I get my husband/wife to be frugal?" If I had the answer to that one, I could be rich and famous! Roy and Lorraine Maxson are very fortunate in that both chose to be frugal, and they were so good at it, they started teaching others how to manage on less. This is the story of a happy frugal marriage.

> THROUGH FRUGALITY YOU CAN HAVE ANY-
> THING YOU WANT, INDEPENDENT OF HOW
> MUCH YOU MAKE OR WHAT YOU DO FOR A
> LIVING. —ROY MAXSON

Cheapskate, skinflint, tightwad. What images come to mind? Do you envision people busily counting and hoarding pennies, eating gruel and living a miserly and miserable life? We see people being smart with their money and doing things that they enjoy—investing for tomorrow, traveling, spending time with their family, owning a home, going to sporting events, and so on, endlessly.

Being frugal or living simply is not the same for everyone. Roy and I enjoy being cheap for a variety of reasons: We have fun doing a lot of different things, we like getting more for our money, we want to have a comfortable retirement, and we want to send our daughters to college without worrying about tuition. Sometimes it's just the thrill of topping each other with the great deals we find. Though some have decided to cut down on what they possess—and we don't feel compelled to own everything advertisers would have us believe we can't live without—we do enjoy having a few nice toys, like Roy's Vette or Harley and my china.

Roy and I are always on a quest to find something that we are good at and can somehow market. One day Roy watched a Phil Donahue show where his guests were cheapskates sharing their tips and talking about their newsletters. He taped it and excitedly showed it to me later that day. We realized that here was something we could do that would allow us to share our knowledge, help others, have some fun, and perhaps make some money from home. Thus *The Cheap Report* (formerly *The Cheap$kate Report*) was born.

By the time Roy and I met we had both done virtually everything we had ever wanted to do before settling down. We were ready for the next step in life—marriage and all that it entails. When we started dating, Roy had pretty well tired of spending lots of money on dates who didn't finish their meals and didn't believe in doggy bags. Luckily for him, I did.

Having been single for so long and having had boyfriends who weren't money smart, I was quite used to dating on a shoestring. Roy sometimes says that he knew I was the girl for him when I packed a substantial picnic lunch for a ski date. I knew that the meals at the slopes were way overpriced, and Roy, of course, appreciated the frugality factor. He is, after all, one of those "through the stomach to the heart" kind of guys.

It didn't take me long to realize how cheap Roy could be, and how frugal I already was. Roy's notoriety among his friends was such that they made sure he was not the last to leave the table at a restaurant for fear that the waiter would lose his or her tip. Once we both became aware of our penny-watching and quarter-diving skills, we challenged each other, and our inherent tightness became even more obvious. In the beginning Roy and I raised a lot of eyebrows. Eventually, friends and family began to see how well our tactics worked for us. They were soon asking Roy for financial advice and both of us how to get a good deal on this or that. They even began to tell us of how they had pulled a "Maxson."

Roy's advice on investing is simple. First of all, investing isn't as difficult or mysterious as many people seem to think. And yes, there is some risk in investing. However, you stand to gain more than you will lose, unless you put all your money into one fund or stock only. It doesn't take a large income to start investing. By investing anywhere from fifty dollars to a few hundred dollars a month, with the growth of the market, our investment portfolio for ourselves and the girls has grown to about $100,000 over the last nine years.

Roy likes to suggest starting with a no-load, Standard & Poor's (S&P) Index 500 mutual fund. Mutual funds offer the expertise of their managers, and a broad range of investments. Mutual funds are the bedrock of our investment portfolio. He doesn't suggest looking for a "grand slam" in net gains. Steady growth is the smartest buy in his book.

You can then branch out and create your own fund of individual stocks. What should you invest in? Don't invest in something you aren't familiar with. Peter Lynch, a well-known investor, often follows his daughters around the mall to see what they spend their money on. He then looks up the fundamentals of the company. Lynch has made excellent investments by watching, researching, and going for it.

Research isn't that difficult; it means reading, watching, and listening. Roy reads and saves articles about any investment he is interested in. He dates and saves the articles—in other words, he follows what is going on with the company before investing. One of the things he looks for is blue-chip companies with reinvestment programs, as well as companies that allow small investments and allow him to purchase shares directly from the company (saving commission fees). Another tactic is to be a "contrarian"—he buys stock in companies he's interested in when they're at their low—taking advantage of a "sale"—which means more shares for your money. Most people tend to buy stocks when they're on their upward swing.

Understanding investing is easy. You can look at magazines like *Kiplinger's* and *Money*, or the business section of your paper. If reading isn't your thing, then try listening to radio shows (check your local listings). Even TV has programming on investing on some of the cable channels (just make sure you're not watching an infomercial).

Recommended reading: Peter Lynch's *Beating the Street*; Mutual Fund Education Alliance's *Investor's Guide to Low-Cost Mutual Funds*—it describes mutual funds and gives an extensive listing of low-cost mutual funds with basic info on each ($15—MFEA, Dept. 0148, P.O. Box 419263, Kansas City, MO 64193-0148); Charles B. Carlson's *No-Load Stocks: How to Buy Your First Share and Every Share Directly from the Company*; and Bill Statton's *America's Finest Companies Directory*—over two hundred well-performing stocks that you can invest in directly from the company, with a one- or two-share minimum purchase; and *How to Become a Multimillionaire on Just $50 a Month* (1 800 779 7175 for more information).

Roy believes you don't have to invest in fancy high-tech companies to make money. Do you like Coca-Cola? or Pepsi? Then invest in them. They're both blue-chip companies, and both are expanding their markets overseas. Oil companies, such as Chevron and Exxon, have been good investments. Many blue-chip stocks have been paying dividends for over eighty years—in other words, they are solid companies.

When we got married we each had substantial debt—most of which was due to enjoying the ease of spending associated with credit cards. As Roy often says, we each lived the excess of the eighties. A portion of the debt was constituted by my student loan and the remaining mortgage on Roy's mom's house. We knew from the beginning that we wanted to buy a house and start saving for our retirement. The main task was to reduce our debt while managing to save enough for a down payment. Perseverance, planning, and economizing helped. As well as, before our children were born, two full-time paychecks.

Part of what makes our cheapskate strategy work is that we both agree to it, and we have different strengths. Roy is especially adept at researching a product and waiting until he finds the best deal. I'm patient enough to do comparison shopping for everyday expenses. While I'm particularly good at seeing the potential of something, despite its present condition, Roy is good at understanding investment jargon, following what is going on in the market, and investing our money. Our strengths provide a good financial balance.

After eight years the payoff has been two wonderful daughters through the expensive procedure of in vitro fertilization, our own home in a nice neighborhood, and enough financial independence to allow me to work part-time and Roy to run our business from home. We each have reliable cars that were nearly new or in excellent condition when we purchased them, we have paid off our initial debt, and we are about one fourth of the way toward investing for our retirement goal.

In whatever we do, we look for a good deal—whether it's grocery shopping, hiring a contractor, or buying a vehicle. The first step is *research*. This is especially important for large purchases. For example, before we actually were expecting our first child, we began to discuss what kind of vehicle we would need when a baby came. Up to that point our cars had been two-seaters or small beater economy cars that weren't well suited to a family lifestyle or safety. Roy spent a lot of time at car lots looking at, asking about, and test-driving different vehicles.

After showing me big, bigger, and biggest versions of all-purpose vehicles, we finally decided on a Ford Explorer. A brand-new one was out of the question. First of all, purchasing a brand-new vehicle is economically unsound—too much of the vehicle's value is lost the moment you drive it off the lot. Second, while we felt the Explorer would best suit our needs, the sticker price was just too high.

Roy began scouring the classifieds and auto papers for an Explorer that was no more than a year or two old and had low mileage and a good price. He found one through a private party for considerably less than a used one at a dealership would have cost. The mileage was good and the previous owner had taken good care of it. It was even still under warranty.

Since it was also more than we had ready cash for, Roy also shopped for a good loan rate. Two weeks after getting the loan, Roy found an even better rate—we changed the loan source and saved an additional $28 per month. Roy is always looking for a better interest rate on loans. If you don't want the hassle of changing lenders, tell yours about the better rate; frequently they are willing to lower the rate rather than lose your business. We plan on making the Explorer last, so Roy makes sure it gets regular oil changes, tune-ups, and other maintenance.

Not only do we look for good deals—neither of us is shy about exercising our consumer power when there is a problem, whether it's a rock in a can of soup or an incorrectly installed appliance. The result: on the small end we've received lots of coupons for free products or refund checks (which we automatically deposit to our investments), while on the larger end, we've been reimbursed or had items replaced that were ruined. One example is a washer that we purchased. The delivery people installed it. The machine worked fine. But unfortunately, the hose that goes from the washer to the drain in the wall wasn't properly connected. When the machine went through the rinse cycle, the water pressure popped the hose out of the wall, flooding the laundry room. The water ruined the linoleum in the laundry room as well as in the adjacent bathroom, and stained the carpet in the nearby hallway and den.

The reimbursement was enough to replace the linoleum with tile in both the laundry room and bathroom (at which time we discovered the toilet was seated incorrectly, which meant we had the builders repair that problem as part of the house's warranty) while the money to replace the carpet was invested. Since the carpet was new, we had it professionally cleaned and decided to save the money for replacement later down the road, after the girls have finished wreaking small-child havoc.

One of Roy's beliefs is that everything we own is for sale. Always purchase with an eye to resale. A top of the line vehicle, loaded, that is kept in mint condition, can return most of your money if you're in a pinch and need to sell it. His Harley is a good example. Some may say that a motorcycle is a motorcycle is a motorcycle. Not so with Harleys.

While other bikes rapidly lose resale value and bring just a fraction of their original price, Harleys keep appreciating. In 1987 he paid $10,000 for his Heritage Softail. Ten years later a new Harley retails for $20-21,000. His '87 has gone up in value as well—now reselling for around $14,000.

Having two young daughters, with whom we want to spend as much time as possible before their school years, means part-time work for us both. We want to be the main influence in their young lives, rather than worry about how someone else's values and caregiving skills are shaping them. This means that spending wisely is even more important right now, as we continue investing for them and ourselves on a reduced income while still taking care of day-to-day living expenses. When they have both reached school age, our plan is to work more hours while they are at school to increase our earnings and invest at our pre-child/pre-part-time rate, with at least one of us available when their school day has ended.

Raising our own children has inspired Roy and me to examine our frugal roots. Since we come from different backgrounds, the driving force behind our cheapskatery is often different. But the eventual goal for Roy and me is the same—a comfortable lifestyle now, with investments for a cushy retirement and an excellent education for our daughters.

Roy and I feel strongly about being self-sufficient. It is doubtful that by the time we retire Social Security will still be around. Its original purpose was to be supplemental income. Somewhere along the line that concept has gotten lost, and many of today's retirees rely on it as their sole source of support. Building a retirement portfolio now helps to ensure that Roy and I will be able to provide for ourselves in a manner that will make us comfortable. We also don't want to be faced with having to continue working when our girls are ready for college, so we invest for their educational needs as well.

Whether it's finding good bargains on everything from new cars to toilet paper, or deciding on where to invest for your retirement, the best way to find the answer is to ask, read, look, and listen. The solutions are out there—in the papers, in books, and in friends.

For Roy and me, being cheapskates is a continually evolving

process. We find new ways to save, set new goals as old ones are attained, and find that the needs of a growing family also mean priorities change as well. It takes effort, especially in the beginning. But the liberating feeling of not being tied to a nine-to-five job, or worrying about nonexistent job security, while seeing our investments build as we continue to enjoy ourselves, is worth the extra planning.

THE *CHEAP REPORT'S* TOP TIPS

1. Always keep a mental list of what you need—and eyes and ears open. Chances are you'll eventually find it along the side of the road, hear of someone getting rid of the very item you need, etc.
2. Take all the little refund checks, dividend checks, recycle refunds, birthday gift checks and put them in your investments instead of your checking account. Pennies, dimes, and dollars add up to a great amount when you add in interest and reinvestment.
3. The person you see in the mirror each morning, yourself, is the first and foremost person to trust as far as where and how you invest your money—no one has your best interests in mind as much as you do.
4. Keep your financial goal imprinted in your mind—constantly review what you are doing.
5. Sometimes quality is the better deal, sometimes cheap—always consider the options and shop around before you make a purchase.
6. Keep your credit clean. A clean credit history allows you to make the big purchases like a house or vehicle, or gives you access to credit when "waiting until you've saved enough" is inappropriate. While paying cash is ideal, it's often not possible for the really big things.
7. Involve the whole household in your frugality—children learn by example and are more willing to live what you are teaching if they are part of the process. Even a spendthrift mate can be partially converted—when his or her side is heard and mutual goals and compromises are made.

8. Find like-minded people. At least one or two. You'll keep each other's frugal fires lit.

9. Ignore Madison Avenue marketing, "keeping up with the Joneses" tendencies, and snide comments from others.

10. Never shop when you're hungry, tired, or rushed.

11. Use cash whenever possible.

12. Always ask for a better price. Whether it's furniture at a yard sale or services from a contractor or a retail shop, more than likely a better price can be had—especially if you have done your homework about the product, you have comparison shopped and you talk to the owner or manager.

13. Before buying brand new, look at secondhand options.

14. Look for coupons for everything—from the grocery store to two-for-one dinners to 20 percent off everything in the store.

15. Subscribe to your local paper—you'll find free stuff to do, garage sale ads, coupons, and lots of good information.

16. Keep holidays simple. Make your own gifts and set a budget.

17. Stay on top of how much things cost—groceries, cars, houses, appliances, etc. That way you'll know when something is a good deal.

18. Raise the deductibles on insurance.

19. Grow your own vegetables and fruits.

20. Always make a shopping list and stick to it.

21. Go to "happy hours" at restaurant lounges or bars. You'll get food for no more than the cost of a soda.

22. Always pay yourself first. At least five or ten percent of your gross income.

23. Never pay for groceries with a credit card.

24. Shop alone!

25. Don't buy prepared foods.

26. Don't play the lottery.

27. No TV shopping.

28. Don't shop because you're bored or have nothing else to do—take a walk, go on a picnic, visit a friend or the library, or even do some of your spring cleaning—anything to keep your money in your pocket.

A GENTLE SURVIVALIST

Laura Martin-Buhler

When Living Cheap News *was first mentioned in the media, I became acquainted with many newsletters of the "survivalist" persuasion. Most of these dealt with how to survive in a post-apocalypse world. The world they described as imminent was so horrible that I could not help but wonder why anyone would want to survive in it. Laura Martin-Buhler's* Gentle Survivalist *was a breath of fresh air. I found her definition of and approach to survivalism refreshing. I suspect you will, too.*

Gentle Survivalists are a unique collection of folks: I myself am a survivor of fallout blown downwind from the atomic bomb tests of the 1950s; a 1960s flower child; a soldier in the U.S. Army; and a student of Native American wisdom. Born naturalists, we share a high level of concern for our fellow beings, and are innately curious about our own process of individuation. Sharing a deep sense of awe and appreciation for all living things, we feel the presence of the Great Creator, like a signature, in and through all matter, inanimate as well as animate. And doesn't everyone know that great artists always sign their creations?

Prophets, Native Americans, and other inspired teachers have

41

always sensed the divine energy that flows through the earth and heavens. When the white man first came to this continent, he did not understand this reality and ignorantly assumed from outward rituals that the indigenous peoples were worshiping the sun, moon, stars, and other natural phenomena, instead of the God they themselves had been taught to worship in their own cathedrals and churches. Besides, there was greater justification for displacing the natives from their rich ancestral lands if they could be portrayed as savages without religion or scriptural knowledge of God.

From our holistic viewpoint, not only plants, animals, and humans, but even the dirt, water, and rocks, are alive and composed of spinning atomic and subatomic particles. As physicists find ever smaller particles of matter, the line between the energy of matter and the energy of our spirits grows finer and finer. Scientists know there is something beyond what they are able to detect with instrumentation, that even their smallest quarks and leptons are reacting to invisible forces. As we approach the edge of this invisible world, we begin to wonder if there is any real difference between the spiritual world and the physical world, or if they are just different manifestations of the same fundamental energy. Isn't it ironic that science has brought us to the reality that matter and spirit only differ in their mass? Essentially this means that the energy that animates our bodies is a form of rarified matter that will continue to exist, regardless of what happens to our material temple.

Einstein's genius felt the signature of God everywhere, sensing that energy, or spirit, was diffused through all things. From this perspective, everything is to some degree, spiritual. This model also implies that even our spirits have tangibility, just in such infinite fineness as to be unobservable to the human eye. In addition to saying that God does not play dice with the universe, Einstein also said, "Everyone who is seriously involved in the pursuit of science becomes convinced that a spirit is manifest in the laws of the universe—a spirit vastly superior to that of man and one in the face of which we, with our modest power, must feel humble."

Gentle Survivalists are aware that all Creation is interdependent and whenever a strand from the great web of life is torn, we all will eventually suffer the loss . . . if not immediately, then in the future by our children's children's children. To see the wanton destruction and abuse of Earth's resources brings us discomfort and eventually disease, as by-products of conspicuous consumption pollute our air, earth, and water. These dangerous imbalances motivate us to align ourselves with social and environmental movements to demand a return to natural order and safety.

As a Gentle Survivalist, I'm not a frugal penny pincher, but I do enjoy saving money on energy and consumer goods wherever possible. My focus is on learning to differentiate needs from wants. I'm aware that all I have, or ever will have, are divine gifts, to be respected and shared with those in need. Of course, I gladly receive gifts from others, but must also feel free to decline an offering if it looks to become an albatross or weighty problem.

Gentle Survival encourages responsible stewardship and loving care of resources for future generations, believing that what is best for the earth is eventually best for humanity. We are sometimes judged as a drag on the capitalistic prerogative to harvest earth's bounty or on technological advancements as we insist that public policy support and complement the natural world; do we really need bigger dams, more nuclear power plants, irradiated foods, and cloned people? Influenced by common sense, Native American wisdom, and ethical appropriateness, we are committed to applying the brakes to all gratuitous scientific technology or other manifestations of selfishness and imbalance.

As Gentle Survivalists often come from a variety of backgrounds and faiths, we may not always agree on specifics, but we do seek to cultivate patience and discover the unifying thread that connects us as brothers and sisters. These common strands reveal our divine origin as children of God with unlimited potential for good and the power to find balance and harmony, even when surrounded by chaos. We stand, as it were, in the peaceful, quiet eye of the hurricane, anchored by faith to timeless truths and wise elders.

Now, I know some of you are waiting for me to get down to basics, to show you how a Gentle Survivalist puts all these lofty ideals into practice. Well, a good place to start is with "stuff." Stuff owns you. For example: Wash it, dry it, fold it, iron it, have it cleaned, repair it, wax it, dust it, pack it, sweep it, paint it, pick it up, put it back, hang it up, file it, store it, insure it, oil it, shelve it, stack it, separate it, rearrange it, protect it, service it, recondition it, untangle it, refill it, polish it, refinish it, remodel it, or display it. Some alternatives are: refuse it in the first place, give it away, sell it, recycle it, compost it, or burn it for fuel.

Paradoxically, the things we think we own really own us, consuming our time and energy. We spend a third of our life sleeping, and much of what is left is spent waiting in lines, watching TV, or working for more things to own and take care of. Very few precious hours are left for service to others or nonmaterial pursuits that lift our minds and spirits. If you feel unfocused and pressed for time, look around your home and identify the things that demand regular attention or maintenance. Are they worth the time and energy expended on them? If not, . . . unload! Take boxes or laundry baskets from room to room, collecting the things you have no need for, or emotional attachment to, and get them *out* of the house. Do the same with the garage, sheds, barns, attics, and basements. Whew! Our devotion to junk and other material security blankets not only detours us from accomplishing our missions here on Earth, but steals time from us that could be spent with those who need and love us.

This energy-consuming, dust-collecting, space-taking stuff can be donated to others in need, taken to thrift shops, or, in the case of reading material, dropped off at libraries, hospitals, care centers, and doctors' offices. You could hold one big "final" yard sale, or clean your valuables one last time and offer them to a consignment shop. Our family has used "free gas money" from consignment shop sales to visit several national parks in California, and also to take an enchanted trip south of the border to Mexico. While others may wonder where we get enough money to go on our far-flung vacations, they could do the same, if they really wanted to. It's all a matter of priorities.

For years I worked for a very wealthy man who was a retired Indian trader. One day I found myself complaining to him about "things" and how they require so much of one's time. His response was simple and to the point, but not one I could embrace. He told me that his own solution was simply to hire someone to take care of his possessions. The choice is up to us: we can become slaves to our possessions, pay a storage company to secure them for us, hire a slave to take care of them (e.g., a housekeeper or caretaker), *or* wisely commit ourselves to a simpler, less complicated lifestyle that frees and empowers us to pursue higher goals, enjoy recreational activities, or travel.

The greatest emotional obstacle to downsizing faced by the elderly is the Depression mentality that dictates every rubber band, paper bag or screw must be saved. Recycled, yes, hoarded, no! Highly prized items such as furniture, organs, and other old valuables are tenaciously saved "for the children." If these perpetually self-sacrificing parents could see the big estate sale their children will have a month after they're gone, they would distribute their worldly goods to those who really need or want them before their final departure, sell the rest, and go on the vacation or cruise of a lifetime, while they can still do it.

In the Native American culture, there are special events called "Giveaways." These usually occur during breaks at large ceremonial dances or other community encampments for spiritual purposes. The family sponsoring the Giveaway saves for many months or even years to purchase or create the presents. These items range from vehicles, horses, blankets, and jewelry to practical household items, silverware, and small appliances. The Giveaway items are not damaged or in any way secondhand junk. Names are called, and some of those so honored are given expensive items that the givers know they need, such as a truck or horse. Others, perhaps not so needy, are given their choice of gifts that may be on a blanket or auditorium stage.

Many tribal chiefs traditionally share almost all they have to show their dedication to the welfare of their people. Becoming a chief's wife is also a selfless position, where one does not really own anything, but is simply a steward over it until the next Giveaway or knock on the door. I was once honored with a blanket at a Giveaway in Oklahoma with the Cheyenne/Arapaho People, and the warmth I received went far beyond the merely physical comfort provided by the blanket.

Since we can't take this stuff with us when we die, why not share our excess? In one tribe I lived with, if the deceased had not given away all worldly goods prior to death, they were burned near the grave after burial. What a great way to deal with the things that the owner could never give away! This practice also reinforces the idea of sharing with others while one has the opportunity of doing so . . . for we never know when it will be too late. The worst nightmare scenarios imaginable play themselves out amongst inheritors when a family member in our materialistic society dies. Just when family and friends should be drawn together in mourning and appreciation for the departed, they are torn apart by the possibility of greedy and protracted legal battles over the estate. Since we are all headed for the exit door anyway, why not spread sunshine while we can by sharing our material goods with those in need? This is the Native Way.

I agree with the great playwright Henrik Ibsen, who wrote: "Money may buy the husk of things, but not the kernel. It brings you food, but not appetite, medicine, but not health, acquaintances, but not friends, servants, but not faithfulness, days of joy, but not peace or happiness."

As mentally competent individuals, we are only truly alive in relation to our understanding and practice of eternal laws of truth, our independence from commercialism, our avoidance of conspicuous consumption and addictions, and our embracing of love, light, charity, and service. If, as the scriptures state, we are to be judged by our works and the desires of our hearts, we probably need to lighten our loads a little. Just as passengers in a hot air balloon throw heavy bags of sand overboard to rise higher in case of unforeseen obstacles, we too, need to discard ballast in the form of material attachment in order to be lifted closer to true happiness.

Remember the rich young man that Christ counseled to give all he had to the poor and to follow Him? This educated young aristocrat of the great city of Jerusalem could have become a great leader or teacher, and his name recorded and revered for all time as an example for others to follow, but instead, bound hand and foot by wealth, family position, and peer pressure, he went away sorrowing. A spiritual door had been opened for him, but he turned away.

By sharing our material blessings, we not only lighten our financial burdens but discover new opportunities for personal and spiritual growth. But getting out from under our stuff is not the only way to enhance our lives; food is another, often-overlooked component of a Gentle Survivalist's lifestyle.

Our ancestors were hunters, gatherers, fishers, and farmers. There were no pilots, cable installers, computer programmers, or telemarketers. Food was either gathered, raised, or killed fresh and served in relative purity straight from Mother Nature's pantry.

Today, most consumers live in close proximity to a large grocery store, where hunting through the butcher's cold case or deli and foraging in the produce section is about as close to the food source as they will ever get. It has been rather shrewdly observed that if all meat eaters had to slaughter their own meat, there would be mass conversion to vegetarianism. Needless to say, that may never happen, but it does show how far most of us are from the real process of food foraging and/or production.

As I wander through the orderly vegetable and fruit displays in our area's new techno-megamarket, I hear thunderclaps and the sound of soft rain as overhead misters automatically spray the vegetables. In the egg and dairy section, I am serenaded by mooing cows and clucking hens. By the meat and fish counter I hear the sounds of the ocean and the piercing cries of seagulls. In the pet section, I am reminded to buy the kitty her cat food with the plaintive meows of hungry kitties and barking dogs. These nature recordings are more than mere entertainment or novelties. I know store managers are subtly trying to manipulate my natural foraging instincts by attempting to make me feel like a self-sufficient primitive hunter/gatherer, or at least like I'm back on the farm, filling my basket with the earth's fresh bounty. The recordings seem to delight most shoppers and their children, but they do nothing but annoy me. I resent any form of sales manipulation, especially on the subliminal level.

As a child, I loved to traipse along the banks of ditches in the spring and summer to find tender asparagus stalks, fruit, and whatever else was free and edible. Today, long hikes in the canyon wetlands, desert arroyos, and mountains gain me pine gum, piñon nuts, strawberries, blueberries, currents, wild garlic, mushrooms, rosehips, juniper berries, wild peas, and other goodies. Amaranth, an ancient source of flour, husk tomatoes, and Jerusalem artichokes are also freely available in our southwestern area. Find out what your area has to offer by visiting the library or contacting other local sources such as nurseries, gardening clubs, and plant experts.

Given the opportunity, I prefer to forage for wild foods, but presently, I am surrounded with development and increasing population density, and must forage where I can. This translates into farmers' markets, roadside stands, natural food stores, and even my neighbors' gardens. Walking to the post office in my desert town of St. George, Utah, I can eat fresh apricots, plums, and fresh figs from neglected bushes and trees, and the pecans that litter the ground. The neighbor's apricots that hang over the wall are freely offered to us, as my pomegranates that hang over his side of the wall are offered to him. This year, a big pumpkin vine has turned the corner from another neighbor's yard, and is developing a huge pumpkin on our lawn, which our friends have generously acknowledged as ours.

One summer in New Mexico, I noticed a For Sale sign at a beautiful old estate. I also noticed that the trees were overburdened with ripe fruit that, except for birds and insects, would all go to waste. I wrote down the telephone number of the real estate agent, planning to ask permission to harvest the fruit. Later, when I somewhat timidly called, I was surprised at how happy the realtor was to grant us permission. Looking back, I realize a large fruit drop is unsightly and makes property look abandoned and uncared for. I learned a good lesson . . . it never hurts to ask.

Another summer, my husband and I accepted a caretaking situation from a friend who was visiting Scotland for part of the summer. The large garden she left provided many fresh offerings for a ravenous pregnant lady, requiring in return only water and the pulling of a few weeds. That experience was the beginning of a serious agricultural partnership with Mother Earth. As I write these words, our current garden is offering us more than we can eat, an excess I am able to share with others.

The following are a few more foraging tips, some of which you might want to try in your area:

1. Put a classified ad in your local paper or advertising circular offering to help harvest organic produce or to weed and tend gardens for a share of the produce. Good advice: Don't be too greedy and they might invite you back next year. This could also apply to fishing, nut gathering, or other heavily harvested food in your area.

2. For the not-so-picky forager, call your local store managers to ask if they need help getting rid of damaged produce or day-old bread and pastry.

3. An unusual source for less expensive staples is your local livestock feed store. Poultry grains and horse oats are of good quality, and much cheaper as bulk animal feed. Twenty years ago, the question of whether or not animal feed was organic might raise a few eyebrows, but today, feed store owners are old hands at dealing with folks who want their chickens and even large farm animals organically fed. You don't need to mention that you're planning to make hot cereal or oatmeal cookies with it!

4. Recently I passed the health food store Dumpster on my daily walk. I saw a big box of vitamin and herb bottles that had been discarded after an attempt to sell them for 50 percent off. It was an excellent brand, but evidently being discontinued. Later, after the store had closed for the evening, a friend drove me and my most athletic son back to the Dumpster where my son quickly hopped in and retrieved the heavy treasure box. We all felt like members of the Butch Cassidy gang after pulling out with more than $770 worth of nutritional products. (Not counting tax!) Not bad for five minutes' worth of foraging! Several friends also benefited from this Dumpster raid as the valuable supplements and herbs were spread around according to individual needs.

5. Take a hike, cutting across foothills and forest—preferably with a companion—and determine if there are any wild edibles that haven't been sprayed. Forget mushrooms unless you have been taught by someone knowledgeable in the field. In the spirit of Euell Gibbons (who wrote *Stalking the Wild Asparagus*), learn about local plants that are often considered weeds or ornamentals.

6. Be a responsible forager, asking for permission when necessary. Be kind to the trees and plants you harvest, leaving enough behind for them to regenerate or reseed. Always leave some for the wild birds and animals that depend on them for survival. Never gather so much in one area that it looks stripped or bare; move along and take a little here and a little there as the animals do.

7. Ask the elderly what wild plants they used to help them survive the Depression. You might learn more from them than you ever expected. Native elders and friends showed me how to gather healing herbs and other helpful plants. I still love the story my adopted Taos grandfather told about his family gathering big bags of marijuana for his grandmother to soak in for her arthritis. It was his way of telling me that there is a good use for everything the Creator put on earth.

8. The most overlooked area to forage is our own gardens, yards, and property. If you have a dripping faucet, brook, or spring, plant mint, watercress, or other water-loving plants that can take care of themselves. In our own yard, we have many plants that require little but water. These include catnip, two types of oregano, peppermint, rosemary, volunteer mammoth sunflowers, lamb's quarters garlic, and Echinacea augustifolia.

9. Consider becoming a modern-day Johnny Appleseed. If you are aware of ditches, reservoirs, or damp areas, try planting mammoth sunflowers, watercress, tomatillos, or other (legal) herbs, trees, or seeds and care for them periodically during their initial growing stages. A few squash or pumpkin seeds can yield enormous amounts of food. Just don't be too disappointed if fellow foragers discover and harvest your plants. True earth farmers and

caretakers know that if we could give as freely as Mother Earth, no one would ever go to bed hungry.

SIMPLE SAVING SUGGESTIONS

As you may have realized, my Gentle Survivalist philosophy is bound up with a host of ethical considerations people may not associate with plain old pragmatic frugality. Foremost among these ethics is the environment. Without the ethic to support their actions, without a deeper commitment to recycling and energy saving, the average person soon loses interest. Like a little boy who collects bottles or cans until he has enough cash to buy a bicycle, and then couldn't care less about recycling, many adults are also briefly attracted to a sparse, energy-saving lifestyle until they have achieved better cash flow, and then all cutbacks (viewed as deprivation) are put behind them as they forge ahead into consumerism and eventual debt. It is an economic given that a person's expenditures will rise to meet the level of his or her income. Few people have the self-discipline to maintain responsible stewardship over increasing wealth. Instead of saving, which few Americans do, new income is spent as soon as it is available.

Advertising, big business, bankers, and money lenders who make their living from ever-increasing consumerism encourage unconscious spending. Spending everything we have is often equated with patriotism, and we are led to believe we absolutely have to keep the economic wheels of this country greased with an ever-increasing cash flow. Actually, the opposite is true; our country suffered its greatest economic nightmare—the Great Depression—as a climax to a wild spending spree that began after World War I. Individually, we also suffer a "great depression" when we begin to feel sucked downward into the spiral of financial distress and impending bankruptcy. Facing embarrassment and credit loss, many decide that a lifestyle of simplicity and energy saving looks very good indeed . . . but only as a means of regaining their former spending level.

There are, however, many folks who hold a deeper commitment to resource stewardship based on concrete internal values. These commitments do not change as their fortunes change, for their actions are based on love of God, their fellow man, the earth, and the innumerable creatures who share this increasingly threatened, unique, blue-green planet. These folks may have great wealth, but they still recycle their trash—not to make a few bucks at the recycling center, but because it is the appropriate response. Earth caretakers, whether rich or poor, feel a spiritual connection to the earth, and act out of love, not for some other external reward. When Gentle Survivalists pick up litter or a broken bottle from a park pathway, it is only a small act of respect, but like a ripple from a rock thrown into a pool of water it expands outward to touch other ripples, so that these Earthkeepers affect all those with whom they come into contact.

Should we throw up our hands and give up when some drunken oil tanker captain devastates nature on a mind-boggling scale, seemingly erasing any contribution we can make on an individual level? Absolutely not! We have been instructed to endure to the end in goodness, or as my Taos Pueblo uncle was fond of saying, "No halfway!" Our relationship with the earth is a reflection of our relationship with the Creator, and we will not be judged by the actions of others. The earth is filled with life, and testifies to a finely tuned and engineered plan. Native Americans have always acknowledged life in all things, even in the hard flinty rocks. I subscribe to the sentiments of Chief Seattle, who said, "Will you teach your children what we have taught our children? That the Earth is our Mother? What befalls the earth befalls all the sons of earth. This we know: The earth does not belong to man, man belongs to the earth. All things are connected like the blood that unites us all. Man did not weave the web of life, he is merely a strand within it. Whatever he does to the web, he does to himself. One thing we know: our God is also your God. The earth is precious to Him and to harm the earth is to heap contempt on its Creator."

To list the many ways in which we might save money seems trite after such expansive thoughts, but the following are a few small ways we can show respect for the Creator who has allowed us the privilege of living on Mother Earth:

1. Learn to accept the seasons and changes in temperature they bring. Total dependence on heat pumps and air conditioning is not only expensive, but often unhealthy. In the summer we open the doors in early morning to cool the house, closing them when it begins to warm up. Our two-story home is cooled by one small, limping swamp cooler upstairs so we have learned to close the shutters and blinds on the side of the house receiving sunshine and use fans to circulate the air downstairs. In the winter we receive solar heat from our greenhouse and by opening shutters and blinds to the sun. We have an efficient wood-burning stove whose warmth rises to heat the upstairs, eliminating most of the need for electrical heating. Besides, cool houses are healthier—with fewer bugs, germs, particulates, and gases from fuel combustion. Each degree lower cuts fuel consumption by 3 percent.

2. Silk is the warmest natural material. Wear it next to the skin to retain warmth. It is especially good as underwear, hat, and glove linings. Wool is warm also, but the weave in silk is closer, retaining heat. Stay warm with layered clothing, socks, long johns, a sleeping cap, and a warm blanket tucked under the mattress cover. In the winter, we often sleep outside on our deck under feather comforters with balaclavas to keep our heads and faces warm. To sleep under bright twinkling winter stars and breathe fresh air is reward enough for bundling up.

3. Sleeping out in the summer is the best alternative to keeping the air conditioner on all night. Houses are made to protect us from the elements. People in arid climates always had flat roofs where they could escape the stuffiness of four walls for a wonderful and refreshing sleep. I remember an old Caddo Indian leader in Oklahoma who had his bed out on a raised platform in his yard. He was one of the last few Ghost Dancers still living and his beautiful songs of long ago drifted with a life of their own on the cool evening air.

4. In the winter, steer away from cold foods such as ice cream or iced drinks and eat warming foods from the oven, or soups to stave off the cold chill of winter. For breakfast during the cold months our

family eats blue cornmeal mush, oatmeal with raisins, buckwheat pancakes with apple sauce, refried beans with eggs, and chili. For dinner we eat hearty vegetable soups like lentil and corn chowder with homemade muffins or bread. Our favorite, "Buhler Borscht," is made of beets, beet stems and leaves, carrots, red onions, red cabbage, vegetable salt, and a dollop of sour cream. Steamed vegetables with grain dishes such as whole wheat couscous, buckwheat groats, or rice are also warmly received in wintertime. If foods are eaten fresh in their season, we'll be more in harmony with the cyclic pattern of nature, stay healthier, and save money in the process.

5. In the summer avoid too much cooked food. Heavy, dense, fiberless foods such as meat, pastry, puddings, and potatoes will only slow you down. Summer is the season for fresh fruits and vegetables of all kinds. Our family usually eats light in the summer months with watermelon, cherries, and cooling mangos high on the list of favorites. The boys make their own high-protein yogurt fruit smoothies and graze on raw vegetables and other uncooked food until evening dinner. My boys are not picky eaters, but if I bring junk food into the house, they will eat it and start *acting* like picky eaters. If you feel bad about the junk food that your family is eating, stop buying it. Once a week, cook a big pot of brown rice and one of beans, using those basics to build your healthy "fast food" meals around. One of our favorite fast food meals is corn with green chile and white corn tortillas torn in little pieces, sautéed in oil with a little water to steam and soften the tortillas. We season it with vegetable seasoning and during the summer we add yellow crooked neck squash—cheese optional.

6. Give up expensive or time-consuming addictions. If you have them, you know what they are. Every hour spent in front of the television set or video game is an hour of meditation, reflection, reading, study, hobby, or income productivity lost forever. Be selective with television viewing in order to make it a worthwhile and enjoyable experience. You might want to do a little exercise while watching your favorite programs.

7. If you think you can live without the latest timesaving gadget, you're probably right. I love my blender, though I could probably learn to live without it, but I would never trade the grinding stone and smooth, handheld pounding rock that my father gave me for the most inexpensive food processor in the world. It is part of our family and performs its work very well, crushing herbs, grinding grain or sprouted wheat, or cracking nuts perfectly with a light tap.

8. Just say "No!" to vending machines and expensive impulse buying. Bring lunch to school or work. Jog or visit libraries, museums, or parks during lunch hour instead of window shopping. If you need to lose weight, make it a high-protein powder/frozen fruit/apple juice/low-fat yogurt smoothie for lunch. Put it in a cold thermos before leaving the house in the morning and if tempted to eat some high-calorie food before lunch to raise your blood sugar level, take a few sips of your smoothie.

9. Refuse and recycle 99.99 percent of all moneymaking offers. *They will get rich . . . at your expense!* Most of us have already learned this from experience. Instead of buying magazines impulsively, read them at the library or exchange with friends, if possible.

10. Wash dark, slightly soiled clothing on the cold setting or by hand, with less soap. Dry clothes on the solar dryer (with clothespins!). If it rains, let the distilled water rinse and soften them further. Iron wrinkled clothing by hanging it on the inside of the shower door while showering. Turn nozzle away from the door so that only steam touches them.

11. We wash our hair with liquid castile soap and rinse with natural apple cider vinegar for shine. For body we use pure aloe vera gel. One of my luxuries is the occasional use of Herbal Hair Conditioner by Nature's Gate. The smell takes me right back to the mountains. Indigenous peoples have long used pounded yucca root for shampoo . . . but it is a lot of work. Apple cider vinegar with a dab of baking soda or cornmeal on a washcloth will clean a dirty or oily face.

12. Put a filled jug of water in the toilet tank to conserve water or use new advances such as clean and efficient self-composting toilets. If a faucet leaks and cannot be fixed right away, use a container to catch and save. Use cooled, mineral-rich vegetable cooking water to water thirsty houseplants. They will show their appreciation with abundant growth.

13. Keep the freezer compartment of the refrigerator filled to prevent overworking the motor, even if it means filling up empty milk jugs with water and freezing them. These ice containers also make great cooler ice blocks to keep your picnic food cold. They have the added benefit of not leaking and wetting everything in the food cooler.

14. Use hydrogen peroxide to lift bloodstains out of clothing. Wash only full loads, and have everyone change out of their good clothes and hang them up when returning from dress-up functions. Mend small tears before they become large ones. To remove oil or grease stains from soft leather, rub in dry cornmeal and brush off. Cornmeal also makes a good dry shampoo for those confined to bed.

15. Always check grocery receipts. Surveys reveal that supermarket scanners overcharge one in every ten times! Eat before grocery shopping and always make a list. Check all charges on your receipt—especially sale items—before leaving the store.

16. When renting a hotel or motel room, call the 800 number first, then the desk number. Be sure to use the telephone first, even if you are just a block away. There are often several different prices for the same room, depending on availability and other factors. Simply call first, and you'll probably be offered a better price than if you show up tired, carrying a heavy suitcase, or with cranky, sleepy children. From the lobby of an expensive Salt Lake City hotel, we called our favorite motel, an older one with tile bathrooms, big bathtubs, and an outdoor Jacuzzi, and were given a room for several dollars less, so we know this strategy really works.

17. Big business always finds ways to convert social sentiment to cold hard cash. One of the worst examples of this is fast food outlets touting their environmentally correct packaging while destroying the rainforests to raise cattle. The same can be said about most nonrenewable resource users. The concept of simplicity will no doubt suffer the same fate. Beware of any form of advertising that promises a simpler, less complicated life if you buy their product.

HE WHO HAS LITTLE AND WANTS LESS IS RICHER THAN HE WHO HAS MUCH AND WANTS MORE.

I believe, in closing, that a few words about simplicity are in order, since this book is a collection of writings by those working under the broad banner of that movement.

I believe that living a life of simplicity is far more than a frugal lifestyle of penny-pinching or finding a great bargain at a yard sale. Simplicity, in the deepest sense, means throwing every form of dark and weighty ballast overboard and, like the balloonist, rising higher toward the light. This process, while often painful, gets easier with practice. As we put priorities in order, we find that our lives are filled with service, peace, and focus.

Simplicity is never as simple as it sounds. It requires a childlike approach to the universe, a sense of awe and gratitude, the discarding of worldly desires, false pretenses, the praise of men, and every other form of vanity and excess materialism. True simplicity requires that we forgive others and stop wasting our personal energy wallowing in past hurts and injustices. To live a life of honest simplicity has implications that extend light years beyond Webster's definitions and calls forth the very best we have to offer.

Laura's newsletter, The Gentle Survivalist *is $20 per year (eleven issues). For a sample, send $1 plus a SASE to P.O. Box 4004, St. George, UT 84770.*

SAVING WITH A SENSE OF HUMOR

✺

Sherri L. Eskesen

When I first read Sherri Eskesen's 429 Ways to Save, I was on an airplane. The book has a lot of good ideas, but interspersed among the good ideas are suggestions so humorous and off-the-wall that I couldn't help laughing. I know the passengers in the surrounding seats would like to have known what was so funny about saving money. I hope they've had a chance to read her book, but if not, here's their chance to read her story.

I moved to California to escape the rat race of the Big Apple. However, I did not realize at the time that along with leaving the high pressure of the city, I would be leaving that huge city income. I thought I could continue my yuppie lifestyle in the laid-back attitude of the California sun. Boy, did I get burned!

It did not take long for me to realize that the trappings of success were just that: trappings. I had a luxury automobile with a monthly payment almost equal to my current rent payment. In the city, clothing, housing, insurance, food, and entertainment expenses were outrageous, but I did not recognize it because they were relative to the income I was generating. After relocating, I continued to live the yuppie life—without the yuppie income. When reality finally hit me, I was too far gone. I had taken cash advances on the credit card to pay the phone bill. Threatening letters and calls from the auto leasing company were stressing me out, and I couldn't even sleep at night. By this time I had two alternatives: either earn more money or spend less by simplifying my life.

The biggest step of all was not realizing that I needed more change in my pocket, but recognizing I needed a change in my attitude. All I had left was my pride, and my landlord was not accepting pride as payment for the rent.

I sat down and wrote a list of all of the things I could do to save money and live a simpler life. I did not want to deprive myself of the things that I enjoyed. I just had to learn how to do things in a way that was more cost-effective. These kinds of decisions are so personal that I cannot advise anyone on where or what they should simplify. I can only relay some situations from my own experience and let you decide the rest on your own.

First of all, you don't have to be in an urgent or desperate situation to get started. Perhaps your motivation is that dream vacation to French Polynesia or your daughter's tuition to college. By reading this book, you already show a willingness to scale down. When I look back today at the way I used to live, I'm embarrassed. I thought nothing of spending thirty dollars a day for the luxury of parking my car around the corner from a Madison Avenue client. Now I feel I'm a much better person for taking the train and contributing more money to the charity of my choice. Not only does my new choice save money but it helps the environment, and it gives me time to read on the train instead of arriving at my appointment aggravated from the freeway.

Like I said before, these are very personal lifestyle changes that each one of us should make on our own. For example, some people would never dream of taking public transportation. The thought of being there with the "masses" is just something that would never appeal to them. One of my little luxuries that I would never give up is my dog. That little critter can nibble away at my budget as well as my shoes. Vet bills, dog sitters, grooming, food, and little treats are something that I will always make room for in my budget. However, spending fifty dollars for a dinner at a fancy restaurant with friends is now a thing of the past. My friends and I can have more fun sharing a potluck, a movie, and a game of Pictionary these days without my American Express card making an appearance.

Scaling back is all a matter of attitude and priorities. When I began scaling back, I fought it every step of the way. I did not embrace the idea of having a generic product in my cupboard because I didn't think I had a choice. I thought I *had* to do it, so I did it kicking and screaming. Now I realize that I did have a choice, and I made the choice to scale back. I could have returned to the corporate rat race, but whenever I was tempted I remembered that no matter who wins the rat race, they're still a rat! If I am feeling down about the used car I am driving with the dent in the fender, I readjust my attitude by reminding myself that I am not sitting in a luxury automobile, stuck in two hours worth of traffic, just to have a luxury car. Those two hours are spent in the luxury of my home or studio . . . creating the life that I have now chosen to lead for myself.

What helped me cope with my initial attitude adjustment was humor. To me, scaling back was not about deprivation or standing in line for government surplus cheese. I used to despise the woman in the checkout line with her fistful of coupons, holding up the line for a "Price Check!" because an item was supposed to be an advertised special. But guess what, now the woman with a fistful of coupons is me! And while I appreciate the irony, I do try to rise above my crazed, coupon-crazy predecessors. I tend to shop when the market is not in rush hour so I can take my time and concentrate on my savings. Additionally, when someone stands in line behind me at the supermarket I warn them, "I have coupons," so if they are in a big hurry they can choose another checker. With the advent and implementation of the scanner, it takes such little time to deduct the coupons that I barely have enough time to read about the "Alien Baby" born to a Toledo, Ohio, woman in the *National Star Global News*. What is most likely to happen is the person in line behind me says, "No problem." Then they are amazed at my before coupon and after coupon bills and are shocked as to how much money I have taken the grocer for. Then I have a big laugh, for who doesn't like getting something for almost nothing?

Once I started making scaling back and saving money a game instead of a chore, it was not only rewarding but addictive. I started getting excited about how little I could really live on. The little ways I could save money began adding up to a big list. Before long I was sharing my list with neighbors, family, and friends. Then they started sending me their ideas and articles. I taught my mother the art of couponing and now she is a better coupon queen than I! My big list of "ways to save" was now in demand.

The *San Diego Union Tribune* got wind that these ideas were about to be published and reviewed my manuscript in the Sunday paper. Within the next few days, checks began arriving in my mailbox for the presale of *Save and Survive in a Difficult Economy: 429 Ways to Save*. What a turnaround! Not only was I saving money but I was *making* money from saving money! The response to my book convinced me that I was not the only person simplifying my life out of choice or necessity. So many people were calling and telling me that their high-pressure, high-paying job was not "worth it." Others were scaling back as a result of downsizing while some were parents who simply wanted to stay at home with their kids—where the real payoff was.

The concept of simplifying one's life was a wake-up call for Americans. Each one of us comes to simplification in our own way, in our own time, and for our own reasons. I am confident that each reader of this book can make up his or her own list of ways to save, and each list will be different. I challenge you to make one based on your own priorities. For example, I love books. Books are a source of knowledge, education, and escape for me, and I used to spend quite a bit of money on them. Now I have focused on ways to keep books in my life at little or no expense. The bookstore has a 50 percent off shelf. Garage sales and thrift stores have lots of books for almost nothing. If you really want a book for nothing, use your library. Even if the library doesn't have it, they can probably get you what you're looking for. Libraries are also my source for videos, cassettes, magazines, and CDs. With every pun intended: the library—check it out!

My point again is that you don't need to deprive yourself of luxuries to live a simplified life. Massages and facials are luxuries by just about any standard. But the way I look at it, if I can cut my grocery bill by a mere ten dollars a week by using coupons, I can get a facial every month. (Note: That's only *five* one-dollar coupons per week if your store "doubles" coupons.) Rationalize it any way you want—I think if my grocery store wants to give me a free facial every month, I'd be a fool not to take it.

Recently, fires ravaged the county in which I live. I sat on a hilltop and watched the fires rip along the canyon. As the fire continued to burn and consume the homes in its path, I began to become concerned about my own home. As the hours passed, the winds picked up and the fire raged closer and closer. It became evident that I had to evacuate my house and go. I had some time to pack and gave some thought as to which things I was going to save. Obviously, my dog and my photographs were my highest priorities. A few handheld heirlooms were next and then some practical clothes to get me through the next few days.

I evacuated my home and watched the coverage of the fires on the news all night long. As the hours went on we heard the names of the streets where my friends' homes were. The flames had taken a path right down the canyon and into my backyard. I knew everything would be gone by morning. I thought about all of the things I would have to replace, yet I was not overly concerned. In a way, it was going to be a relief and an opportunity to unclutter my life from all the things I had accumulated over the years. I was satisfied that I had everything that was important to me. My family, my friends, and my dog. If my house burned down and I had nothing, I was still the same person.

When I returned the next morning, I was shocked. The flames had stopped two hundred yards from my back door! Yes, I can say that I was relieved, but it gave me a perspective on the disproportional emphasis we put on inanimate objects. Many of us place so much importance on the things we are accumulating . . . all of which can be wiped out in an instant. The things that are really important to us are the simple ones. The emphasis in our lives should be directed toward such things as education, relationships, values, and commitments. These intangible things are the most dear to me and cannot be destroyed or consumed by mere flames.

I dropped out of a high-tech marketing career to go into a no-tech artist/writer career. I can clearly remember the day I received the signal that shouted *"Get out!"* I was attending a trade show and describing all of the exciting features and benefits of a state-of-the-art, auto configurable, 32-bit EISA adapter. The gentleman who had a keen interest in this product began speaking technobabble about his office network environment. My eyes just glazed over. It was not that I didn't follow his technobabble; the trouble was, I did. It's just that I had no interest in this stuff whatsoever. Reality hit me like a ton of silicon chips: I was not living my dream. When I was in high school my dreams were to become a veterinarian or an artist. I followed the academic path to vet school but got a job in the computer industry. Ten years on the path to "success" I realized I was not going to be a vet or an artist this way. I was not living my dreams. That's when the misery set in. I was "successful" in my computer career, but it was not what I wanted to be successful at. It was becoming more and more of a chore to get to that 8:00 A.M. meeting.

I went back to college and took Biology and Ceramics. For nearly a year now I have not had to dread an 8:00 A.M. meeting. Now by 8:00 A.M., I have had my coffee at home and already produced a few vases in my studio. I can't wait to get to "work." I "work" weekends and evenings, too. I don't consider what I do work because I love what I do and am living my passion. What does all this have to do with living a simpler life and getting back to the basics? Just ask any artist what it is like not to have a regular paycheck. You never know if the gallery will sell your work, if the agent will push your story, or if the client's check will clear the bank. Living a life that is uncomplicated by huge financial burdens gives me the freedom to create without pressure.

This type of simplified lifestyle benefits not only artists and writers. Having less "stuff" to pay for, insure, store, keep track of, fix, protect from theft, clean, or move unencumbers us all. Having less stuff allows us to focus on the top of our personal priority list, rather than someone else's.

Call this movement what you will—new frugality, voluntary simplicity, practicality, parsimony, back to basics—undoubtedly you will encounter some resistance from your family, coworkers and friends. Your kids may put up a fight when you say no to the movie theater, but they will certainly not refuse going to the video rental store for a few films. Friends may think you are being "antisocial" when you opt not to attend the weekly happy hour at the local pub. However, if you suggest a BYOB wine and cheese party at your home, they will probably think that you are an innovative entertainer, not a tightwad. At work, how about suggesting a breakfast meeting instead of lunch? Breakfast is always less expensive than lunch, and then the meeting is out of the way for the day (though, God, I hated those 8:00 A.M. meetings!).

The above examples are ways that you can scale back without depriving yourself of necessities or recreation, but every now and then a "splurge" may be in order. Treating your spouse to a well-deserved anniversary dinner and theater tickets is an example. One of my splurges may be actually buying the book new from the bookstore instead of getting it from the library. When the "splurges" are occasional, they will definitely be more deliberate and appreciated.

Below I have outlined some ways that can be helpful to you in getting back to your basics and helping you focus on a simplified way of living.

- Identify your *goal.*
- Modify your *attitude.*
- *Assess* your current living situation.
- *Restructure* your finances and lifestyle based on your *goals.*
- Gradually *implement* these changes into your daily life.

Writing down your goals on paper makes them more real. Very often an idea remains just that when it is only in your head. Go ahead, write it down, no matter how crazy you or others think it seems. Though you currently live in a high-rise apartment in a bustling city, your simplified life goal may be to live in a cabin in the Adirondacks. If living in a cabin is your goal, write it down.

It is also helpful if you share your goals with others who are supportive. Cut out a picture of your dream cabin from that issue of *Field and Stream* sitting on your desk. Tape it to the refrigerator, scan it and make it your screen saver at work, or whatever. Do something visual to remind yourself to remain focused on your goal. Friends and associates may stimulate conversation about your goal and help you achieve it. The pennant from Pepperdine posted in your cubicle may inspire an associate to say, "I have an uncle who is a professor at Pepperdine University, perhaps I can have him arrange a tour for you."

Resolving to change your attitude comes from within. Putting new thoughts to paper and then verbalizing them will help you eventually realize them. Associating yourself with peers who have similar attitudes about scaling down and living a life that is back to basics will reinforce your new attitude. Association with people having similar attitudes will give you ideas on how they are "making it." Discuss your new attitude about the new frugality with your spouse and coworkers. You may get a cynical response, but more than likely, you will stimulate a conversation that will get them started rethinking their current lifestyles as well. Who knows, you may even discover allies.

Assessing your current situation will be easy. When it comes to the financial aspect, I highly recommend keeping track of where your money goes. For three months write everything down to the penny. The easiest way to do this is with a computer program by Intuit called Quicken. With this program you can categorize all of your income and expenses in an organized and effective manner. If you are so inclined, you can even use its helpful budget feature.

You have to be honest with yourself when you assess your current situation. This stage allows you to look at your life and your finances as they are. There is no judgment to be made here. Just look at the three months as the way things now are.

The restructuring phase is where you can begin to apply judgment. This is where you look at your calendar and expenses and determine if you are spending your time and your money in ways that will help you achieve your goal.

Let's go back to the goal step for a moment. If your goal is to become a writer, how much time and money did you spend over the last three months working on it? Did you spend money on a writing workshop or on a new suit for the office? Did you spend time writing or working? Going on to the restructuring step, you will realize that the suit you have is good enough and spending a Saturday afternoon at a writers' workshop instead of Brooks Brothers is time spent helping you reach your goal and simplifying your life.

You will implement your ideas and strategies at your own pace and within your own comfort level. You will have to make a conscious effort to implement change. If you want to scale back your calendar, schedule it. If your last Saturday afternoon was spent at the mall shopping for your daughter's friend's birthday present, realize you could have spent an hour with your child making a gift (e.g., a special card with homemade movie tickets for a film festival and popcorn at your "home theater." Be creative).

Schedule a day to get back to your basics. This is so important. Block out a whole day for writing, singing, painting, working on the garden, whatever. Many of the simple things you love to do may not only save money for yourself and your family, they may generate an income. Implementation of such goals can lead to teaching a pottery class at the local community college, tutoring students with their math homework or painting murals for local businesses. The possibilities are only limited by your desires and imagination.

Getting back to basics has more than just financial rewards. A life unencumbered by keeping up with the Joneses will set you free from the rat-race snare. Below are some tips from my book, *Save and Survive in a Difficult Economy: 429 Ways to Save.*

I. *Teach a class highlighting your talents or skill.*

While I was studying at the University of California, San Diego, there were several students and adults who wanted to take some recreational classes in the craft studio. Classes and studio time was not outrageously expensive, but the extra cost was prohibitive for those on a budget. Several driven students found a way to take the class by offering their services to the Center in exchange for the class or studio time.

One such doctoral student taught beginners how to make pottery on the potter's wheel. Not only did sharing her passion with others bring her pleasure; she was paid by getting studio time and instruction from senior teachers. An adult student, continuing his post-graduate psychology work, was an amateur potter. This enterprising student/potter offered to perform the time and labor intensive work of firing the three studio kilns. This provided him with several benefits: He was able to learn about his hobby while doing, he did not have to pay for his studio time, and his kiln sitting time was well spent while he studied.

So what does this all have to say about simplifying your life? Well, for example, if your work is your passion, you are being paid for leading a fulfilling life. Doing what you love makes your life a lot less stressful and more enjoyable overall.

2. *Contact the National Foundation for Consumer Credit to obtain assistance with budgeting at 800-388-2227.*

Consumer Credit Counselors is a non-profit organization whose goal is to get people back on their feet financially. Clients are assigned a counselor who will assist in assessing their current financial situation. In my area, local branches offer workshops on budgeting and money management. Consumer Credit's forte is assisting clients who are having trouble meeting their credit card obligations.

After assessing your income and expense worksheet, an experienced counselor will work with you to determine the amount you can reasonably pay to creditors each month. After determining a rate, Consumer Credit Counselors will contact your creditors and negotiate a repayment plan for you to meet your obligations. All creditors have their own set of rules regarding acceptance of new payback plans. Most often, banks will not refuse a reasonable offer for payment. If not, their alternative is having you go bankrupt and not seeing anything back at all. You lose your credit rating and integrity; the bank loses their money.

In many cases the bank will lower or eliminate interest charges while you are continuing to make payments through Consumer Credit Counselors. In addition, they will freeze your account, which will prohibit you from going further into debt.

3. *Use Quicken or a computer-based finance tracking system.*

I cannot stress the importance of using a tracking system that shows how much money comes in and how much money goes out. More importantly, your system needs to show where the money goes. There is no magic here. It is a very simple thing to do and so very few people actually do it. So how does adding one more task of tracking money simplify your life? Tracking, managing and knowing where everything goes reduces stress and helps you plan and prioritize for the things that are important to you.

My friend says she does not like to be constrained by a budget. I think of it in opposite terms. I think of my budgeting and tracking as a tool, which allows me to do what I *want* to do with my money. Budgets aren't meant to be restrictive. They can help you allocate for what is really important to you.

4. *Don't keep up with the Joneses.*

Keeping up with what's hot for the sake of being hot is foolish. How boring life would be if we all wore the same suit, drove the same car, traveled to the same places and listened to the same music. Buck the trends and have the courage to try what's not hot. You'll save lots of money and perhaps create a new trend.

5. *Ask yourself three times "Do I really need this?" before purchasing.*

Think. Avoid the urge to impulse buy. When you buy on impulse or out of desperation it really can complicate your financial life. If you are using the spending plan that was recommended above, you will know if you **need** something because you will have planned for it. Conversely, you'll have to decide when you should buy something you hadn't planned on. For example, you know you are going to need new tires in a few months. Right now your tires are okay and you don't plan on spending $350 for new tires until winter. In a circulated flyer you see the tires you will need on sale for $275. Is this a worthwhile time to adjust the budget to save seventy-five dollars? It may very well be, and that is where a spending plan can be a very useful tool. But you must remember to ask yourself: Do you need it? Once I bought several deodorants on sale at the supermarket because it was selling at such a great price. I thought, at that price, I can live with a new brand of deodorant. When I used it, I didn't like the perfumed smell or the way it was applied. Even though it was a good price, cans of this product still sit in the medicine chest. It was a deal that was the pits!

6. *Use common cents!*

I once knew a person who would travel seven miles in his car to save two cents on a gallon of gas! Need I say more?

7. *Shop using unit pricing.*

When you are in the supermarket, hopefully shopping from a well-prepared list, you must take your time to look at unit pricing. Unit pricing tells the consumer how much you are paying per ounce, per pound or per count on a particular item. It is easy to look at the pricing and want to grab the cheapest can of coffee off the shelf. When you shop using unit pricing, that can of coffee may only have 11.5 ounces in it and cost $3.50. Another can sitting next to it on the shelf has a price of $4 and has 16 ounces in it. It doesn't take rocket science to figure out that the $4 can of coffee is actually cheaper. Most often, you don't even have to do the calculations, just look closely at the price marked on the shelf. It may take just a few seconds longer, and you may only save a few pennies . . . but big money is only lots of little pennies all piled up.

8. *Make saving chic.*

My greatest kick was going to a black-tie gala fundraiser and auction. As part of my volunteer work with the local animal center, I participate in fundraising activities. One very generous donor offered some beautiful estate jewelry to be auctioned off later in the evening. One of my jobs was to model the estate jewelry and to encourage bidding on the item. The event is always a black tie-and-limo event. I had to get just the right dress to complement the jewelry. But I was not about to pay a fortune on a dress that I would wear for one night. To the thrift shop I went. It took several trips to numerous locations before I found the right one. Twenty dollars later, I had a designer dress that was probably only worn once or twice before. What a joke it was to model $5,000 worth of jewelry in a twenty-dollar dress! I had a great time, the dress looked perfect, the animal center got their price for the jewelry and a woman walked out with some outrageous jewelry and a man walked out with $5,000 less and a tax deduction.

To top off the fun, I can probably return the dress to the shop to resell again and make back a few dollars from the same dress!

9. *Get rid of "mooch" friends.*

We all know one, a mooch. This is a person at the office who is always borrowing a few dollars at lunchtime and never pays you back or returns the favor. These people are sometimes your own family and friends. It is not always easy to get rid of mooch friends, but you don't have to be the moochee. Simply say no. Practice. Say something like, "Gee, I was hoping you could spot me this time, because I haven't had a chance to go to the ATM." Use the same line *every time.* Sooner or later, they'll get the hint. If they haven't taken the hint, buy them a copy of this book.

10. *Check out technical schools for auto repairs and salon services.*

People learning their trade at a technical school or college are often looking for auto bodies or human bodies on which to hone their skills. You must keep in mind that no warranties will be involved with the service provided, so you must be able to live with the outcome if it is less than favorable. For example, you may have a second car that you want to sell, but the fender is crunched and the paint is dingy. Often for only the price of materials, your car will look better, and you may be able to get a better price. The same holds true for beauty schools. Call several of them in your area and inquire if they have certain times for student services. Remember that you have to live with the outcome. Then again think about all of the times you spent $20 or many, many times more at the salon and hated what they did to your head!

One great deal was had by a girlfriend of mine in need of some major dental work. Even with her dental insurance, she still would have been required to pay several hundred dollars in deductible and co-payments. Through the grapevine we learned that a dentist friend was moving to this state from another area and had to take the dental boards for California. Keep in mind that he was already a dentist, and had practiced for several years, yet he had to prove his skills to the state he was relocating to. The boards consisted of both written and practical exams. After passing the written, the practical had to include actual work performed under review of his peers. My friend was an eager and willing subject. She had several crowns made and all of her dental work performed at no charge! Additionally, the exam was performed over several days so the dentist paid for her travel, hotel, and meals while she had a weekend in Los Angeles. He passed his exam and she got her teeth fixed at no charge.

11. *Don't be penny-wise and pound-foolish.*

Saving a few dollars here and there is time consuming. Very often we will go to the trouble of saving twenty-five cents on a can of peas, yet lose hundreds of dollars when shopping for a mortgage, health insurance or autos. What happens most often is that the legalities, contracts, and stipulations regarding the purchase of big-ticket items are so overwhelming that we ignore the details and sign on the bottom line. What is most crucial here is that you take the time to become an educated consumer. Ignorance is not bliss when purchasing a big-ticket item. The more competitive bids you get on insurance, mortgages and autos, the more you will learn and the better you will feel after you finally decide to make a large purchase.

If you don't have an eye for detail when shopping for big-ticket items, do yourself a favor and hire a professional or bring someone along who will help explain. Don't be afraid to ask questions, and there are no dumb questions. Even after the sales representative has explained something three times and you still don't understand the answer, wait until you have time to consult someone else. Pay a professional for their consultation, e.g., accountant or attorney. Yes, it will cost you up front, but it may save you hundreds, if not thousands of dollars later.

12. *Entertain at home.*

Entertaining at home is a great way to cut back on your expenses, yet still maintain a social life. Dining out has more hidden costs than just the price of the meal. What about driving downtown to the restaurant? There's gas, sometimes tolls, parking or valet charges. The price for a bottle of wine at a restaurant is so inflated that you could have a better quality bottle of wine at home for less cost.

Potluck is a fantastic way for friends to get together and have a few laughs without putting the burden on one cook. Have everyone bring his or her favorite dish for everyone to share. You supply the buffet table and beverages. Sit back and relax while you and your guests help themselves to the variety of food. Home is more relaxing than a restaurant any day and you don't have to tip the valet!

13. *Do it yourself or barter services from other professionals.*

Doing it yourself is probably the best deal you can get for any service with the exception of brain surgery. Just think of all the services you have paid for in a three-month period that you could have done for nothing. (Yes, it usually includes cleaning). Car wash, window wash, housekeeping, painting, manicure, and oil change to name a few. Many of them are time consuming and only you can figure what they are worth in terms of your time. Some of the do-it-yourself jobs around the house require some skills, but most home improvement stores have plenty of free, quality advice. The home store in my neighborhood even has free classes on gardening, tiling and plumbing. Best way to get these kinds of jobs done is to change your attitude about it being a job. Think of them as labors of love for your investments. You will also have the satisfaction of seeing your handiwork and accomplishing something gratifying.

If you are not the do-it-yourself type use the barter system with professionals. Know your skill or talent and offer it generously for the service you require. Don't think that your plumber will be offended if you offer your bookkeeping services. Just be sure that you work out the details of your arrangement before any work has been done on either side.

There are organizations that specialize in matching up people who barter their services. You can belong to one for a fee, but who knows?—maybe you can barter that, too.

If you would like 416 more tips from "Save and Survive in a Difficult Economy: 429 Ways to Save" send $8.59 in a check or money order made payable to:
Sherri L. Eskesen
429 Ways to Save
P.O. Box 231603
Encinitas, CA 92023-1603

AMERICA'S CHEAPEST MAN?

■

Roy Haynes

When the media first noticed me, I got a letter from Roy Haynes saying he was "the Cheapest Man in America." And I didn't even know there had been a contest! Nevertheless, after reading some of his tips, I realized he had me beat hands-down (you'll never find me separating two-ply toilet paper, for example). Here's his story, and you'll notice it's the shortest one—he's frugal with his words as well as with his money!

I am grateful to have had the opportunity to appear on several talk shows as an advocate for living within one's means and the benefits of a low-maintenance lifestyle. As a result of these appearances, and because of my unconventional approaches to saving money, the media have bestowed many monikers upon me. They have described me as everything from "an ingenious underachiever" to "the epitome of a tightwad." I have been dubbed "The Wiser Miser," "A Huge Scrooge," and my favorite, "The Solution to Pollution." It was on syndicated national TV, ("The Danny Show" in Chicago) that I was officially crowned "The King of Cheap." Royalty? It was no coincidence that when I was featured on television's "A Current Affair," the same episode aired a segment on Willie Nelson, the American icon who was dealing with a bankruptcy caused at least in part by his lavish lifestyle. I hope to give credibility and encouragement to those who share my philosophy of living with respect for thrift, self-reliance, and American hardiness.

HE WHO IS PLENTEOUS PROVIDED FOR FROM WITHIN NEEDS
BUT LITTLE FROM WITHOUT.

—GOETHE

Americans are considered the richest people on earth. If this is true, why aren't we more content? Could it be that the never-ending quest for wealth in the form of material possessions is just not the answer we're looking for? As some folks work sixty-hour weeks just to make ends meet they are stricken with ulcers and heart attacks. Is it worth it? Other runners in the weary race to accumulate goods are finding themselves abruptly laid off from the jobs they counted on for life. In these days of payoffs and layoffs far too many have built themselves prisons of plastic, one signature at a time. The irony is that consumers are working overtime and indiscriminately spending (with a "shop till you drop" attitude) on items whose production is depleting the earth's resources. Should we not reject an idea that is self-defeating and ignore the "call of the mall"? We put a price tag on a piece of furniture, but what is the value of peace of mind? It seems to me that if individuals put their lives in perspective, and place emphasis on quality time rather than bigger and shinier throwaway consumer goods, the result would be a happier, more balanced life.

SAVING IS A VERY FINE THING—ESPECIALLY WHEN YOUR
PARENTS HAVE DONE IT FOR YOU.

—WINSTON CHURCHILL

My outlook can be attributed to my very humble upbringing in one of New York's inner-city housing projects. Despite my father's dedication to hard work and long hours there were few extras my family could afford. As a teenager, while my peers were busy with their after-school activities like playing basketball and chasing girls, I was busy working part-time and gathering soda pop bottles for the deposit refund. As time progressed I learned to cut corners and to get by without indulging in any whims. Soon, I had saved enough money to be the first family member to claim proud ownership of a car. I believe this to be the beginning of my unique path from housing project to homesteader.

After barely graduating from high school I toiled at a few entry-level jobs. The positions hardly paid enough to cover my expenses: clothing, meals, and carfare. During this time both my parents passed away before either had reached retirement age or had ever taken a real vacation. And no, their deaths did not bring any capital my way. Faced with the harsh reality of being completely self-supporting in a city known for its high cost of living, I developed a talent for stretching a dollar and creating something out of nothing. Rather than buy a spool of thread I would use dental floss for sewing purposes; I clipped coupons, reused paper towels, checked all public phones and vending machines for loose change, and even separated two-ply toilet tissue to make it last longer. Every little bit helped, yet as prices skyrocketed, I was still hardly able to keep my head above water financially. This was in 1980 and Florida had a reputation as being paradise. A friend was driving south on vacation and the Sunshine State was beckoning me. Realizing taxes were lower there and there was no need to spend money on winter clothing or snow tires, I decided to go along. What did I have to lose? I sold my few possessions and took along a cassette player, a pair of dumbbells, twelve hundred dollars, and a pocket full of determination.

Shortly after arriving in Fort Lauderdale I rented a small furnished apartment near the beach. Since rent was affordable, the lack of space was well worth the sacrifice. I landed a part-time job at night, which allowed me the freedom to spend carefree days on the beach and discover the better bargains in town. I never met a buffet I didn't like!

> DISHONEST MONEY DWINDLES AWAY, BUT HE WHO GATHERS MONEY LITTLE BY LITTLE MAKES IT GROW.
> —PROVERBS 13:11

Lisa came into my life. At that time she was a down-to-earth college student majoring in finance and waitressing at night to pay her own tuition. It wasn't long before Lisa moved in, and we split the expenses. She soon adjusted to my slightly extreme ways and was no longer repulsed by reused greeting cards or receiving flower arrangements that I obtained from the local funeral homes. After all, it's the thought that counts! She even got to accept that "a night at the movies" meant staying home and watching a videotape borrowed from the library. Things were going well and Lisa got a job upon completing college. Matters were somewhat complicated when it was determined that I needed approximately five thousand dollars' worth of dental surgery. To alleviate this expense, Lisa and I decided to marry. Now I was covered under the benefits of her job's insurance policy. God bless America!

The wedding ceremony was very low-key, but some friends did splurge on rice, which they threw. Needless to say I swept it up, collected it, and cooked it with dinner the following night. At this point Lisa knew not to expect an extravagant honeymoon, but she was stunned when we boarded a cruise ship, ate the dinner the passengers were given as a Bon Voyage party, then quickly left the ship before it set sail. You guessed it—the dinner was free!

Now my part-time job was supplemented by the one day a week that I worked for a local moving and storage company. This was hard work in the Florida heat, but it paid well. Also, I often got to keep items of furniture that were in good condition but no longer wanted. Of course I sold these for additional money. Around this time Lisa began to question me. When I unplugged all electric appliances not being used was I being fanatical or fiscally responsible? When I filled my ketchup bottle at home with the handful of packets obtained at fast food restaurants, was I resourceful or ridiculous? Did the fact that I only bought clothes from clearance sales and appliances from scratch-and-dent sales make me a skinflint or a smart shopper? Whether prudent shopper or penny-pincher, my flat wallet soon turned into a fat wallet. Lisa was not 100 percent in accord with my bizarre methods of saving money, but she had to admit the end result was viable—only six months elapsed before we made a down payment on our modest home. We furnished it with "contemporary leftovers."

Our lives were virtually stress-free, but the atmosphere in south Florida was changing. Our neighbors, once laid-back, were being replaced en masse by an unsavory element: pretentious and often dishonest fortune seekers. We were not impressed, and, while they were striving to compete with the Joneses, we were satisfied to keep up with the Homer Simpsons. The novelty of the tropics was, for us, beginning to fade. An opportunity arose for Lisa to go on a business trip to Vermont. Since her employer was footing the bill, I went along. We fell in love again, this time with a state. The mountains were breathtaking, and the people seemed genuine and homespun. This was something we hadn't seen in quite a while and found very refreshing. Upon our return home we decided to relocate from the increasingly hectic lifestyle of south Florida to the uncomplicated life in Vermont.

As of this writing we have fulfilled our dream. Lisa has pursued a career in Vermont, where we now reside, and we have discovered that Vermont is indeed more than a state. It's a state of mind.

The transition has been a smooth one, and, though we are not "farmer-wannabees," we now have the back-to-basics lifestyle we longed for. Our Florida home is presently being rented out, and we still have the option to vacation there. We now reside with our dogs in our cabin on a few remote acres in the mountains. Lisa continues to be motivated to earn an income from her career while I put in less than twenty hours per week "treasure hunting" for discarded items I can fix up and sell through the classified ads or flea markets. We turn trash into cash to provide adequately for our needs without depending on any bureaucratic agencies. Most of our cooking and heating is done on our wood stove with logs that I obtained by helping a neighbor clear his land—proof that the barter system is alive in Vermont. I appreciate each day as a gift—never knowing when this life will end, and I make well-being, rather than money, my reward for working. The marketing trendsetters of Madison Avenue would not approve. While I feel no hostility to luxury, I don't feel deprived living without the latest fads and fashions. While I'm not completely opposed to complex modern-day toys like high-tech video games, at times they do seem intimidating. For me they do more to frighten than to enlighten. How comfortable will you be when tradition is broken and the next generation's children are sending their Christmas lists to Santa by e-mail?

Nowadays my strong ideals may differ from others, but personally a taste for the plain and functional serves me better than overindulgence in consumer products. I make a point to do more with less. (And I choose to reuse.)

But I must admit to a certain delight in receiving a freebie of any kind, while I remain somewhat oblivious to the blank stares I provoke when others react to my eccentricity. For me, frugality is the obvious and practical way to live as I cherish the old-fashioned principles of independence, nature, concern for family, and living simply so that others may simply live.

ROY'S TIPS

1. Use plastic hotel shower caps to cover food in the refrigerator.
2. An old garden rake with the handle removed makes an excellent rack for kitchen mugs.
3. Use six-pack plastic rings in dresser drawers or on hangers to hold socks, belts, gloves, etc.
4. Use toothpaste to clean jewelry, take stings out of insect bites, and spackle small holes in the wall.
5. Frequently overlooked tax deductions are prescription glasses, prescription contraceptives, and job searches.
6. Cotton shoulder pads taken from women's blouses and sweaters make excellent pot holders.
7. Old shower curtains can be used as tarps for painting and for covering woodpiles.
8. To seal small holes in a leaking garden hose, use the glowing point of a heated ice pick.
9. Sharpen razor blades on the striking part of a book of matches to make them last longer.

10. Do you really need cable TV, designer jeans, and optional phone services?

11. Judge your own success by how much you enjoy life.

12. You can often find secondhand baby equipment, used sporting goods, and casual clothes at thrift stores that are as good as new, but much cheaper.

13. Use sheets of fabric softener or soap wrappers placed in drawers, laundry hampers, and wastebaskets to combat mustiness.

14. When you are grocery shopping, check the bottom shelves for the best buys. Stock clerks don't like to bend, either.

15. Natural insect repellents for the home are bay leaves and slices of cucumber. Place them wherever you see insects crawling—on window sills, in cupboards, near baseboards, etc. I learned this one growing up in Brooklyn.

Here's what others are saying about my helpful hints:

"They made my day!"—Dirty Harry

"I loved them and hated them!"—Dr. Jekyll/Mr. Hyde

"I really flipped over them!"—Mary Lou Rettig

For more money-$aving tips, send $4 (whadda bargain!) to Roy Haynes—"Steals and Deals," 150 Dorset St. #147, S. Burlington, VT 05407.

How I Learned to "Live Cheap"

Larry Roth

In some respects my childhood was a very fortunate one. I was the oldest of four children, and being both imperfect and difficult to control, I suspect I was something of a disappointment to my perfectionist, controlling parents, who had remained childless for the first five years of their marriage (and probably wished they had left well enough alone). As a result, I spent a lot of my childhood with my grandmother. I don't mean to criticize my parents. I've heard horror stories from people who were reared in abusive and alcoholic homes, and I am very thankful that I did not have to cope with such horrors. This world guarantees no perfection. There are no perfect parents, and there are no perfect children. All in all, I think I wound up with a pretty good set of parents (besides, it's too late to trade them in now). And in all fairness, it is easier to be a grandparent than it is to be a parent. Grandparents have "been there, done that." And they know the world won't end if every one of life's little details is not accomplished perfectly and on time.

My grandmother had truly "been there, done that." Born in rural Sweden, she emigrated to the United States at the age of fifteen. She worked as a maid for a family first in Omaha and then in New York.

She married my grandfather, who was from Transylvania,* when she was twenty. She survived the flu during the 1918 pandemic, though she suffered a miscarriage as a result of it. She and my grandfather homesteaded in southeast Colorado after the First World War. The farming venture was not successful, though they eventually expanded their homestead to 960 debt-free acres, which they sold in the 1950s. When the Dust Bowl hit in the 1930s, they moved to Oklahoma City. My grandfather first drove streetcars and then buses. My grandmother again worked as a maid. They practiced the frugality that by then was second nature. They bought a house. Eventually my grandmother was able to stay home. They moved into the American middle class. In 1947, my grandfather bought a Packard. In 1950, he bought a second.

In 1955 my grandparents set off on a trip to Montana to visit my uncle, their younger son. They never made it. In western Kansas, in those days before seat belts and air bags, the trip came to an end in a grinding crash with a semitrailer truck. My grandfather died but, miraculously, my grandmother survived. She was severely injured, and, though she never recovered completely, she lived another nineteen years. And in those nineteen years she would teach me a lot about the history she had seen. She would teach me to question conventional wisdom, and she would teach me to avoid debt.

I can't say I was never profligate. In fact, I can't even claim that I now only spend on necessities. I eat out and I travel, for example, but I have always questioned conventional wisdom, and I have avoided debt, mortgaging my future only in the cases of homes and cars. And my practices have served me well.

In 1982, as a result of the Reagan revolution, I lost a federal job—probably the best job I ever had—here in Kansas City. I learned just how unstable a life can be if it is tied to dependence on a salary and an employer. I moved to Los Angeles without so much as a one-cent

*Transylvania is one of those unfortunate territories that has at times been part of Hungary, the Ottoman Empire, and Romania. When my grandfather emigrated, it was part of Hungary; it is now part of Romania. To further confuse matters, my grandfather was an ethnic German (though he was probably never in Germany).

raise but with new goals: become financially independent and return to Kansas City, which I had come to regard as home. Though I had always been frugal, I was now motivated by a job situation I hated. I shifted into hyperfrugality.

After two years, in 1984, I left that job and the federal government for private sector employment and higher pay in Austin, Texas. Though I remained frugal, I bought into the corporate culture a little too enthusiastically. I had to travel on my own time, meaning I would put in a full day at my desk in Austin, go to the airport, catch a red-eye, fly to (usually) Baltimore, attend a meeting, catch a red-eye back, and report to work the next day. Why did I put up with this? Well, first, the company convinced me that their stated policy ("We don't pay you to sit on an airplane") was right. Second, everyone else accepted the policy. It was only after I finished a meeting in Baltimore early one Friday and changed my reservations so that I could catch an earlier flight that I began questioning this policy. I ran into one of our vice-presidents at the Dallas airport while we both waited for our connecting flight to Austin.

"What are you doing here this time of the day?" he asked.

"I finished my meeting, and I couldn't see any sense in not catching an earlier flight," I said. I think he knew I was wondering what *he* was doing in Dallas during working hours. And I couldn't help but notice he was flying first class while I had to wedge my six-foot-seven-inch body into a coach seat. I wondered why a company that demanded so much from its workers was so lenient with its executives. Then it occurred to me that I was cramming my body into space made for a midget on my own time, and my employer took it as a given that *I owed them my time and discomfort.* Four years later, in 1988, that job, too, ended, and I wound up being transferred back to California. Though I was in a job situation that was, for a while, actually tolerable, I stuck to frugality, and I started writing as a sideline business.

The story of how *Living Cheap News* got its start has been told so often that even I don't want to hear it again, but there's a part of the story I have never before written. And I've told it only to a very few really close friends.

In late 1991 I was involved in a major proposal effort for my employer, Company L. The dollar value of this proposal exceeded a billion dollars. By a lot. My boss put me in charge of making sure the subcontractors' part of the proposal, more than half the dollar value of the whole shebang, got in on time, in a format we could use, and was analyzed, audited, massaged, and squeezed into the proposal we would send our customer.

Company L, like most major government contractors, shut down between Christmas and New Year's Day. This was no secret, but it did seem to be a source of envy with many of our government customers. To "punish" Company L for being so lenient during the holiday season, many government agencies requested that proposals be completed and submitted by the end of the year, which meant, in reality, they would have to be done a week earlier. And these government requests are *always* issued late, and they are *always* a mess. Requirements for government programs—especially billion-dollar government programs—are confusing, and the government employees who issue these requirements, bless their pointed heads, follow one rule above all others: When in doubt, put it in.

So we people in the trenches had to inspect these things, pass the "real" requirements on to our suppliers, and put the thing together in an artificially abbreviated time frame. During these proposal efforts, our jobs truly become our lives. We went full-speed seven days a week. Some people even brought sleeping bags, futons, and the like to the office and literally lived there.

A couple of days before our Christmas break of 1991, I shipped our part of the proposal out. As I was loading the packages on a dolly, I caught my shirt on something and ripped a hole in it. In spite of the loss of a good shirt, I was elated. I'd done a hell of a job, and everyone knew it.

I wound down over the Christmas holidays, and I came back to work in early 1992. One day during the first week of January, in an early-morning staff meeting, it happened. One second I was sitting there, ready for the challenges *du jour.* The next second I was somewhere else, looking down on the meeting and myself through something like a porthole. And a voice inside my head asked, "Is this *really* the way you want to spend the rest of your life?" I snapped back into my body, and I don't think anyone else in the room noticed my "momentary absence." But, once the question was in my mind, I had to admit the answer was, "No, this is *not* how I want to spend my life." But I was, after all, forty-three years old, and I didn't know how to change course.

Was my experience in that staff meeting some sort of New Age kundalini? Or should I ascribe it, as Scrooge did Marley's ghost, to "an undigested bit of beef, a blot of mustard, a crumb of cheese, a fragment of an underdone potato?" Do you believe it? For that matter, do I believe it? I have no answers. But I can tell you this: It happened on some level—in reality or in my imagination—and though it would take three more years, that experience set me on a course that would take me out of Company L and corporate America.

It would not become apparent for some months, but Company L was changing as well. It was out with the old, people-oriented management style and in with a cold new style of management that viewed employees as expendable at best and enemies of management at worst. As the working environment deteriorated I became more convinced I had to leave. I did the numbers and concluded I didn't need this foolishness anymore. I left February 3, 1995; I was completely moved into the Kansas City house five days later. I was forty-six years old and out of corporate America. My journey back to Kansas City had taken almost exactly thirteen years. The job I left paid well—more than $70,000 a year—and I would have stayed in it had it been the slightest bit enjoyable, but no amount of money was worth the toll that job was taking on my life and my mental and physical health. Within a year of my leaving, both my supervisor (at age fifty-three) and the man who took my job (at age forty-nine) had open-heart surgery. Stress does take its toll.

And a funny thing happened on my way out of corporate America. My annual income initially plunged to around $30,000, but my taxes plunged nearly 90 percent. Nearly 40 percent of my income had been going to Social Security taxes, federal income tax, and that great tax sinkhole, California. My income went down, my taxes went way down, my standard of living improved, I'm *still* able to save about a third of my income, and I don't live a deprived life. While no one can predict the future, I consider myself far more likely to live to collect a pension than either my former supervisor or the man who wound up in my old job. And I owe my lifestyle change to frugality.

Had I not been frugal I would still be at the beck and call of some insensitive idiot. I would still be in California working in a dark cubicle in a "secure" building with a poorly planned parking lot. I would be wasting countless hours and gallons of gasoline commuting to and from my townhouse. I would be counting the days until I could retire. I would be wishing my life away. What Lincoln had done for the slaves my frugality had done for me.

As for how I became financially independent, I did it the old-fashioned way. I saved my money. I bought bonds—some Treasuries, some corporates, some municipals—thus putting the money I saved to work for me. Why bonds? Well, for one thing I knew I wanted a second income—an income I could depend on if I had to (or, as actually happened, when I decided to) live without a salary. This was the best route for me, given my goals. It may or may not be best for you. I am not a financial advisor, and I am not pushing bonds as the path to financial independence for everyone, but I will take this opportunity to give you a brief primer on bonds.

A bond is a loan. You lend money to an entity—a business or a government, for example. You get interest, which is usually paid every six months, on the money you have lent. Assuming you did not pay more than the face value of the bond, and assuming the borrower does not default, your principal will be paid back when the bond matures.

There are some risks. The borrower could default. People who want to limit the possibility of this happening buy U.S. Treasury bonds, which are as safe as the government's credit (in fact, if the government's credit went down the tubes, money as we know it would have no value). Other options are highly rated corporate and municipal bonds. But a high rating is not infallible; people who lost a bundle in the Washington Public Power System default in the early 1980s held triple-A-rated bonds. Some unrated municipal bonds are quite good (a rating costs money, and some of the smaller issuers forgo the rating and pay a higher interest rate). A good source of unrated bonds is Miller and Schroeder (phone: 800-328-6122). But remember, some unrated bonds are unrated because their issuers know they could not get a good rating, so be careful with these things.

Another risk is the bond could be called, or paid off early. I had some 15 percent tax-free bonds that were like my favorite children. These were yanked away from me at their earliest call date (I did own them ten years, though). One consolation when your bonds are called is they are usually called at a price over par. In other words, they'll pay you more than face value when they pay your bonds off early.

If interest rates go up, and you have to sell your bond, you will lose money. On the other hand, if interest rates go down, the value of your bond will go up. My advice is that you never invest money in bonds if you can't just leave the money there.

A final risk is your principal may be eroded by inflation. This is an argument you will hear from the anti-bond crowd. If inflation runs at 5 percent a year, goes the argument, you'll need 63 percent more just to replace your principal at the end of ten years. Well, maybe. But keep in mind that, if you've already bought your house and you spend sensibly (especially if you buy used whenever you can), you'll find inflation a hobgoblin you can control.

If you want to take advantage of the magic of compound interest for an IRA or Keogh plan, consider Treasury Strips. These are bonds that pay no interest over their lifetime, so they sell at a healthy discount, but they compound until they mature, and you don't have to worry about reinvesting the interest.

My decision to write about frugality came in 1989, when a thirty-three-year-old friend of mine who had been going to night school for years completed her B.A. degree. She was offered a paralegal job paying $20,000 a year. At that time, a starter home in the Bay Area, where both my friend and I lived, could easily run $300,000. The starting pay for a college graduate was totally out of kilter for the area. While I was happy I had gotten my start twenty years earlier, I began calculating the price increases I had absorbed. My salary had increased five times, but my housing costs had increased more than eleven times, and a new car was six times what I paid for one in 1971. It occurred to me that Americans could not continue to survive their expenses outrunning their means for much longer. These observations prompted me to write *Living Cheap*. The timing was uncanny. The book came out just as the roaring eighties were becoming the downsizing nineties. The book didn't make me rich, but it established me as a writer. Two years later I began *Living Cheap News*.

Frugality is no longer a necessary way of life for me. But it remains my choice. There is (or was) a television ad for Suave shampoo in which a woman tells the audience she once used Suave because it was inexpensive. When she could afford to, she tried other, more expensive shampoos, but she found none of them worked better than good old cheap Suave. For me the same is true of frugality. It works for me. If I can do something cheap or expensive, why choose expensive?

Have I made financial mistakes? You bet I have! And still do. My mistakes are the sources for some of my best advice to others. I try not only to learn from my mistakes so as not to make the same mistake twice, but also to keep my readers from making the mistakes I made. No one is perfect, and mistakes are a part of life. Our approach to our mistakes must be to get over them, forgive ourselves, and recover from them.

As I grow older, every once in a while I catch an unexpected glimpse of my hands. And I see my grandmother's hands. She is gone, but her genes live on. When I debate whether to buy something, I ask myself, as she advised, "Do I really need this?" And so her ideas live on, too.

My Ten Tips

1. Never buy new if used will do. Quite often, you can find a used item for ten percent of the cost of a new item. Buying recycled things you can use is also kind to the environment.
2. Know the true value of your hard-earned dollars. So you make $50,000 a year. Really? After taxes, your fifty grand is more likely

to be around $30,000. A method for determining how much money you must earn to have a dollar to spend is, first, find your total tax rate using the following formula (use decimals—i.e., for 15 percent, write 0.15): *total tax rate* = federal tax rate + [(1.00 − federal tax rate) × state tax rate] + FICA

Then, using the following formula, get the bad news. To have $1.00 to spend, you must earn: $1.00 ÷ (1.00 − total tax rate)

3. Don't suffer from taxophobia. Remember, a tax deduction is not a rebate. If you are in the 28 percent tax bracket, you must spend $1 for every 28¢ you save in taxes. If this sounds like a good deal to you, send me $100. I'll send you $28. What the heck, I'll send you $29.
4. Remember, little things add up. If you can use a postcard instead of a letter, you'll save 12¢ in postage. Do that three times, and you've saved more than the price of mailing one first-class letter.
5. If you have time, shop garage sales and auctions. If you don't have time, shop thrift, resale, and consignment stores. You will be amazed at how much you can save and pretty soon you'll consider paying retail prices for new goods a ridiculous waste of money.
6. If you work for a company that has a newsletter that lets employees advertise items for sale, use it both to buy and sell.
7. Make your newspaper pay for itself. Clip coupons. Look for items you need in the classified ads. And shop grocery store and sale brochures (but only for items you need).
8. Practice guerrilla shopping. Combine coupons (or double coupons, if possible) with store "loss leaders." I have bought Hamburger Helper for as little as 19¢, though it usually costs me about 50¢ (I would never buy it at the regular price of $1.79). I've actually gotten money back on some items.
9. Stock up when things are on sale. I might spend $50 on groceries one week and nothing for a couple of weeks, depending on what is on sale.

10. Beware of "Wholesale Shopping Clubs." We all normally assume that if we buy in massive quantities our per unit price is less. Sometimes this is true, but sometimes it isn't. Check the per ounce prices at your neighborhood stores (where you can use coupons) as well as at Sam's and Price/Costco (which don't accept coupons).

The Best of Living Cheap News *was published in 1996 by Contemporary Books. It should be available in most major bookstores and your local library. For a free sample issue of* Living Cheap News *and a flyer on back issues and current products, sales, specials, etc. (including closeout specials on* Living Cheap *and a special price on my personal favorite,* Beating the System*), send a stamped, self-addressed long envelope to Living Cheap Press, 7232 Belleview Ave., 2nd Floor, Kansas City, MO 64114-1218. Please understand that Living Cheap Press gets a tremendous volume of mail, and requests for sample issues that do not include a stamped self-addressed envelope will receive no response.*

Zen and the Art (and Science) of Dumpster Diving

John Hoffman

John Hoffman first hit the national limelight with his book, The Art and Science of Dumpster Diving *(Loompanics, 1993), in which he told how he uses soap, shampoo, towels, bath mats, cologne, shaving cream, deodorant, watches, furniture, jewelry, and food he salvages from Dumpsters. And that was just the first page! While I have not become a Dumpster diver (yet), I will confess to having acquired much of my office furniture, some of which is very high quality, from America's curbs on garbage collection day. John's motivations, as you will discover, are political and environmental as well as economic. He has some pretty strong political beliefs, which he is not afraid to express, as you will also discover. You may not agree with everything John says, but I guarantee you'll be amazed at the things he's found in America's trash (including his wife's wedding ring)—he even wrote this article on a computer he found in—you guessed it!—a Dumpster.*

People and businesses throw away perfectly good stuff. They throw away whole mountains of clothing, furniture, household appliances, books, and even (this will shock you) yummy and usable *food* such as boxes and boxes of slightly-bruised melons, tomatoes, oranges, apples, you name it.

I retrieve this good stuff through a process known as "Dumpster diving." I use the stuff I find myself, or I sell it, give it away, barter it, or find something else to do with it. Sometimes I use the cool junk that I find to pull pranks or I use Dumpster-dived documents to embarrass the powers that be (which I loathe and oppose) such as the time I went on television and humiliated two major bank corporations with documents I found in their trash. There's all kinds of good stuff out there just *waiting* for you, with nothing standing in your way but one teeny-weeny social taboo:

Oooooh. Dirty. Unclean. Forbidden.

Sinful, even!

That's about as simple as it gets, and if I stopped right now and left you with nothing but those words and you—believing in those words—were to go out and start poking around in Dumpsters and talking to other folks who do likewise, I am certain you would figure out everything yourself without any further help from me. You might even learn a few tricks that aren't included in my book or video, because Dumpster diving is like that. Its length and breadth encompasses all the goods and services of our society and—in some ways—all the values and myths of our society as well.

My book, *The Art and Science of Dumpster Diving*, was described in *USA Today* as "an artifact of our civilization." The fact that my book shows you how to get just about anything you want or need for free is certainly an important selling point—yes, it is true (though I would prefer that local libraries purchase copies rather than people such as yourself, for whom the book was written, for whom *The Ultimate Dive* video was produced—ask not for whom it was produced, it was produced for thee!)—but, beyond those very important albeit parenthetical points, this book is a cultural milestone for our civilization.

Yes! Think about it! It has always been possible, to a degree, to eke out a living by scavenging the discards of entities more powerful than yourself. Supposedly, according to some, human beings started out in this fashion; competing with hyenas for scraps of zebra and giraffe, which had been killed by lions, smashing open bones to suck out the marrow, gnawing upon tattered chunks of hide. For eons it was like this, and thus evolution has gifted all human beings with a brain attuned to the activity of scavenging, to hunting and gathering.

Obviously, our human civilization has evolved and invented cool stuff like cars that run on petroleum; light-as-a-feather Styrofoam, which is used one time, thrown away, but lasts and lasts practically forever; and things of that nature. Even as our civilization evolved in this manner, certain human beings have always managed to survive through highly advanced forms of hunting-gathering, depending on *the discards and droppings of society itself* rather than those of the natural world. One example of this would be ragmen, who were the Dumpster divers of yore, back in the days before people threw away so much good stuff somebody had to invent trash cans the size of small automobiles just to hold all of it.

In the "urban jungle," however, many human beings have adapted their basic scavenger skills to forms of activity that involve very little actual scavenging, except in the highly abstract. Panhandling, for example. Stealing hubcaps. Writing bad checks. And, of course, running for public office to gain access to bribes, graft, free postage, etc. Human beings have basically taken their scavenger instinct and directed it toward human society itself.

Note how commonly the word "opportunity" is used in conversation and mass media. All of us, to some degree, wait for goodies ("opportunities") to fall out of a metaphorical fruit tree. We watch the modern equivalent of cave bears (Democrats or Republicans—pfffft!) snarling and fighting over some prize, and we hope when they are finished some scraps will be left for us. The goodies might be a tax break, a job promotion, a good deal on a used truck, whatever, but my point is that we are *still* scavengers and hunter-gatherers. The only major difference between modern times and 40,000 B.C. is that we hunt and gather mostly off each other instead of nature.

Still, alongside the mostly "abstract" bent of modern scavenging activity, there have always been "true" scavengers, such as ragmen and junk dealers *à la* Sanford and Son. In the Old Testament Book of Ruth we have the story of Ruth and Naomi, who kept themselves alive by scavenging the wasted portion of crops. ("And she went, and came, and gleaned in the field after the reapers, and her chance was to light upon a part of the field belonging to Boaz. . . .")

So some of us are "abstract" scavengers seeking a promotion or a bargain, and some of us are "true" scavengers literally picking through waste, throwing road kills into the trunk of their automobiles, and so on, but we are all scavengers. Seeing oneself in this light—I believe— helps to cultivate a successfully frugal attitude. Huge and powerful forces outside of our control spew forth goodies that can be used and consumed by us if we are quick and enlightened. The key is understanding that everything comes down to *taking advantage of opportunities*. You can't force the big and evil corporations to issue coupons for cheap orange juice and you can't force your neighbors to throw away their precious coupon books, but you can take advantage of opportunity when you realize the trash can in your mailroom is bursting with great coupons for orange juice.

But now we have a new milestone.

At some point (I think it was about November 1965), our civilization passed a marker upon the highway, and was totally unaware of it, except perhaps for one mad visionary who saw the radiant monolith while obtaining Dumpster-dived food for his unborn child, who was to be called John (that's me).

Suddenly it has become possible not merely to *survive* by digging around in the waste products of society, not merely to keep body loosely connected to soul, to stay alive for another hard and gritty day, but to *live like a king* upon the opulent discards of human civilization.

Consider this: If you were a barbarian king, what price would you be willing to pay for a television? How much gold, how many wagonloads of wheat would you be willing to trade for a magical device that can tell you about events in distant lands, that can sing for you, perform dramas, share the knowledge of scientists and philosophers?

Obviously, a barbarian king could be as rich as Solomon or Midas, and yet a modern television would be unattainable. Even if a television fell through a wrinkle in space/time, the poor barbarian king would have no place to plug it in, much less local television stations to provide programming. And yet modern Dumpster divers recover televisions every day.

Many decades ago, untold numbers of people died from scurvy, which is simply a lack of vitamin C, and yet modern grocery stores throw away tons of oranges simply because the fruits are a little bruised, a little discolored.

In the 1930s my mother—a little seven-year-old girl who barely spoke English, whose primary language was Czech—cried as though her heart would break while two country schoolteachers cut a pair of boots from her frozen feet. She had missed her bus and walked the several miles to school. My mother wasn't crying in pain, she was crying for the boots. But today I can go out and find truckloads of boots, shoes, socks, sweaters. Sometimes people throw away stuff without opening the damned package. That's how I got my underwear . . . except for the brown ones, which were issued to me by the Army.

So we have this milestone. Is it a good thing or a bad thing? Speaking as a foaming-at-the-mouth revolutionary who looks forward to the day these United States will disintegrate in a fashion similar to the Soviet Union, I think it's a really *good* thing. I have labored to promote Dumpster diving through every available medium because I want people to withdraw from the system and *not* buy goods, *not* pay taxes, *not* cut down more trees to make more furniture when all the furniture you need can be obtained near your local college the week those wasteful little frat pukes go home for vacation. I am very hopeful that, when people take my advice to *dive Dumpsters* in order to find perfectly good stuff *for free* instead of paying money for everything, then those individuals will commit their extra time, money, and energy to activities they truly enjoy and desire, such as art and activism.

Because I dive in Dumpsters, I have extra energy (time, money, resources) to pursue activities besides work, work, work. This is not to say that I don't work. As a matter of fact, I have a job in the health care industry. I am a member of a union and have full medical and dental benefits and vacation days, sick days, and a job that is not terribly hard, pays me well, and which I find stimulating. I'm always happy to promote Dumpster diving on television, radio, newspaper, whatever, and I adore my friends in the media (especially the friend who brought me to Hollywood twice and rode me and my wife around in a fancy limo—all because I'm the Lord God Master Dumpster Diver of the Universe and all that), but, to a degree, my message has been slightly distorted by the media. Inspiration and urban legend status have resulted, so I'm not complaining, mind you, but I have *never* advocated trying to find *everything* in Dumpsters *or* quitting your job to become a Dumpster diver. Quitting your job to make a living doing your own thing, well, that's different, and that's something I work upon each and every moment, more or less.

Dumpster diving has allowed me the surplus time and energy to become a well-known civil rights activist in Seattle and to write a novel called *Love Children of the Cartoon Cult*, which is in the hands of a major Madison Avenue publisher at this moment. My wife plays the viola in an orchestra instead of, for example, working another job to make ends meet.

But, invariably, the media have scanned my simple message and then babbled stupid things like: HERE'S THE WACKY GUY WHO FINDS EVERYTHING IN DUMPSTERS! HE WON'T BUY THINGS! HE EVEN FOUND HIS WIFE'S DIAMOND WEDDING RING!

Well, O.K., it's true about the ring. It was at the bottom of a discarded garment bag, with some trinkets and junk, and now my wife wears it as her wedding ring. But I have always tried to encourage people to *supplement* basic simple frugality with the incredible bounty found in Dumpsters, not to live off Dumpsters entirely. If me and my wife hadn't *found* her a wedding ring, I would have gotten around to buying her one.

Eventually.

I do buy some stuff at yard sales. And I do go to the grocery stores and snap up the "loss leaders" and hunt through bargain bins for stuff like clam chowder at ten cents a can. (I still can't believe it. I bought every last can, all twenty-four of them!) I use coupons and I even find ways to get major corporations to send me stuff in the mail for free. All of these tricks and more are mentioned in *The Art and Science of Dumpster Diving*. I call my lifestyle a "totally integrated lifestyle of frugality," which simply means that one thing leads very naturally to another. Sometimes I find myself in the middle of a "chain reaction" that goes on for days, weeks, months, or years as goods are traded for favors that lead to more goods, more value, more fun.

The other people in this book have so much wisdom to share, and you should listen to them—though, personally, I think that whatever does not kill me *strengthens* me and therefore I'm damn sure not going to stop eating meat, drinking soda pop, or watching television. Also, when I hear advice about using aluminum foil a dozen times or making your own French fries from whole potatoes, I have to stop myself from snickering, slightly. People who are moving throw away rolls of aluminum foil—they throw away unopened bags of sugar, working blenders, china cups, super-dooper knives you can order on television, everything—as well as stuff from their freezer like, well, plastic bags of frozen French fries.

Personally, I recycle and get the maximum use out of things, but one of my main problems is trying to use up all the stuff I find before it goes bad. I don't use the same Christmas card over and over, as some have suggested. Why should I? I find boxes of new Christmas cards all the time, more than I could ever use. I think patching shoes is great—for those people who don't have unlimited amounts of Dumpster-dived shoes.

I do, however, become *pissed off* that people don't recycle even when the appropriate bins and barrels are placed right in front of their stupid face and they still can't tell the difference between brown, clear, or green glass because they're *idiots*—but I personally regard my wasteful society from a viewpoint of a big, happy, trash-digging dog.

People just keep throwing away stuff.

And that's good for me. *Woof!*

Dumpster diving is not the beginning and end of a more simple, enjoyable, and affordable lifestyle, but it can be the keystone or cornerstone of such a lifestyle. Different individual circumstances will determine how well you can take advantage of the "waste stream" and fish out valuables. But, along with Dumpster diving, you will want to consider the approaches of the other contributors to this book. Personally, I've eaten lots of road kill, though I couldn't write the book on the subject. I use coupons, too, but only for those items I haven't found *behind* the store in abundance. So I embrace many other approaches, to some degree, and you can do the same thing.

My book and its basic attitude (some might say attitude *problem*) may represent the "lunatic fringe" of the simplicity movement. But that's just fine with me. Today's lunatic is tomorrow's prophet and visionary.

So you wanna be a Dumpster diver, huh? Or maybe you're already a Dumpster diver, but—since Dumpster divers are wise, observant, and open to things—you won't mind a few more tips and some weird trash diving tales.

Well, Dumpsters are mostly full of garbage. Simple, huh? What we're doing is mining—seeking nuggets or veins of goodies amid a relatively worthless "urban ore" of, well, crap. Along the way there will be cheap thrills and many titillating insights about the human condition. (But you need to be careful about those kinds of things because, after all, this is how Ted Bundy got started and a Dumpster diver needs to be like, well, a lotus, which derives its nourishment from the reeking muck of the swamp but rises above the muck, pure and white. Ohhhmmm!)

First, you need the right equipment: boots or shoes with thick soles that are going to protect your feet, since alleys are full of broken glass. Durable, nondescript clothing. Keep in mind that we aren't going to be burning this clothing afterward. I tell you, if you aren't the kind of person who would be willing to pull a hundred-dollar bill out of a pile of dung with his or her *bare hands,* you might as well *give up right now* and go back to *saving aluminum foil* and *making your own French fries.* Dumpster divers are the kind of people who know darn well you can cut the moldy colony off a piece of cheese and eat the rest of the cheese. It isn't going to kill you, damn it!

Sorry, sorry, sorry. . . .

I get so worked up sometimes.

I mean, really, it's that life-in-a-plastic bubble yuppie attitude about dirt and germs that assures me a steady supply of slightly dinged and damaged goodies, but all the same, this attitude makes me rant. The modern Dumpster—Behold!—was designed specifically for the purpose of keeping vermin *out.* Dumpsters are *not* full of rats and cockroaches. Sometimes there might be some flies or bees (especially around sweet, sticky grocery produce) but, generally, Dumpsters have lids and they are emptied pretty regularly. Despite the title of my book, I seldom have to "dive" inside a Dumpster. I mostly reach into Dumpsters just as you might reach into the trunk of a car. I do not get all covered with slop and filth. So, as I was saying, generally you can wear stuff like jeans and sweatshirts. I try to avoid distinctive words and logos upon my Dumpster clothing.

A kind of "ninja effect" occurs when you dive Dumpsters. Not only will people ignore you, not only will they pretend you don't exist, but often they will make a sincere effort *to erase you from their minds.* In all the years I've been diving Dumpsters I have never, never been arrested and only rarely have I been scolded or confronted. (Now, I have been arrested for other stuff, like sitting down in front of a bulldozer, plus that whole "aggravated criminal property destruction" thing at Seattle's Municipal Building, but, well, that's a different story.) Still, I try to cultivate a nondescript appearance while Dumpster diving, so somebody can't say, "Well, it was a green-haired guy wearing a bright blue shirt with a clown on it and the words 'Back Jack.' And camo pants, winter pattern. Yes, very strange, that guy . . ."

Now, about gloves. Truthfully, I don't always wear gloves. You just don't enjoy the same sensitivity and dexterity you experience with bare flesh. Something comes between you and the thing you desire to get at and experience, an unnatural barrier. It's like showering with a raincoat! But you should wear gloves, and I bet you will. After a while (you don't believe this, but it's true), most Dumpster divers give up on the gloves.

Flashlights are essential for night diving, but keep the light below the rim of the Dumpster to avoid disturbing people. *Never* use a lighter or matches to illuminate a Dumpster. It is good to have a "dive stick" to poke around with and pull things toward you. This allows you to avoid climbing into supersized Dumpsters to go after booty. Dive sticks are simply broom handles, mop handles, or similar pieces of wood with a nail or screw in one end, hook fashion. You don't always want a stick, especially in new territory where people who are not used to your activities might become paranoid, wondering what you're doing in an alley with a pair of black leather gloves and a *big stick with a nail in it.*

So use your stick in familiar territory, where people are used to seeing you.

Next, you need a bag to carry off your loot. A duffel bag is good, or a small gym bag. I like to carry a pocketknife to slice bags open, but of course you can tear open trash bags with your hands. A vehicle is extremely valuable for reaching a big territory and carrying off large items. A bike with a large basket is good, too. Hardcore Dumpster diving certainly requires a vehicle, preferably a truck. Keep a few empty boxes in your vehicle. Not only are boxes handy for containing your booty, but they provide an alibi. Repeat with me the number one Dumpster diving excuse:

I was just looking for some boxes . . . !

Now, you may be starting to think Dumpster diving is going to take a lot of time and effort. Not so! I suggest people Dumpster dive on their way to work or returning home. A nice evening walk is good for you and pleasant, too. Wouldn't it be more fun if you found a six-foot halogen house lamp needing nothing more than a new bulb? A funky old *Whole Earth Catalog?* Or maybe an extremely private and personal videotape of people doing it?

(Hey, different strokes for different folks.)

Personally, I'll Dumpster dive almost any time. Once, I retrieved a perfectly good apple and bologna sandwich from a trash can inside the King County Jail. Hey, a revolutionary needs to keep up his strength. My point is that whenever I see trash, rubbish, garbage, waste, discards—call the wonderful stuff what you will—my instinct is to poke around and see if there is any good stuff. All the same, the point of Dumpster diving is to *save* your energy, not to *waste* your energy. So it's good to develop a route near your home, or in areas you frequent. The trick is to find Dumpsters that consistently pay off, and keep hitting those Dumpsters. From time to time you may find yourself in a new area, or you may want to recheck some old Dumpsters to see if anything has changed. The trick, really, is just to be out there looking around.

Seek and ye shall find!

Watch out for glass and gooey messes. Avoid getting into Dumpsters where you might step on sharp stuff, where heavy articles can shift and hurt you, or where you could, well, *get caught.*

In some cities, Dumpster diving is against the law. Then again, in some cities sitting on the sidewalk is against the law, which has never kept me from planting my ass on the asphalt right in front of the boys in blue and then letting my half dozen lawyers straighten out the resulting mess. For free. In all of my writings about saving money I've never mentioned that, in an average year, I receive tens of thousands of dollars' worth of free legal help. Also, if you were to calculate the value of "free advertising" I receive in the mass media, the monetary figure would be—I am quite sure—in the millions.

But my point was that "anti-Dumpster-diving" laws are about as important as jaywalking laws or sidewalk-sitting laws in those rare cities where they exist on the books. Just don't slam lids loudly, don't make a big mess, and avoid confrontation. Usually you won't have any problems. If you are confronted by a police officer, be very polite and try to worm out of things. The police seem to have different attitudes in different cities. In El Paso, for example, the cops will almost hold the lid open for you while you rummage. In Seattle, though, most Dumpsters are locked, and our city's finest have major attitude problems, which is why some of my friends and I confronted them in September 1994 on Broadway, which resulted in tear gas, televised beatings, a lawsuit by three innocent bystanders for false arrest, mistreatment, and blah blah blah during what came to be called the Broadway Police Riot.

So check local laws.

Obey all laws!

Cross on the green, not in between.

If a cop knocks out one of your teeth, put it under your pillow and the Tooth Fairy will give you some money. If that doesn't work, I suggest you sue the blue bastards, because filing a complaint won't get you anywhere and the city prosecutor won't do diddly-squat to his corrupt cop buddies, that's for sure. No justice, no peace, *screw* the police.

Um, where was I?

In cities like Seattle, which have Dumpster locks, most of the time all the locks can be opened with one key. So even slackers working lowly McJobs often have access to "garbage keys" which will open up virtually every Dumpster in the entire metropolis. What, I ask you, is the point of locking up all those Dumpsters?

Keep them open, I say!

Watch out for heavy lids suspended in the upright position. I wouldn't want you to get smashed in the head for no political gain or purpose whatsoever.

And, for goodness' sake, *don't drink and dive.*

You may be asking yourself, "What the heck made this guy John Hoffman this way? How can I become more like him? Would he consider letting me have his baby through artificial insemination?"

As I hinted, I was something of a Dumpster diver before I was ever born. In fact, I'm a third-generation Dumpster diver. My parents did it, and my grandmother on my mother's side took it up late in life. So that's how I got myself three generations for promotional purposes, and not merely two.

Improvise, I say. Adapt and overcome. The meek shall inherit the earth, but Dumpster divers will accessorize it.

My parents gave me a foundation of knowledge about Dumpster diving and simple instinctive frugality. In my highly acclaimed book I merely wrote down what I had learned from my wise and wonderful parents, telling my own anecdotes and adding my own opinions about certain things. All my life I watched as my mother provided down-on-their-luck neighbors with food, clothing, and useful household items through sheer brilliance. Nowadays, seeing me utterly consumed with various political activities, people have been known to ask me if my parents were "radicals."

And I've answered like this:

"My mother ran a free store out of her garage, and she set up a food distribution network for grocery store produce we salvaged. When I worked at a Godfather's Pizza, each night I would bring home a couple gallons of leftover sauce and about twenty pounds of pizza dough, in addition to the usual surplus pizzas. My mother set up a pizza route to redistribute the wealth. Does that make my mother a radical? a political activist? or what?"

In 1979, while I was in sixth grade, I became intensely politically minded and conscious of issues like class, oppression, distribution of resources, et cetera. It happened like this. The area of Minnesota where I grew up was prime farmland and situated amid beautiful lakes frequented by tourists. Then a nasty power company got a wild hair up its rich collective ass to run a high-voltage power line across all that beautiful land in order to bring distant city dwellers electricity generated by a filthy nuclear power plant somewhere in the Dakotas. The fact the farmers didn't want a power line running across their nice land made no damned difference. Working hand-in-hand with the government, the power company was going to pay the farmers what they (the power company) felt their land was worth and erect a high-voltage power line that would have God only knew what health effects on people and animals.

(Leukemia, as it turned out. Mysterious tumors in cattle and brain cancer in humans, stuff like that. But all the evidence of ill health effects was considered "anecdotal" back in 1979, which basically means only "wacky" scientists believed in that stuff, not mainstream scientists. But now it is generally accepted that a high-voltage power line can have ill effects on organisms living in close proximity. So when somebody tries to tell you that the CIA smuggled cocaine into Los Angeles, that the Reagan campaign team made a deal to keep the hostages in Iran, and so forth and so forth, don't just dismiss it as wild conspiracy stuff. . . .)

The farmers rose up in righteous fury. In the middle of the night they bombed, shot, unbolted, and did many other brilliant deconstructionist artsy things to the hated power lines. They marched on the state capitol building and, upon a cherrywood table, when nobody was looking, one of them whipped out a pocketknife and carved the words WE WANT A MORATORIUM NOW.

Which meant, of course, *stop the freaking power line.*

I remember how one day I was riding the bus to school and, as I went past the Holiday Inn, I saw more police cars than I had ever, ever, ever seen in my life all in one place—and I still have yet to see so many, all in one place. These were Minnesota State Patrol cars sent to oppose and arrest my neighbors for defending their own land against a faceless, evil corporation.

I had a notion that I knew who some of these deconstructionist farmers were, even though my parents never expressed their thoughts about the matter in front of me. The way I saw things, the American Revolution was taking place around me—and if I didn't do something drastic, run off and volunteer, somehow, the whole thing would be over before I could get a piece of the fight. My father had fired on Japanese planes at Pearl Harbor and later participated in the violent and bloody "island hopping" campaign. He was the toughest, bravest male human being in the whole world, and I wanted to be just like him, which appeared utterly impossible.

So I told my father of the plan I had hatched to go off at night and try to find one of the revolutionary farmers, to join them in their struggle against the evil power line. To my amazement, sadness, and profound disappointment, my father was opposed to my little scheme. So I cried my eyes out and threw a temper tantrum, naturally. But, at some point, my father made my understand that, even though this regional conflict with the power line appeared to be the greatest and most important struggle I would witness in my life, there would in fact be *other* great struggles to follow. My duty was to learn all I could and prepare for those unknown future struggles that would involve the whole nation, not merely one small region of Minnesota.

And this is exactly what I have done my whole life. I have studied and prepared for revolutionary struggle. At some point I obtained a degree in English, *magna cum laude,* and at some point (September 1990),

I joined the United States Army, and all along the way I've sought out every form of knowledge that might arm me in the Great Unknown Struggle to Come, Whatever It Is. This was how I became familiar with arcane books of the lunatic fringe marketed by my publisher, Loompanics Unlimited. But I would have to say it was my wonderful wife, Tina, who helped me to understand my Dumpster diving skills were something I needed to share with the world at large.

It was my senior year in college, and my father had been struggling with an awful cancer throughout his body. I have no doubt the cancer was helped along by all the little pieces of scrap metal he carried in his spinal column after being damn near killed by a Japanese grenade. But let's just keep the record straight and note that even World War II was a fight between powerful elitist interests and not between, for example, American and Japanese foot soldiers, which is to say *cannon fodder*.

Oh, excuse me. There I go again.

Before my father died, I tried to offer him some hospital food. He started to eat but couldn't finish.

"I can't eat," he whispered.

"Have just a little more," I urged.

This type of exchange went on for a little while, until finally I said, "Well, then, do you mind if I have this stuff?"

He didn't mind.

So I ate what turned out to be his last meal.

"I hope," I told him after a while, "that I haven't been a terrible disappointment to you. I mean, I'm not very good at sports. I've never even learned how to dribble a basketball and here you played the Harlem Globetrotters—"

"No!" he whispered. "You're not."

"I . . ." I asked, timidly, "I haven't disappointed you?"

(I wasn't mentioning the stuff about hanging out with anarchists and advocating the overthrow of the United States government and all that.)

"No," he whispered. "Not at all. I'm very proud of you."

After a while I said, "I think I'm going to marry Tina."

"Marry her!" he agreed, nodding weakly. "Yes."

When my father died, Tina came home with me. It was a bitterly cold night, but, for some crazy reason, my brother and I pulled up the car and went Dumpster diving behind Ollie's Warehouse Foods. After all, Ollie's was on our route home and tribal custom decreed that we were to hit the Dumpsters when passing by. Even the death of our patriarch wasn't going to stand in the way of that ritual. (Tina had, of course, seen the fruits of my Dumpster diving in our college town. On our first "Dumpster date" we found an antique Pepsi-Cola sign, which an appraiser once valued at $300.)

So there we were behind Ollie's Warehouse Foods, which was the third or fourth successively larger building Ollie's had occupied in my lifetime, growing fatter and fatter selling overpriced food to struggling families. It had been at the very first Ollie's that my father, Willard, had Dumpster dived back in November 1965 to provide food for his new wife and unborn child. Though the pickings at this grocery store Dumpster were usually rich, on that cold night the wasted goodies were particularly obscene. While my steady girlfriend watched, amazed, my brother, Jed (a.k.a. "Slash"), and I heaved and panted and loaded our old beater of a car with delicious booty, our breath visible in the air.

"I wish Dad was here!" Jed laughed. "Oh, he'd be happy."

Later that night, Tina helped my mother to process the goodies. My mother told Tina all kinds of Dumpster diving stories and tales of the Great Depression.

"John," said my future wife, "you should write a book about Dumpster diving."

"Who," I laughed, "is going to buy such a book? Anybody who would want a book like that would be too cheap to buy a book like that, so consequently no publisher is going to publish it, so what's the point of writing it?"

But the idea took hold to such a degree that I snapped a picture of Tina and my brother in front of that night's Dumpster goodies. Later, as fate would have it, that photo "sold" my publisher on the concept of a Dumpster diving book. In fact, they literally retrieved the manuscript for *The Art and Science of Dumpster Diving* from their trash container! This has become a kind of urban myth in publishing circles.

At this point, I don't need to tell you that I think my departed father is playing a role in all of this, or at least having a heck of a laugh.

For the past several years, I have been intensely involved with the problems and issues of cities, as you might expect of an urban hunter-gatherer. Once I helped take over an abandoned building with a group of modern "homesteaders," until Seattle's finest came and threw us out. I was one of the "initiators" of the October 22 Coalition to Stop Police Brutality. But my dream is to obtain a farm like the farm where I grew up, with hogs to eat grocery store and restaurant discards and a constant garage sale of Dumpster-dived goodies to bring in extra cash. But I will approach these matters with the intense political consciousness that I first developed during the Power Line Uprising of 1979. My farm will be a haven for radicals of every type and stripe, a launching point for one (nonviolent) attack after another upon the system, which—as I think I may already have mentioned—I oppose and despise.

So now I would like to share ten Dumpster diving "hot spots" with you, places where you can find just about everything you could possibly want or need, assuming your needs are simple.

John's Dumpster Diving "Top Ten"

1. Thy neighbor's Dumpster. All the items produced by our society are eventually in people's homes and then eventually in people's Dumpsters. Since most Dumpster divers are looking for things to outfit their homes, other people's homes are the first place to go looking. Apartment complexes are best, the sort of places where twenty or thirty people use two or three Dumpsters. At any given moment, one of the people is probably cleaning out a closet or moving. (Just before the beginning of the month is a good time to look, because that's when people move.) Believe it or not, you generally find more stuff from the middle class than from rich people. Besides clothing—which is frequently discarded in boxes, sometimes even in dry-cleaning bags!—you might turn up dishes,

appliances, books, school supplies, and, of course, intensely personal and interesting documents.

Some people who Dumpster dive claim they don't snoop. I think they are lying. Looking through pictures and letters is the best part of residential diving. But I don't recommend, for example, trying to utilize discarded checks, credit cards, house keys, and the like. I've been known to push the line (just a little) when I find things like discarded gift certificates and, frankly, if I found something incriminating to a politician—any politician, Democrat or Republican, it doesn't matter—I would use that stuff any way I could in a white hot second.

2. Rude food, Dude. Many of you will draw the line at eating something from the trash (or you *think* you'll always draw that line, just like you think you'll always wear gloves and you'll always politely disagree with folks who throw bottles at police officers) but for those of you who want to maintain your personal "welfare as you know it," the eating of food every day is essential regardless of whether you can actually afford it. So I've taken all the many dozen pages of "food stuff" in my book and condensed it into one compact bouillon cube of distilled advice.

Grocery store produce is plentiful, not disgusting and one store can keep dozens of divers supplied year after year. Expired milk is not always sour and can be quickly consumed or used for making other goodies, like yippie yogurt (see Abbie Hoffman's *Steal This Book*). Plus too much other good stuff at grocery stores to list here, but have fun with those unlabeled "mystery cans!"

Bakeries throw away tons of two-day-old goodies that, if stale, can be revived with a few drops of water and a quick spin through the microwave. Fast food places keep food on the "hot rack" and then throw it out. Everybody knows about pizza places that do this kind of thing, but just about all other fast food places do it as well. The problem is finding the "good stuff" amid all the other "crap and scrap" from the diners. So places that only, or almost only, deliver are good places to dive. Remember when dealing with prepared foods to cook the hell out of it to avoid getting a disease.

Candy stores are, well, a sweet deal, and stale candy is better than no candy at all. Movie theaters throw away nice clean giant garbage bags of popcorn, but you can't really stay alive eating popcorn.

Once again, residential folks throw away much perfectly good food. Freezer stuff, when moving. Boxes and cans, never opened. After Halloween, I like to get discarded pumpkins that have never been carved (sometimes they've been Magic Markered) and extract the seeds for roasting, the rest of the pumpkin for pie or eating squash-style.

I'd like to leave you with the thought that all fruits and veggies grow in dirt fertilized with, well, eons of dung. The eating of animals and animal products is and always has been a bloody, ugly, nasty business that most folks have been isolated from through middlemen who kill and slay upon their behalf. Our government regulates exactly how many insect parts and rat droppings are allowed in food and, well, there's angry men filled with spit who work in food service and other things you shouldn't think about every minute of the day but, rather, keep trying to do that pure-minded lotus thing. (Ohhhmmm!) So, really, extracting a nice clean wax-paper box full of slightly imperfect apples from the confines of a Dumpster is no big deal.

All the same, just remember this: Never, *never* use somebody's discarded turkey baster to baste your turkey.

Always get a new turkey baster.

3. Bookstores! When books do not sell, booksellers send the covers back to the publisher and discard the coverless paperbacks by the thousands. When books are discounted down to one-fourth of their original price, they are thrown away because booksellers would rather discard the world's greatest literature than drop their price down to fifty cents, rummage sale–style. Likewise, you can find magazines in this manner. Don't forget to flip through the magazines you don't feel like reading and find stuff like coupons for free packs of cigarettes, though.

4. Discount stores throw away lots of nice clean boxes, so they're a good place to go when you really *are* looking for boxes. You can

also find all kinds of slightly imperfect household goodies. Once, for example, I found two dozen dysfunctional lawn sprinklers. There's lots of cool "tinkering stuff" available in these places as well as things like in-store displays (giant Easter bunnies, etc.), which are fun and funky, especially for kids.

5. Toy and novelty stores. My mother used to say the difference between new toys and old broken toys was about forty-eight hours. Toys, like baby clothes, are obscenely expensive. But even little cars that "won't go no more" are still fun in the sandpile. When I told my father that my toy machine gun wouldn't go "pop pop pop" anymore, he told me that I should run up to my imaginary enemy and vigorously smash him over the head with my dysfunctional weapon, just like a real soldier would.

6. College areas. I've mentioned that college kids are wasteful and, as you might have guessed, one of the best times to dive is the end of a semester, especially in the spring. But colleges themselves have lots of interesting facilities—the kitchen, the library, the academic offices—where you can locate all kinds of good stuff. In other nations, revolutions frequently begin on college campuses, but in the United States these institutions of higher learning are more like a refuge for impractical individuals who can't—after all these years—make their socks match, and so starry-eyed high school graduates think their profs are *geniuses* because, you know, Einstein couldn't make his socks match, either.

   There are books here. Lots of books. If you like books, you will certainly like campus Dumpster diving. Everywhere you go on a campus there are books, books, books. And software. Nowadays you find lots of software on a campus.

7. Florist shops are a great place to obtain flowers. Not all the flowers you find are wilted, either, especially around holidays like Valentine's Day when huge amounts of flowers are discarded as surplus. Once I found 144 red roses and gave them all to the same girl. I was a freshman. She was a senior.

   The rest is college legend.

8. Photocopy centers. These places throw away lots of useful office supplies. Once, for example, I found almost fifty thousand envelopes with a glue that didn't quite seal. These were "parchment-style" envelopes—very nice—and I used the two thousand-count boxes I salvaged for about a year. If I had that dream farm of mine instead of an apartment, I'd have all of them stored and I'd be using them until the year 2000. Some friends of mine took another few thousand envelopes off my hands, but I couldn't salvage everything.

In fact, the sheer surplus of Dumpster material is one reason that I wrote my book. There's just too much, and we Dumpster divers need to increase by about tenfold just to get a grip on all the wasted wealth.

Oh, there's also lots of interesting information flowing through a neighborhood copy center, and many of these "imperfect" copies end up in the trash. You might be shocked to find out what kinds of things your neighbors are doing.

9. Photo processing centers. As these places make copies of photos, they continuously adjust the light and color. Many "imperfect" photos are discarded in big, slightly damp and chemically smelly bags. Following this tip, my loyal fans from all over America have sent me pictures of naked women which—in some cases—the customer himself or herself hasn't seen because the images were too "hot" and the store won't "handle" stuff like that.

(Thanks, all of you! Now can somebody explain to me why beautiful women will bare their breasts for even the most scruffy-looking individual with a Harley-Davidson motorcycle?)

Often you will find pictures of people that you know. Dumpster diving is like having a person hand you photos from his or her album, saying, "Here's a shot of me with my niece. Oh, here's an ugly shot of me in the hospital. Here's a shot of me in a string bikini. Here's me exposing one breast. . . ."

10. Private organizations. If you are fiercely opposed to a particular organization, its Dumpster is a quick and simple place to find information. As long as this book will be some kind of historical

record, I'd like to relate a truly incredible incident involving this kind of activity and, in a sense, the promotion efforts for *The Art and Science of Dumpster Diving.*

In my book, I related an anecdote in which an ideologically motivated young woman managed to use Dumpster-dived information to harass—and eventually shut down—a clinic that was involved in abortions. (I should point out that I myself was not involved in this incident, but rather I was describing something that I had heard about firsthand.) Now then, while promoting *The Art and Science of Dumpster Diving* I found myself on a Chrisssstian radio station down in Texas, talking to a guy who personally knew Randall Terry of Operation Rescue.

Me? I was trying to promote my book. As Saint Paul said, I am all things to all men. So, when talking to tabloids I emphasize the "weird and wacky" aspect of my book. When I communicate with investigative news folks, I discuss *that* particular angle. Some have approached the book as literature, which is nice, since I'm certainly trying to build upon *The Art and Science of Dumpster Diving* and publish more works. So I'm happy to discuss the book as a work of literature that can be read purely for amusement and enlightenment. In any case, on that radio show I was happy to discuss the ideologically motivated young woman, whom I called Mrs. Spooner, whose life revolved around stopping and opposing abortion. I was discussing the woman in an *objective* sense. I was *not* taking a position either way. For my wife and me, a baby would be a gift from God, but I also like to be able to associate with both liberal and conservative friends, to have dinner at their homes without plates being hurled—

"This is incredible, folks!" cried the Christian radio guy who personally knew Randall Terry. "Tune in after the commercial and we will discuss how these Dumpster-diving methods might lead to *a whole new season of rescue!"*

What, I wondered, had I gotten myself into? Why, it was only a week or two before that I had been doing that nice anarchist radio show out of Detroit. Somehow I had always promoted

Dumpster diving *in general* without aligning myself with the far left or the far right, because—believe it or not, folks—I don't care what sort of political opinion a person might have. I simply want to put all these free discarded goodies in people's hands.

About a week after my Texas radio show, a woman went into Dr. Jack Kevorkian's trash and pulled out an incriminating document. This woman, according to the media, had been associated with Operation Rescue.

Coincidence? I think not.

Lots of crazy stuff has happened since my publisher rescued *The Art and Science of Dumpster Diving* from the circular file. My book (and new video) have reached a lot of people, changing their perceptions and behavior. Oddly enough, the media reports associated with my works have reached many, many more people than the works themselves have. In the process, to some degree, I've helped to transform our civilization. I believe that my wife and I will soon be blessed with children, and in our lifetime (certainly in *their* lifetime) we will witness sea and space colonies. And another revolution upon the North American continent.

Dealing in a *sensible* fashion with our resources is something we must do if we want clean air and water, if we want to avoid killing all the other life on the planet. But I think people are more likely to engage in Dumpster diving because *they can get all kinds of good stuff for free.* Thus, by motivating people to act in their simple short-term interest, I've aided the long-term interest of the planet and the human race.

What is *extreme* today is *mainstream* tomorrow.

Thanks, and remember, JUST DIVE IT!

The Art and Science of Dumpster Diving can be ordered from Loompanics Unlimited, P.O. Box 1197, Port Townsend, WA 98368 for $12.95 plus $4 postage and handling. You will get the mind-bending, gene-altering, paradigm-shifting 150-page Loompanics book catalog free with your order.

The video, The Ultimate Dive, *can be ordered for $20, postage and handling included, from Suzanne Girot, P.O. Box 269, Felton, CA 95018.*

Once again, please save your money and ask your local library to obtain these materials. Always be nice to librarians. They made me what I am today. (My eternal gratitude to that nice hometown librarian who warned me to use a fake name when requesting subversive materials through interlibrary loan.)

There is a Web site "inspired by" The Art and Science of Dumpster Diving. *Check it out at http://www.mindport.net/~stephen/dumpster.html.*

What Happens When a Missouri Grandmother Gets Riled

Cal-A-Co

I first read about Cal-A-Co in a now-defunct newsletter. Her story intrigued me. She insists on anonymity, and, in her own modest, persistent, and insistent way, she is making a difference in the world of recycling. Here is her story, and don't ask me to reveal any more about her. My lips are sealed.

QUESTION: What did the trash barge that went to sea, the trash train that came to the Midwest, and the Earth Summit at Rio have in common?

ANSWER: They riled up a mid-Missouri grandmother!

That hearty soul entered this life in 1937. She grew up in a one-room house next to the county dump in a rural Michigan community of immigrants. She saw firsthand how successful the simple life could be.

After high school graduation she moved to the town where she was to attend college. The college was in its second year of coeducation. There were no dormitory accommodations for women. Local residents made their own arrangements to house out-of-town female students. Within a month's time this seventeen-year-old moved from a home without running water or modern appliances to the $150,000 house of a doctor's family. It was 1954. She soon realized that the foundation for happiness was not grounded in the accumulation of dollars.

It was with the mindset of a pioneer that she married and moved to her first Missouri home, an eight-by-ten-foot smokehouse with a lean-to room added to each long side. Soon three children completed this family. At times their only income was from the husband's job— driving a school bus for sixty dollars per month. Rent took thirty of that.

They lived in the country. A garden was essential. So was a cooperative spirit. There was no money for gas to run to town for rummage sales or thrift shops. They received hand-me-downs.

That same vivid imagination that once made tiny tops from the gears of discarded alarm clocks now conjured up little dresses from men's white shirts, house slippers from worn blue jeans, and curtains from the edges of torn bed sheets. Strawberries and fresh butter on toast made a shortcake substitute. Double-yolk turkey eggs, culled from a hatchery, were boiled, added to milk gravy, and served on toast. Every smidgen of food was used. Small amounts of leftovers were added to oatmeal cookie dough or blended and added to chili. Day-old bread was served a hundred different ways. The home thrived on inconspicuous reuse.

Fast-forward twenty-five years. All three children had moved to homes of their own. This now single mother had gone back to college and become employed in a job that required travel. Work assignments varied from five days to six weeks. She traveled throughout eastern U.S.A. She discovered, regardless of geographic location, two constants: overflowing Dumpsters and people wanting to improve their lifestyle.

In spite of verbal reprimands for too much camaraderie with her employees, this supervisor continued to empathize and share ideas with workers who were trying to make ends meet on a very limited income.

As she moved from one city to another she kept in touch with these employees by letter, often sharing frugal ideas contributed by new workers. Much of the same information was going to several different people. It soon became obvious that a newsletter was an acceptable alternative to writing so many individual letters.

It was 1992, the year of the Earth Summit in Rio. Closer to home, this was also the year the trash train from New York was trying to unload its fetid cargo in Missouri. A few years earlier, a barge loaded with New York trash had been sent on a similar mission. This wasn't the first time New York had exported its garbage. When the trash returned to New York people were assigned the unpleasant task of sorting through the stinking refuse to remove recyclable items in an effort to reduce the volume.

What a dilemma! A more practical solution seemed to be to encourage each individual to take another look at any item he or she was about to discard. *Another Look . . .* that word combination seemed so appropriate for this endeavor. The next step was to find a trademark and patent attorney to verify that the name was available.

Meanwhile, a thrift newsletter from Washington state mentioned the possibility of this reuse newsletter's publication and supplied an address. Inquiries quickly came from across the country, inspiring our hero to go ahead with her plans. At the time the name *Another Look* had not been cleared so the first issues went out with only the slogan, "An Adventure in Grassroots Ingenuity." Eventually "Another Look Unlimited" was registered and the newsletter is now distributed as *Another Look Unlimited® News.* But most of us only get to design one newsletter in our lives, and she couldn't let this one go with just a name. Thoughts next turned to designing a logo. Smokey the Bear had accomplished so much in preventing forest fires; a teddy bear seemed appropriate for the Keeper of Landfills. After all, landfills are the final resting places of so many teddy bears. The teddy bear (a female) needed a name, too. That was easily solved by using the first letters of Callaway and Cole, two counties in central Missouri. With thoughts of a whole empire being built around this character, her new alter ego, "Cal-A-Co" could not do it alone. Remembering that frogs and butterflies develop another look during their normal life cycles, a frog (Footz) and a butterfly (Flutter) were included in the logo's unending circle.

Thought was also given to the importance of keeping the identity of the force behind the newsletter confidential. Her salary was crucial to getting the publication up and running, and her employer might not approve of her endeavor. While Cal-A-Co did the actual writing, friends at home carried the bulk of the load by copying, assembling, and mailing the newsletter.

In 1995 the editor changed employers. She is currently working as a nanny for her son and his wife. This frees up time for more writing and keeps her in one location where, with the help of friends, she has been able to do nontraditional recycling by gathering rummage sale and thrift shop surplus, which is then sorted and distributed to appropriate charities. This has also allowed time for her to attend a local clown school. Her clown's name? N. Vira Myntyl, of course!

Another Look Unlimited® *News* is a no-frills newsletter that encourages "working together to find, trade, use and sell reusable discards thereby reducing the flow to landfills while improving quality of life on this planet."

Before I proceed, I must offer three notes of caution:

- Ask before removing anything.
- Clean up any nails or debris you generate.
- In today's world of hazardous waste, Dumpster diving is considered to be dangerous. Please get discards before they reach the Dumpster.

FINDING REUSABLE MATERIAL

Wherever there is activity, discards appear, and removal is expensive. The result of a survey printed in the December/January 1993 issue of *Workbench* magazine reports that thirty-two percent of 2,400 builders surveyed said they spend between $250 and $500 on disposal costs for *each house.*

Furniture factories discard the scrap from quality lumber because it is not cost-effective to work with these individual pieces. Remember, too, any older television, radio, and phonograph cabinets you may run across are made of real wood, not pressed particle board. Glass installation businesses are an excellent source of rough lumber. Sure, their business is glass, but the crates used for shipping glass are made of quality wood. Other sources of reusable materials are bedspread and coat factories, which discard scrap batting suitable for filling stuffed toys and pillows.

TRADING REUSABLE MATERIAL

Get acquainted with the crafters in your area. If your civic club is looking for an educational project, suggest a craft exchange meeting where ideas, patterns, and supplies can be exchanged.

Communicate your needs to friends, relatives, and pen pals in other locations. Large pine cones are plentiful in the South. Tiny tamarack cones can be found in Michigan. Kansas has craft-quality wheat straw.

After (or instead of) a rummage sale, organize a clothing exchange. Some churches have weekly clothing giveaways.

USING REUSABLE MATERIAL

Take another look at each item about to be discarded. Visualize a garment as fabric pieces for a quilt or doll clothes. Can shelves be added to that TV cabinet to make it a storage cabinet? Use any plastic bottle (not just detergent bottles) as a base for a doll. A two-liter bottle, with the bottom cut out, fits perfectly over a one-pound round oatmeal container. These dolls make inexpensive treasure keepers for little girls.

Small tile samples are great for refrigerator magnets. They can be removed from the display card by putting them in a mircowave for a minute or two. Pull the tile off while glue is hot, then use a glue gun to apply a small magnet to the back.

Not all reuse projects are small. Bill Reeks[a] had a mess of broken trees after a storm. This inspired him to harvest the lumber by building a single-operator sawmill, from scrap. It cost less than one hundred dollars for parts, including the large band-saw blade. People from every state and some foreign countries have contacted him seeking information on how he built it.

One crafter had small dabs of water-based paint in several colors. Masking tape was used to mark off rock shapes on a concrete wall. Three children mixed their choice of colors and painted a very attractive "rock" wall.

SELLING REUSABLE MATERIAL

Check out your local shops and craft malls. In addition to these, many communities have craft fairs on a regular basis. Check into remote stocking at distant malls. Sell from your own yard if zoning allows. One woman used scrap two-by-fours to make wishing wells. During one Mother's Day season she sold one hundred. Little League teams, 4H clubs, or other groups can raise funds by selling birdhouses, wind chimes, quilts, etc. made of discards.

MAKING REUSE A BUSINESS

Some individuals have developed businesses through the prudent use of discards. Phil Donley[b] used to get paid to haul off discarded privacy fences near Dallas, Texas. It didn't take him long to recognize this weathered lumber was a desirable commodity. He uses the good boards to build furniture with the popular Southwestern-weathered look. He also builds birdhouses, garden benches and numerous other outdoor projects that he markets through his Texas Weathered Wood business.

The Workin' Man,[c] another small business, provides a service that helps keep used clothing out of landfills. It acquires clothes that have been removed from rental service because of minor spots or stains. Once these have been industrially cleaned and, when necessary, repaired, they are sold as work clothes.

COMMUNITY REUSE PROJECTS

Reusing discards is not limited to individuals. Lincoln County, Missouri, was faced with a mess after the 1993 flood. Instead of the traditional dozing/landfill approach, they opted to hire thirty people to dismantle the damaged houses. Salvaged materials were sold at discount prices. Landfill space was spared. While traditional demolition costs about $3,500 per house, Lincoln County's average was $2,400 per house. Much of that went to pay the thirty workers, most of whom were homeless as a result of the flood.

In Tutwiler, Mississippi[d], a group of quilters converts scrap fabric into quilts that are sold nationwide. Each quilter gets a percentage of the profit.

A woman in Pennsylvania began making what she called Ugly Quilts[e] from any available fabric. Other people became involved. In one year over five thousand of these quilts were distributed to homeless people.

The Madison, Wisconsin, area has a project known as Wheels for Winners.[f] In 1992 a local resident noticed discarded bicycles next to Dumpsters. Now volunteers refurbish donated bicycles. Any child in Dane County who wants a bicycle can earn one through community service.

Exodus Ministry of Missouri[g] is a nonprofit organization helping ex-offenders. They rely heavily on donated goods from the public to furnish and maintain the four apartments where their clients live. Response has been so good that they have opened a thrift store where surplus items are sold to the public at very low prices.

The ReUse Center[h] in the Phillips neighborhood of Minneapolis, Minnesota, is another example of what can be done when a community recognizes the value of "discards." Opened October 14, 1995, the ReUse Center was developed as a positive, pride-building alternative to a garbage site. Its retail store focuses on harvesting valuable building material from the waste stream by way of donations, which it sells at low cost. To date, an estimated fifty tons of usable material have been diverted. Profits from sales go toward paying "livable" not "minimum" wages to staff. Classes on repair are also offered through the center.

REUSE READING

Books and other publications with emphasis on reuse, instead of traditional recycling, are making their appearance. In their book, *Choose to*

Reuse,[i] coauthors Nikki and David Goldbeck define "reuse" as the re-utilization of an item in its current form. Recycling, in contrast, refers to the processing of goods to provide raw materials for new products. *Choose to Reuse* is a valuable resource for individuals as well as businesses.

In *Building with Junk and Other Good Stuff,*[j] author Jim Broadstreet shows how to incorporate discarded lumber, concrete, pipe, floor coverings, windows, doors, light fixtures, and appliances into your building project. Information on finding and storing the stuff is also given.

Farm Show[k] is a bimonthly, tabloid-size publication with no advertisements. Each issue is chock-full of articles and pictures of projects made from discarded items. Most articles include the name and address where the author/inventor can be contacted. *Farm Show* began publication in 1977. It has over 175,000 subscribers in the U.S.A., Canada, and other countries. The $13.95 annual subscription rate (for the United States) includes a copy of the 434-page "World's First Encyclopedia of Best Ideas Born in Farm Workshops," featuring over 1,200 inventions and ideas.

One is not likely to read about the Earth Summit at Rio these days, but Cal-A-Co & Friends and *Another Look Unlimited®* continue to gain recognition nationally. Through such publicity they have become acquainted with JoAnn Cayce's Charities,[l] of Thornton, Arkansas. For Christmas 1996, JoAnn distributed gift bags to six hundred needy children in her area. Cal-A-Co & Friends helped by bringing surplus clothing and toys from central Missouri. They have also shipped craft and sewing supplies, clothing, and housewares to the Widow's Mite Mission[m] near Flagstaff, Arizona. Several local charities and various individuals in several states have benefited from Cal-A-Co & Friends' distribution of discards.

Cal-A-Co & Friends are always interested in hearing of others who are benefiting from the use of discards. Through *Another Look Unlimited® News* a nationwide network is being developed. Interested people can learn from each other, and people in an area of need can benefit from items discarded in areas of plenty. The profit from newsletter subscriptions helps pay for transfer of reusable supplies.

"Together We Can Brighten the Country Where We 'R'"

1. There are many uses for thermal drapes (with the "rubber" coating on back).

   Carry an old one in your vehicle for a ground cover when you're changing a tire.

   Put one under your sleeping bag when you're camping to keep your body heat from going into the ground.

   Cut one to the appropriate size, and use it under the draw sheet on a patient's bed.

   Place one between blankets for added warmth. This is especially beneficial if you lose your power.

   Use one to recover a crib mattress. Cut and sew pieces together to form a snug-fitting envelope about 5 inches longer than the mattress. Slip it over the mattress so seams are at the sides. Fold each end as if it were a package and hand stitch in place. This is water repellent, and tough enough to last for years.

2. Adjustable ironing boards can serve many uses.

   Place one next to a patient's bed to keep supplies handy.

   Adjust one to the correct height for children to do their finger painting on—then take it outdoors and hose it down afterward.

   Set one up at window sill level so "Kitty" or "Doggie" or your whole menagerie can see out.

   At the proper height one will make a good portable typing or sewing table.

Cal-A-Co's newsletter, Another Look Unlimited® News, *is published monthly by Cal-A-Co & Friends, Dept L, P.O. Box 220, Holts Summit, MO 65043. Subscription rates are: U.S.A.—$15/year; Canada—$20(U.S.)/year. For a sample, send $1 plus a large (#10) SASE.*

a. Bill Reeks, Lum-BR-Jak Sawmill, 7104 B U.S. Hwy. #231 North, Cromwell, KY 42332. Phone: 502-274-3361.

b. Phil Donley, Texas Weathered Wood, 10805 County Rd. 2426, Terrell, TX 75160. Phone 214-524-5716.

c. The Workin' Man, P.O. Box 14024, Nashville, TN 37214. Phone: 615-883-1530.

d. Tutwiler Clinic Outreach, Quilts P.O. Box 462, Tutwiler, MS 38963. Phone: 601-345- 8393.

e. Quilt Group, Box 1049 RR 1, Hop Bottom, PA 18824.

f. Wheels for Winners, 4547 W. Beltline Hwy., Madison, WI 53711. Phone: 608-273-4787.

g. Exodus, P.O. Box 104313, Jefferson City, MO 65110-4313. Phone: 573-761-7493.

h. The ReUse Center, 2216 E. Lake St., Minneapolis, MN 55407. Phone: 612-724-2608.

i. *Choose to Reuse*, Ceres Press, P.O. Box 87, Woodstock, NY 12498. Phone: 914-679-5573.

j. *Building with Junk*, Loompanics Unlimited, P.O. Box 1197, Port Townsend, WA 98368.

k. Farm Show, P.O. Box 1029, Lakeview, MN 55044.

l. JoAnn Cayce Charities, P.O. Box 38, Thornton, AR 71766-0038.

m. Jim and Betsy Frazier, The Widow's Mite Mission, HC33 Box 432, Flagstaff, AZ 86004.

A QUEST FOR PARADISE

✺

William Seavey

A few years ago, Money *magazine recommended moving to a less expensive part of the country as a way to trim expenses.* Money *was way behind William Seavey, who not only advocated such relocations, but founded the Greener Pastures Institute to assist those looking for a cheaper "Eden" in the western United States. Recent demographics have documented a tremendous outflow of people from California to other western states, primarily Oregon, Washington, Nevada, Idaho, Colorado, Arizona, and Montana. Ironically, though he has assisted many other "Eden-seekers," he has yet to find his own permanent pastoral paradise. Although he has suffered some unfortunate financial and personal reversals in the past couple of years, at age fifty he is still young, and things now seem to be looking up for him. His book,* Moving to Small Town America *(Dearborn Financial, 1996), has had some very favorable reviews, and he has recently relocated the Greener Pastures Institute. But I'll let him tell you his story.*

I grew up in Southern California, a region that today comprises fourteen or so million people and more than one hundred individual cities. The area went through a terrific boom after World War II, as GI's moved there, started families, and fueled housing construction. An ambient climate and a burgeoning aerospace manufacturing economy ensured that millions would move there. The lure of Hollywood was, I suppose, another big factor in these migrations.

Today Southern California has, in the estimation of many, lost much of its original allure. A survey in the *Los Angeles Times* in the late 1980s clearly revealed how great a slide residents felt the region had undergone in the previous fifteen years. But the worst was yet to come.

In 1991 I predicted in my newsletter, *Greener Pastures Gazette*, that housing values would fall by up to fifty percent. They very nearly did just that in many areas of Los Angeles. Smog officials resigned en masse—in effect admitting that they had thrown up their hands over the problem of America's worst air. And thousands of illegal immigrants, crossing the Mexican border since the 1970s and before, were creating an expensive welfare state. The roots of our nation's angst and anger about illegal aliens was being born right in the Los Angeles area.

My disenchantment with Southern California dates back to the mid-1960s. I chose to go to school at the University of Iowa, turning down acceptances at both USC and UCLA. For two summers I worked in a national park, quite happy to be breathing clean air and communing with nature. Even back then I never liked freeway driving and thought Southern Californians in general were not very neighborly and too materialistic. It didn't occur to me at the time to try to help Southern Californians and other fed-up urbanites change their lives by moving to smaller towns in rural areas, particularly in the West, but after living in Eugene, Oregon, for six years in the mid-1970s and Bend, Oregon, in the early 1980s, the stage was set. Oddly, it took moves out of both of those rather idyllic places for me to begin to formulate a true understanding of the implications of modern urban life not just for Americans but for others in a rapidly urbanizing world (in 1900 there were only eleven cities with a population of one million or more in the world; there are now more than three hundred).

Let's take a look at this urban dilemma. The Gold Rush of the 1840s, the opening up of the Louisiana Territory, the Homestead Act of 1862, and other factors encouraged thousands of Easterners—already overly urbanized—to head west. Like people who move today, many left families and friends on a quest for elusive opportunity.

To leave the big city and some if not many of its comforts necessitates a line of thinking that clearly is a component of the "new simplicity movement." Living in places where countryside abounds but employers are few forces one to become more self-reliant and resourceful. Those who bring money to the country may not modify their urban lifestyles to a great degree except as pressured by their neighbors, but those who do not have much money to start with may well have a challenge or set of challenges indeed. If the city breeds a gallery of rigid nine-to-five lifestyles, the countryside is often something of an open slate or empty palette on which to fashion a simpler life (which, unfortunately, *can* get complex in the early goings).

For example, urbanites talk of choices, but in some respects, it is the countryside that offers them. The kind of home you may build or rent in rural areas is infinitely more versatile than those generally available in cities. There are log cabins, old farmhouses, mobile homes, straw bale homes, underground homes, and A-frames as well as the more usual frame and brick houses. Many of today's rural areas, I might add, do not suffer from lack of entertainment thanks to satellite and cable TV or shopping thanks to the ubiquitous Wal-Marts and all sorts of trendy specialty stores. And, if you don't like what's available where you live, the city may well be a short, inexpensive commuter flight away.

It's common wisdom that your dollar simply stretches further in the country, and that's especially good news to those who are shrewd enough to earn the same pay there via telecommuting, the Internet, or investments and Social Security. A study in *American Demographics* reported that rural residents spent an average of $3,000 to $4,000 less annually than urban residents. Housing is where the big savings are. In many areas, the money you have to use as a down payment in the city can buy or build a small castle in the country because land, material, and labor costs—if there are fewer unions, which there generally are—are usually much cheaper.

But country living is not for everyone, and, as I hinted before, a simpler life can get complicated fast. I live in the country today, but not in a town or state that was my first or even my second choice. I lived in Bend, Oregon, for six years. At that time the population was 17,000. My family and I did rather well there. But six months into our stay in Bend, we almost went back to Los Angeles. (I've written this story in an as-yet-unpublished book, *Oregon or Bust.*) Then I got work as a night janitor for the local city government, and I started a resume-writing service that did well. It was in Bend, after we had lived there more than two years, that the Greener Pastures Institute, my relocation service, was born.

Still, we had our ups and downs. Bend wasn't the boomtown it is today. Winters were cold and income was down. One winter we had to pack all of our things and move to Reno, Nevada. We found work there, but when we returned to Bend I found only a succession of dead-end, part-time jobs. My wife did not work, and I was wearing myself out. After a flue fire and a car accident on icy roads, we left Bend for good, and it was back to Los Angeles.

A few years later, my second wife and I, living in a small suburb of Los Angeles, bought an RV and spent several months scouring the Pacific Northwest, looking for a new locale. I was also determined this time to buy land on which to build a mortgage-free house. I had heard of a technique called straw bale building and soon learned of workshops being held in a subdivision of Ponderosa Village, a small town in eastern Washington state. I was familiar with Ponderosa Village and its founders, with whom I'd done business over the years. A visit there in 1994 confirmed that it appeared to be a place where we could build according to our desires, expand the Greener Pastures Institute, and live a cooperative and, we hoped, simpler life with like-minded neighbors.

For a year and a half we planned, with professional architectural help, our house. We started building outbuildings, we put in a garden, and so on. We got involved in the politics of living in a small community, which often turned out to be divisive and frustrating. But we had a dream, and we were going to stick with it.

The straw bale technique was becoming so popular that nearly twenty-five people planned to attend a hands-on workshop to help build our house. People would be coming from as far away as Pennsylvania and Canada. The stage was set for a triumph of American ingenuity. Or disaster.

Although others in the community were planning to build with straw, our design was the first to hit the county permitting process. For some time, Ponderosans and others had been providing the county building official with videos, books, and other documents on the technique and he seemed interested in this type of construction. Unfortunately, there was a movement afoot in the state and county at that time to put more pressure on owner/builders. For example, regardless of the size of one's acreage, individuals were being forced to develop their land on unrealistic time frames and make expensive improvements. Not long before the building workshop, the county building official got cold feet. He sent the plans to the regional International Conference of Building Officials in Bellevue, Washington, which questioned the structural viability of the straw bale method. They nitpicked the 207 pages of plans prepared by my architect, who had even hired an engineer!

It was clear no house would be built anytime soon, and we didn't have the resources to wait. We canceled the workshop, and our dream of living in our own paid-for house in the country came crashing down. We put the land, with foundation supports, septic tank, well, and outbuildings, up for sale. (As I write this, it's still for sale, and there are many recriminations over why it hasn't sold, who was responsible for the fiasco, and whether it could all have been handled better; perhaps I'll be able to write a book about the experience one day.)

In the meantime, I learned that the straw bale building technique was being firmly embraced in a small gringo development in Baja California, Mexico, where I had owned a small lot for years. So we transported all the materials we could to Mexico—windows, window frames, tools, miscellaneous lumber, etc. We were able to pour a foundation and put up an outbuilding the winter following the Ponderosa Village fiasco.

But the stresses of two building projects, having to leave Mexico to promote my book, *Moving to Small Town America*, and being virtually broke at that point (we were living in a hostel) did my six-year marriage in. My wife went back to Michigan. I faced loneliness and an uncertain future along the central California coast.

So far the brass ring has eluded me. I have lived the "simple life" in rural areas as much out of necessity as by choice. (Simple, that is, meaning a life with few material possessions rather than a life that has avoided complicated twists and turns here and there.)

Today I live in an unincorporated area of a few thousand people just outside the boundaries of a small city of sixty-eight thousand on the central California coast. There are three businesses on Main Street that start with the word "Paradise." I am engaged to marry a woman who, fortunately, has her own home, which is nearly paid for. She also has a business that can provide for me when my own income is uncertain (the Greener Pastures Institute fell on hard times when the Ponderosa Village project failed). I work as a substitute teacher in two school districts, and I like the steady if unspectacular pay. I hope to continue to write about quality-of-life topics and eventually reinvigorate the Greener Pastures Institute. But it may never be what it once was—with reporters from such media icons as *USA Today*, the *New York Times*, *U.S. News and World Report*, and even the *Charles Osgood File* beating a path to our door. A few years ago we were hot. Maybe we will be again. Maybe not.

I may be too old, too discouraged, and too tired to try pioneering again. If the Baja house gets fully built, I will at least have a cheap getaway (I pay a yearly "lease" of $395 on my land) from the pressures of capitalistic, downscaling, urban America. (For now it *is* a livable alternative.) But my dreams of living in rural Oregon and Washington, where I spent nearly fifteen years of my life, are history.

Today I eat very well, have more than adequate shelter, and do work I enjoy. It's something of a challenge to adhere to some of the "simple life" principles I have espoused. There's not a whole lot of incentive to grow your own food when big nearby supermarkets and farmers' markets can supply all your food needs relatively cheaply. I'm selling my used car (I've never owned a new one) because my fiancée has two, one of which is nearly new. When we travel we stay in hotels, though I'd probably be just as comfortable in hostels and RVs, or car camping. The clothes I bought in thrift stores during my second marriage are wearing out, and I'll replace them with new stuff from department stores.

I am living today more like those who bring money to the countryside than those who arrive here and have to earn it any way they can. (But my fiancée did have to earn her living—she started an in-home day care business twelve years ago). I don't entirely trust my circumstances, however, because I sense that Americans' credit card indebtedness, stock market speculation, balance-of-trade deficits, employer flight, and so on are setting the stage for a potential global depression. I remain fairly well prepared to go back to growing some of my own food, buying used instead of new, and even fleeing the United States and its excesses if need be.

I'm still very happy not to be living in a big city, but I confess it might have been a lot easier on me not to have made *leaving* such a cause célèbre. In Los Angeles, I was known as "the Guru of Get the Hell Out." I just hope those I tried to help had an easier time of it than I have!

I've been trying to move to the country to live better for most of my adult life. I'm still working at it. You may find it ironic that I am giving you advice on how to do what I'm still in the process of doing, but perhaps if you can learn from my successes and failures, your path to the country will be easier. The following are my tips for you if you, too, decide to go on a quest for your own paradise.

William Seavey's Ten Tips for Eden-Seekers

1. Plan. Plan. Plan. Give yourself all the time you think you'll need—and then add some more. Moving from the big city to a smaller town or a rural area is a total lifestyle change. It will affect every aspect of your life. Know what you're getting into, from the local job/business climate to the variations in the weather.

2. Don't be surprised when you move to your Eden and find it's different from what you expected. You can't possibly know everything about your new home without living there (as opposed to just vacationing there). If there's any way you can do a "trial move" of at least a month (perhaps joining a home exchange program, for example), do it.

3. Get there debt free. This means buying your house or land outright, have your business start-up expenses saved, have your car paid for, etc. Chambers of Commerce will hate me for saying this, but unless you are one of the fortunate ones who will actually have a better-paying job or business in the boonies (taking into consideration the difference in the cost of living), don't put yourself under the pressure to have to earn enough to pay off debts you bring with you.

4. Move somewhere you know someone. It's just so much easier to have friends or relatives—a support system—nearby. It's not that you can't or won't make new friends. It just won't happen overnight. Join a church, club, or fraternal organization pronto. For a while you may be looked at suspiciously by others, who will wonder what "big-city lifestyle" attitudes you might have brought with you.

5. Don't expect your new place to be a panacea. Small towns have all sorts of problems of their own. These may not be as insurmountable as smog, gridlock, and murders, to be sure, but you'll get to fight about street improvements, a Wal-Mart coming in, developers buying farmlands, and "corruption at town hall." If you like democracy, you will find it to be a lot more accessible.

6. Give yourself at least five years to get acclimated. Most of the places I'm still sentimental about are places I lived in for that long or longer. There seems to be a five-year threshold for people who move to smaller places. A year is just not long enough to determine whether you will want to call a place home for many years to come. On the other hand, if nothing is working out after a year, it may be best at that point to cut your losses.

7. Try to live the simple life. Not just because this is a book and a chapter about all that, but because being resourceful, down-home, self-reliant, thrifty, etc. is what made America great and what continues to make the countryside and its inhabitants great. The denizens of the big cities are giving us all a bad image countrywide and worldwide, by pandering to the lifestyle of instant gratification.

8. If you're married, stay together. If you're single, consider marriage. A prerequisite to moving, which is so tough on marriages, is a good primary relationship. If you're not married and move to

a small town, you're setting yourself up for even more struggles. I was always happy to see married couples in my resume-writing service in Bend, Oregon. I knew that if the economy faltered, with any luck at least one would have a job. And, of course, the kids need both Dad and Mom.

9. Be aware of con and rip-off artists at all levels. Just because you're in the "country" doesn't mean people are less sophisticated than you. Or that, by virtue of being country people, they are more trustworthy (though they may be). In reviewing our efforts to build a house on our own land in eastern Washington state, the bottom line was many people promised things they couldn't or wouldn't be held accountable for, and in each case they took our money and delivered much less than we expected. In some cases, they delivered nothing.

10. No matter what you think, there is no one utopia, Shangri-la, or Valhalla, though there may well be a place that suits you fine. Avoid the temptation to keep looking when you're already rooted in a pretty outstanding locale. I've met people who can't seem to settle down because they're always looking for the greener grass. Often it's better to keep watering and fertilizing the grass that's right under your feet.

William Seavey's book, Moving to Small Town America *(Dearborn Financial, 1996) can be found in most libraries and bookstores. For a sample copy of the Greener Pastures Institute's six-page newsletter, send $1 plus one 32¢ stamp to GPI, P.O. Box 2916, Santa Maria, CA 93457.*

LIVING THE GOOD LIFE—RENT FREE

Gary Dunn

Bill Seavey, whose selection preceded this one, and I have had an ongoing "friendly" discussion about which lifestyle, urban or rural, is preferable (I'm decidedly a city boy, myself). I also know many people who have tried the country life and found, after they had spent a lot of time, energy, and money to get there, for them there was no "there" there (as Gertrude Stein said about Oakland, California). Gary Dunn, through his Caretaker Gazette, offers a way for you to "try it before you buy it" when it comes to country life or even life in another part of the country you may be curious about.

Many folks constantly battle against rent or mortgage obligations with the feeling, When will this ever end? How can I get out of this rat race and kick back and start enjoying life again? Well, one way to do this is by becoming a caretaker. Not a caregiver (people who help other people, usually the elderly), but a property caretaker!

For those who are not involved in the caretaking field, the word "caretaker" may have numerous meanings. However, for the growing number of people who are dedicated to the caretaking and land stewardship professions, a caretaker is a property caretaker: a person helping a landowner care for his or her property in exchange for compensation. Caretaking is a very old profession, rooted in the British tradition of land maintenance. In 1868 the *Times* of London defined a caretaker as "a person put in charge of a farm from which the tenant has been evicted." Today that definition has expanded to cover a multitude of landowner/caretaker relationships. The number and diversity of these relationships has increased during the nineties, from babysitting someone's home as a housesitter when the property owner is away to a position as an estate manager, with full salary and benefits. As wealthy property owners continue to own numerous homes, there will be a corresponding demand for caretakers who can watch over these properties.

Not only homeowners are in need of caretakers, but farmers, ranchers, estates, corporations, camps, parks, lodges, and nature preserves all employ caretakers.

The demand for property caretaking continues to increase across the country. Vacant properties are an invitation for theft and vandalism, and with property crimes on the rise, many owners, even those in rural locations, are finding that it's cost-effective to hire a caretaker to watch over their property. Security and maintenance issues are among other landowner concerns, so having a caretaker on the property can minimize these risks as well.

More people than ever are looking for caretaking opportunities. They have discovered that caretaking is an interesting and varied profession, offering unique rewards. People wanting a lifestyle change, retirees seeking a second career, and city dwellers searching for new job opportunities have discovered caretaking. Many newcomers to the caretaking field have spent their entire lives in cities or suburban areas. They're motivated by the desire to live a simple, rural life and enjoy the challenge of living in harmony with nature. Successful caretakers are self-reliant types who enjoy an independent lifestyle, free from the constraints of a nine-to-five job and the constant scrutiny of supervisors. Working independently, they manage their own time and fulfill their caretaking responsibilities at their own pace.

While many landowners seek experienced caretakers with specific skills (e.g., maintenance, security, farming, ranching, or animal husbandry), others are willing to take on and train people with general backgrounds. As with most other occupations, such traits as honesty, common sense, and flexibility are key prerequisites. For caretakers who live and work alone on the property of an absentee landowner, the ability to function independently and fulfill one's responsibilities without daily guidance and instruction from the landowner are important qualifications.

Although a love of nature and solitude is important, having hobbies and interests (e.g., reading, writing, painting, photography) that can be pursued in what are often remote areas is extremely helpful. Many caretakers pursue their own independent careers in writing, music, crafts, telemarketing, and other fields while they stay on the property and watch over it for the landowner.

The duties and responsibilities of a caretaker are as varied as the landowners and caretakers themselves. Caretaking can give one the opportunity to work in dozens of areas: groundskeeping, land stewardship, farming, organic gardening, forestry, ranching, horse and animal husbandry, and fisheries. While some landowners just require a presence on their property to keep trespassers away, others need pools cleaned, gardens tended, animals cared for, and houses, roads, and pastures maintained. Plumbing and electrical work may be part of a caretaker's duties—or the caretaker may be responsible for hiring competent repair people. Overall, property owners are looking for honest, reliable people that can be safely entrusted with their property.

Caretaking can be an inexpensive way to experience life in a specific geographical area. Housing is provided by the landowner, enabling the caretaker to live without incurring rent or mortgage obligations. Caretaking also enables people to leave the rat race behind, along with the crime, pollution, and other problems associated with urban blight. Some positions come with full salary and benefits if there are additional responsibilities to be performed on the property. Estate manager positions can start at $50,000 per year or more, with full benefits.

Anyone can be a caretaker. Some property owners prefer to hire a single person, while others might want a couple or family. In order to get a better understanding of a caretaker's lifestyle, we have profiled a number of caretakers to get a firsthand look at what it's all about.

When Cynthia was a child, she certainly didn't think she would be a caretaker when she grew up. After graduating from college, Cynthia wanted to try her wings at writing a novel before getting involved with a teaching career. The question was, What could she do to earn a living while writing her book?

"I figured I needed something to tide me over for only a year or two that wouldn't force me to work an eight-hour day. I walked over to the employment office at San Jose State University, where I discovered a job I'd never thought about—a not-so-highbrow caretaking position. Although the wages were low, $300 a month, this job also offered living quarters. It doesn't take much to get by if you don't have to pay rent or house payments.

"So I went for an interview, and that was the day that altered the course of my life. I was lucky for two reasons: I stumbled upon a Garden of Eden to caretake and there was no competition for this kind of work. While my friends went on to legitimate careers, I turned into a country girl, and life became very simple."

Cynthia's first caretaking job was working for a wine-making family doing housecleaning, chauffeuring, and cooking. For this work she received her own cottage smack dab in the middle of their vineyard. "I couldn't have bought this kind of environment on a teacher's salary. Which reminds me, with my first paycheck I had enough left over to buy six chickens, four geese, three rabbits, and a partridge in a pear tree. Just kidding. And an electric typewriter."

That was twenty years ago, and Cynthia is still friends with the winery owners today. The typewriter, however, has faded out of the picture and been replaced by a computer.

Cynthia has certainly found the right niche for herself. The artist's complaint has always been that there isn't enough time or energy to create because one also has to earn a living. After a full day in an office or factory, the last thing one wants to do is sit down and compose a symphony, paint a picture, or write a book. Not to mention the importance of focus. It can be hard to concentrate on a project when one is being inflicted with data from another job. Cynthia has been able to pursue her craft because of her caretaking jobs. In addition to her vineyard caretaking, she has lived in a cabin in the mountains, a cottage on a small ranch, a mansion, and she's had her own house at a resort. The resort position was in Big Sur, located along the river. There were two small cabins, each with its own hot tub to tend. Being the only person working the resort, Cynthia was responsible for taking phone reservations, greeting guests and showing them to their cabins, cleaning the cabins, laundry, banking, gardening, and mowing the lawn that ran alongside the Big Sur River. She would get up at 5:00 A.M. and write until check-out time, which was noon. By then she was ready for some physical labor, after being bent over her computer all morning, and went to work cleaning the cabins and doing the laundry. Check-in time was 5:00 P.M., so she had a couple of hours for a break, which usually meant a drive down the road to the post office, followed by lounging over cappuccino in the sun, often with a fellow writer friend who was caretaking the Henry Miller Library. What an ideal situation for a writer! In fact, Cynthia says she can't think of any drawbacks.

"Caretaking can be a uniquely intimate job, however, in that you live and work in your employer's home environment. The benefits can be numerous once you've learned to walk the fine line respecting the privacy and 'space' of your employer."

Cynthia has enjoyed the use of the swimming pools and hot tubs she's maintained and the tennis courts she's swept. She's had a complimentary membership to a country club, and driven a Mercedes, an Explorer, a Cadillac, and a truck.

"Even the work itself is a benefit, as far as I'm concerned. After a morning of writing, I get the kinks out running errands, grocery shopping, cooking—and there are no interruptions so that I can think about the book I'm working on, even as I'm working for someone else. I get to own my own brain!

"Yet the biggest benefit for me is *time* to write. And I've found that the people I work for like the idea that I'm using my free time for writing and not escaping off the property somewhere."

Landowners know that, with a writer caretaker, they have someone who will be there to watch over the property. This makes a very amiable situation for both parties!

*   *   *

When Bruce and Kristen Weaver got married they made not only a great couple but a great caretaking team.

In 1993 Bruce, Kristen, and their son moved to Prescott, Arizona, to take positions as year-round resident caretakers of Camp Charles Pearlstein, a summer camp surrounded by the biggest Ponderosa pine forest in the world. They were full-time salaried employees, and were provided with a large home, health and dental insurance, and an annual bonus. The camp hosts 250 people during the summer months and operates weekend retreats in the off-season. Bruce's duties included light construction, plumbing and electrical work, groundskeeping, and building maintenance. He coordinated with the camp director on annual facility needs and budget concerns. Kristen participated in the general care and upkeep of the facility, and recently assisted in caretaker duties for a self-sufficient home and garden, called God's Garden. In the off-season, they provided security and winter upkeep, while maintaining positive relations with the Forest Service and local subcontractors. Bruce was also responsible for implementing a recycling and composting program, planting fruit trees, creating new garden areas, and building a handcrafted log cabin to be used as a nature center to educate children about the indigenous plant and wildlife. Bruce says, "I love being my own person of spiritual intentions, and love being able to work for people who allow my creativity to just flow. I also love the winter meditation time, which allows me to be alone with nature."

While reading a recent issue of the *Caretaker Gazette*, they were intrigued by another caretaking opportunity for a seminar and retreat center in California. They were impressed that the previous caretaker had been there for the last eighteen years and they decided to apply for the position. Bruce and Kristen were flown out for an interview and soon after were offered the position. The family has just arrived at their new location and are starting to settle in. They plan to turn their backyard into an heirloom garden called the Garden at Four Springs. They will be growing food for the guests who stay at the retreat as well as for themselves. Once again, they will be creating beauty and enjoying the caretaking lifestyle!

*   *   *

On the landowner side of property caretaking, there are a growing number of farmers, ranchers, homesteaders, camps, and nature preserves that are utilizing the services of qualified caretakers. The average age of American farmers is fifty-five. There are a large number over sixty-five who will retire and have no sons or daughters who want to take over. They are increasingly turning to caretakers to maintain their land. The benefits are significant: A good caretaker can ensure that property is cared for even when the owner is no longer able to do it himself, and the land is preserved for future generations rather than being sold off to developers.

As you can see, caretaking can be an inexpensive way to explore other areas of the country before settling down in a specific location. Many caretakers who have a dream of living in another area caretake someone's property there to get to know the area firsthand. Autonomous caretaker positions may include winter-keepers at lodges and camps, managers for "gentleman" farmers and ranchers, or caretakers of resort properties during off-seasons.

For those who do not yet own land of their own, caretaking enables them to learn the survival skills that will prepare them for their own property. For many people caretaking evolves into a lifelong career. Solid backgrounds in caretaking and excellent references from previous employers ensure that they remain in great demand and are able to find positions throughout the United States.

There are a number of things to consider when applying for a caretaking position. The prudent caretaker sets out to develop a working relationship with the landowner, his or her prospective employer. If the landowner's goals and philosophies are stated in the caretaker-wanted advertisement, prospective caretakers should consider whether these are in harmony with their own beliefs. While skill and experience are important, most landowners are initially concerned with character references. When answering an ad, a neatly prepared resume should be accompanied by photographs of oneself (and family, if applicable) and references. Landowners often request a personal letter, in which the prospective caretaker discusses such things as interests, goals, and reasons for desiring a caretaking position. It is helpful to be as open and honest as possible. Information regarding any special skills or interests should also be included.

How does one get started in caretaking? Where does a landowner go to find caretakers? Well, there are a number of answers. One way to find help is by word-of-mouth. That requires being in the right place at the right time. Another way is to try the help-wanted sections of various newspapers across the country. From time to time, you'll find a caretaker-wanted ad in the classifieds. The best way to find caretaking positions is through the only publication in the world that covers the property caretaking field: the *Caretaker Gazette.* Published since 1983, the *Gazette* works as a two-way street. Subscribers can respond to the more than eighty caretaker-wanted opportunities throughout the United States and foreign countries in each issue or they can run their own situations-wanted advertisements to attract property owners.

Subscriptions are $24/year from: The Caretaker Gazette, 1845 NW Deane Street, Pullman, WA 99163-3509. Phone: (509) 332-0806.

You can also e-mail Gary at garydunn@pullman.com or check the Gazette's *Web site at: http://www.angelfire.com/wa/caretaker. Gary will send you his flyer,* Report on Caretaking, *if you send him a large SASE.*

EATING OFF THE LAND

Suellen Ocean

Most of us who live with or near oak trees have a problem every autumn. Raking, bagging, and disposing of all those acorns! Suellen Ocean took a different approach. She asked, "How can I make use of all those acorns?" The answer, she discovered, was to turn them into food. She wrote Acorns and Eat'em, *giving others the benefit of her research on how to make acorns edible and what to use them in. To me this is the best of all frugal worlds—taking something that is not only free but something of a nuisance and making it an asset. Here's her story and a few of her very simple recipes.*

I'm not sure whom I'm quoting, but I once read, "It's not how much you have, but how much you appreciate what you have, that makes you happy." It's a bit embarrassing to sort of invite you into my thoughts and share with you all the silly things I do. I didn't necessarily do them to save money. I didn't have any to save.

It's not that I grew up "poor." I didn't know what poor was until as a young adult I looked around at urban America and said, "I'm outta here." I let go of possessions and literally headed for the hills. I even changed my name. It was a rebirth of sorts and was good for my soul. People laughed at my name, my clothes, my ideas, and even the food I ate. I didn't care. The day I changed my name I stood on an empty beach on an overcast Christmas Day, feeding whole wheat bread crumbs to seagulls. It was the most peaceful Christmas I've ever had.

Looking back to those days when I was very young and naive, I remember deciding, in the dead of winter, that to live off the land was a virtue. I walked out of my cabin and into the forest, where all I found were shriveled berries. The next day I marched my two little boys through the woods to an apple tree I'd seen from the car. Their faith was strong, and maybe they didn't know any better. It was fun to play in the forest and pick fruit. We ate as we picked and we each carried home fresh apples. For the next two days, we enjoyed the apples. I watched the boys' complexions turn rosy, their cheeks the color of the bright red blush on the apples. I knew I was on to something.

In those early days I appreciated watching others go about their simple living. I learned from my landlord, who knew how to grab opportunity. With his old recycled logging truck, he salvaged redwood trees that the timber companies had left behind. I can still see that old truck coming around the corner hauling huge old-growth redwood trees. Back in the late seventies, the environmentalists had begun speaking out, but their movement was young and the timber companies did as they pleased, taking what was easy and leaving the rest for resourceful people like my landlord. He had a mill, and with it he milled up the most beautiful redwood paneling. I'll bet his eyes popped with excitement when he rolled his truck into the forest after a timber operation and saw all those trees lying there. A loss to the forest, but a "find" for him.

What fun would it be to have lots of money? It may mean no more lolling in the appreciation of "the find." A box of glasses bought for a nickel apiece at a garage sale brings me satisfaction—it's a score. I stare at that box of glasses in my pantry like a kid stares into his bag of trick-or-treat candy. Not only did I save money by buying those glasses, I saved resources by not buying new ones. "I hate glasses," I told my husband last year. "They break too easily." And they do. Who wants to pay over a dollar a glass and have it break? But at a nickel apiece, those glasses glisten like gold. At an estate sale my neighbor bought fifty-two boxes of canning jars for thirty dollars—she's proud she saved money, but she also knows I lust after those jars. In the end, it's the hunt, the deal, the score.

I guess it's a reverse culture. Those who have lots of money act nonchalant about spending it. It's a game, a game of excess, a game to impress. "There's more where that came from—we're rich and decadent." It works the same way with us simple-living folk. "I'm sharper than you are at the rummage sale. . . . Look what I found in the corner for a quarter. . . . I'm more conscientious than you. . . . I reuse what others cast out. . . ." Yet there's a sense of relaxation in going the simple-living way. Spending too much money can be very stressful. A friend of mine told me that every dollar is a vote. Each dollar drops a ballot into the box. Twenty votes for oil drilling, one hundred fifty votes for rubber factories, twenty-seven votes for cutting timber. . . .

You don't have to be broke, you don't have to be greedy, you just have to have "money-consciousness." If you are careful with your money, you may never have to be broke and you may well afford to be generous, a most desirable trait, since we all know you can't take it with you when you're gone.

If you want to take up skiing, for instance, you need to know that people often buy skis, use them two or three times, and then give them away to the Goodwill. You can pick them up for about ten dollars. Sweaters, wool caps, and ski poles can also be found at the secondhand stores. You may have to shop longer to find good used ski boots; they're out there but you have to hunt. Don't forget to shop for the bargain ski resorts. Some ski areas cater to families and they offer lift tickets for about half price. These places are likely to be less snooty, and they won't even notice your older ski gear (if they do they'll probably declare, "Awesome vintage!")

After skiing, you can curl up by the fire with a book that you found through the interlibrary loan system. The library may charge you a dollar to find a book, but it's only a fraction of the cost of new ones. When you run across an ad for a new book, request it from your library. If they don't have the book, they'll search the country until they find it. You can read hundreds of dollars' worth of books on the cheap this way.

As a practitioner of simple living, you need to be on the lookout for food. Harvest apples from abandoned trees, berries from wild bushes, wild grapes growing by the riverside, and nuts like walnuts and almonds. Develop warm, sharing friendships with other hunter-gatherer types. Watch for gardens that have gone unharvested, then knock on the gardener's door and ask if you can pick some vegetables. They'll probably say, "Yes, please do."

In 1979 I started preparing acorns for food. I was inspired by the Native American people, for whom I have a strong respect. History shows that their agricultural skills were ingenious. They grew and harvested roots and tubers and used reeds and grasses for making baskets and cooking utensils. They were resourceful people, and in areas where the oak grows the acorn is their staff of life. Every spring the biggest celebration of the year was held — the acorn festival, which lasted three days. The idea of three days of feasting and playing music with friends and family is wonderful.

Acorns are tended for us by nature; all we need to do is participate in the harvest. The plump food is simple to remove from the shell and easy to grind and rinse. Preparing a few pounds of acorns is an excellent way to get a taste of wild foods and, at the same time, to fill our bodies with a local, regionally distinctive produce that hasn't been trucked and probably hasn't been sprayed.

I doubt anyone knows how long the acorn of the oak tree has been used for food. It has in the past been used in delicacies ranging from Moroccan and Spanish oils to distilled spirits. I often wonder how could the staple food of Pomos and other Native Americans be so overlooked by modern inhabitants? As I walk through the forest and in twenty minutes gather what feels like ten pounds of big brown acorns, I know that no matter what happens, I probably will never go hungry in my neck of the woods. Learn to live off the land—you never know when you may need to.

Most people expect living off the land to be a bitter or tasteless experience, but once you taste acorn bread or acorn cheesecake, you may never go back to the supermarket. There are acorns just about everywhere in the United States. In parks, on school grounds, or along the roads and by the riversides.

It was a difficult process, figuring out how to eat acorns, but it turned out to be quite simple. The tannic acid in the acorns is water soluble, so you just have to shell the acorns, then grind and rinse them, draining the tannic acid off. You must leach acorns (soak and rinse the tannic acid out). This is very important because the tannic acid is bitter and could cause digestive upset. Acorns from different species of oaks contain different amounts of tannic acid. So some acorns are less bitter than others, though all require some amount of leaching. I grind acorns in the blender, then I cover the acorn meal with water in large-mouthed, quart-size canning jars, which I keep in the refrigerator. I leach them this way for seven days, pouring off the old water and replacing it with fresh every day. Taste a small amount of the nut meal each day; you will know they have been leached enough when the bitterness is gone, leaving a mild, nutty flavor.

Acorns stimulate conversation. Prepare a big bowl of acorn dip for your next social gathering and you will get a lot of attention. I make cakes, pies, smoothies, soups, pancakes, burritos, cookies, and more. It seems that whatever I add acorns to is improved tremendously.

Make sure that you have an awareness of the wildlife (deer, squirrels, birds, mice, chipmunks, etc.) that depend on the oak trees you're gathering from. Take some for yourself, but leave plenty for the animals.

There are other ways to save money aside from acorns, and one of the best is to cook. It's a lot of work, but a good cook in the house is worth his or her weight in gold. Even when you're traveling, you can bring your own home-cooked goodies. Celery and peanut butter, homemade cookies, hard-boiled eggs, and sandwiches will save bucks. Take a break from driving and stop at a park or rest stop that has picnic tables. Enjoy your meal and make sure you bring lots of fresh water and homemade lemonade. Fresh fruit like oranges, apples, and bananas are great. When you do arrive at your holiday destination, the kids will be so full you can make them happy with a pack of gum, leaving you more money to spend on souvenirs.

Here's another way to save money: Get your vitamins from the foods you eat rather than from costly supplements. Vitamins and minerals can be obtained by eating a good diet with a wide variety of fresh and unrefined fruits, vegetables, oils, and grains. Think of the money you'll save on doctor bills! Sometimes the nutrients are "locked up" and the food needs to be juiced or cooked to retrieve them. If you cook greens, for example, you should try to steam them and if you must cook them, drink the cooking water or add it to soup or vegetable broth. Here are some essential vitamins and minerals and their sources:

- *Vitamin A:* Carotene is broken down to vitamin A by the liver and the intestinal mucus lining. Sources include carrots, chard, kale, spinach, string beans, broccoli, yellow squash, sweet potatoes, yams, apricots, dandelions, endive, lettuce, parsley, prunes, tomatoes, turnip greens, watercress, peas, celery, asparagus, butter, margarine, eggs, and fish liver oils.
- *Vitamin B_1:* unrefined peanut butter, wheat germ, cereal grains, dry beans, nuts, peas, soybeans, lentils.
- *Vitamin B_2:* cooked leafy vegetables, nutritional yeast, yogurt, milk.
- *Vitamin B_6:* blackstrap molasses, wheat germ, nutritional yeast, wheat bran.
- *Vitamin B_{12}:* milk, eggs, cheese.
- *Vitamin C:* bell peppers, pimentos, papayas, rose hips, parsley, garlic, cucumbers, apples, cabbage, carrots, grapefruit, lemons, onions, apricots, celery, oranges, cranberries, pineapples, tomatoes, spinach, rhubarb, turnip greens, radishes, watermelon, watercress.
- *Vitamin D:* eggs (preferably from hens that received sunlight), cod liver oil, vitamin D milk (including any soy or rice milk that has added vitamin D), and papayas. You also get vitamin D when you're out in the sun, a process assisted by the natural oils in your skin, which means the vitamin D isn't absorbed as well after a shower since you've washed most of the oils off.
- *Vitamin E:* fresh grains, fresh nuts, fresh seeds (heating, freezing, and long storage destroys vitamin E), unrefined vegetable oils, fresh wheat germ, celery, turnip greens, lettuce, parsley, watercress, spinach.
- *Calcium:* yogurt, blackstrap molasses, soybeans, milk, mustard greens, turnip greens.
- *Magnesium:* fruits, vegetables, soybeans, nuts, grains, cooked spinach, cooked chard.
- *Potassium:* whole grains, nuts, fruits, vegetables.
- *Iron:* egg yolks, wheat germ, nutritional yeast, whole grains.

If you can, buy whole wheat spaghetti products. Whole wheat still contains the wheat germ and the bran, yet it's often hard to find whole wheat pastas. If we avoid the refined pastas, the manufacturers will get the point. When you do use white flour products, make sure the rest of the meal includes foods rich in B vitamins. Try to do the same if you eat white rice and degerminated corn meal.

I feel that I must mention gardening, though it's not always as easy or inexpensive as it may seem. Rain washes away valuable minerals that plants need, while some areas are so hot and dry that either the plants don't grow or they need shade netting. Deer and wild animals will invade your garden, as will slugs, snails, and, in some areas, fire ants. You need some bucks to garden. Dirt and manure alone just don't cut it. You need implements, good seeds, minerals, etc. You will probably get back more than you put in, but you have to work at it. It's like baking bread—you have to keep an eye on it, baby it. There is nothing like your own fresh-grown food. Ever had a fresh artichoke? or French fries made out of fresh turnips? Delicious! Even if you just have an old bathtub that you grow a few things in, grow some parsley and a couple of tomato plants. The art of gardening will nurture your soul and keep you in tune with the rhythms of the earth. Feel the presence of the angels of wind, water, and sun.

You don't have to live in the country to have a garden but if you'd like to move to the country, there are different ways to achieve the dream. Some people will work and save for years to do it "right." Others just move out and do it cold turkey. You're lucky if you can be somewhere in the middle. Those who work and save big money are often old and tired by the time they reach their goal. Those who go cold turkey grow old and stressed trying to make it in the country with limited resources. Develop a cottage industry or a career that will fit into the area you're targeting and get it well off the ground before you move.

I became frugal because I wanted to survive the twentieth century and live harmoniously with nature. I believe there is too much waste and too much apathy in our society toward the conservation of valuable resources. I wrote *Acorns and Eat'em* because I believe strongly in resourcefulness and wanted to share my ideas with others.

A good frugal rule of thumb is: Use everything up, whether it be cooking oil, shampoo, toothpaste, laundry detergent, or pancake syrup. Don't waste a thing. Don't throw things out that you can use later. Paper bags, plastic bags, tin foil, wrapping paper, ribbons can all be used again. Like I said before, it's a bit embarrassing to share my frugal secrets with the world. I was rather amused to be asked to contribute to this collection, which included an author known as "the cheapest guy in America." When I told my sister that I was participating in an anthology with various frugal folk, her response was, "Oh, like the people who save lint?" I ignored her and held my head up proudly as I watered down my soap dish. It's amazing what you don't need. During tight times, I was always astounded by what we could do without. My mother, who used to save little pieces of soap and melt them into liquid, is still an inspiration to me. She continues to make her own envelopes.

I always have food to eat. You can make a gourmet meal out of tortillas covered with shredded carrots and alfalfa sprouts. And of course, though everyone makes jokes about beans, they are cheap, and a wonderful food. Mix them with rice and you have a complete dose of protein.

Well, as of this writing, I am still compelled to be frugal. But I don't feel "poor." I just made the most delicious batch of homemade bread and ate some with a big salad. It was delightful and as I ate it my mind was calculating how cheap it was. . . . I couldn't help it! If I were rich, I'd probably be shopping for bargain horse ranches. (I already have two bargain horses . . . but that's another story).

SUELLEN'S TIPS

1. Be content with yourself as a frugal person. Respect what that means.
2. Be courageous and see through advertising.
3. Understand that frugality leads, not to miserliness and a joyless existence, but to comfort and prosperity and even generosity.
4. The older secondhand products are often better made.
5. Take care of your health; you will save on doctor bills.

6. Grow a garden. Even if you live in an apartment in a city, you can grow a windowbox garden.
7. Enjoy the simple pleasures in your life, whatever they are.
8. Expect to receive beauty from within, not from commercial products.
9. Watch your utilities. Turn the lights off, be diligent.

FAVORITE RECIPES

The following are recipes from *Poor Jonny's Cookbook*. I began it in 1979. For eighteen years I've saved recipes that were valuable because I made them for next-to-nothing and they're healthy. These are some of my favorites:

Rose Hips
Rose hip juice is classy. Round up beautiful wine bottles with corks and save them for your yearly rose hips project. A bottle of rose hip juice is an excellent holiday gift.

Wild rose hips contain twenty-four to thirty-six times more vitamin C than equal portions of orange juice and sixty times more C than lemons. Rose hips are also a rich source of other vitamins, minerals, and bioflavonoids. Early stages of research are indicating flavonoids may actually dissolve deposits in the bloodstream and prevent heart disease. During World War II, the English extracted vitamin C from rose hips and B vitamins from hops. There is a saying, "England's magnificent strength was maintained by her hips and her hops."

Even Peking Man, though now extinct, gathered rose hips. This evidence was found in excavations of cave dwellings occupied over 300,000 years ago.

Rose Hip Juice
Rose hips have several stages of "ripe," ranging from crunchy to mushy. When to collect them is a matter of taste. In mild climates they can be gathered for months, but in colder climates they should be gathered before the weather rots them. They are easy to pick off the bush by hand, or, using a rake, knock the higher ones off and then gather them from

the ground. Remove any leaves or stems clinging to them, then rinse and freeze the berries for later use.

For every cup of rose hips use two cups of water. Simmer just enough to break down the fibers. Five minutes on a very low simmer will do. As soon as you think the fibers are soft enough, quickly turn off the heat and cover. The flavor is better if you don't overcook. Let it sit for about an hour.

With a potato masher break up the skins and release the seeds from the rose hips. Using a plastic strainer with holes small enough that the seeds don't fall through, strain the juice into a large pitcher, adding more water. One cup of rose hips can require anywhere from four to seven more cups of water to retrieve all the pulp from the strainer. It depends on how strong you like your juice. You may want to filter the juice through a much finer strainer (sometimes there are little hairlike fibers that annoy a sensitive throat). Sweeten to taste.

Rose Hip Jelly

Rinse rose hips. Soften them over heat with just a little water. Cover the pot, but keep an eye on them—don't let them burn. You just want to soften them enough to be able to get the seeds out. Using a potato masher, mash the rose hips completely, adding more water if necessary to make the juice the consistency of tomato juice. For every cup of rose hips, add one cup of water to make the juice. Strain out the seeds and skin by pushing the pulpy juice through a colander. For jelly you'll need:

> 6 cups prepared rose hip juice
>
> I cup honey
>
> I package low- or no-sugar pectin

Add the pectin to the six cups of juice and mix thoroughly.

Bring to a full rolling boil, stirring constantly (turn down heat if in danger of burning).

Boil one minute.

Remove from heat. Remove foam (skim it off with a spoon). Stir in honey.

Fill jars. Screw bands tightly. Turn the jars upside down for five minutes to make sure there is no leakage. If the jam is not to be eaten right away it should be processed in a canner. Though rose hips are highly acidic, and this lessens the chance of spoilage, even acidic food should be processed in a canner if it's going to be stored for any length of time.

Sprouted Wheatberry Bread

This is an ancient way of making bread; it is loaded with enzymes and B vitamins.

Soak two cups of wheatberries in water, covered, for twenty-four hours. Drain. Keep covered until they are just barely beginning to sprout—about two days. If they sprout too much, they become too sweet. Using a food grinder, grind finely. Shape this dough into a round loaf on an oven-proof plate. There is no need to grease the plate; when the bread cools it will come right off. Put about two inches of water in a large pot and place a steamer or a metal measuring cup at the bottom to hold the plate above the water. The loaf stays out of the water, but the boiling water steams it. Cover and steam. After twenty minutes of steaming, take the lid off and let it cool. Wrap the bread in plastic and store in the refrigerator for immediate use or freeze for later.

Spicy Sprouted Wheatberry Dish

Chop up sprouted wheatberry bread (recipe above) into large chunks and place in a large bowl. Add a couple of chopped tomatoes, some chopped onion, garlic, basil, thyme, oregano, and a couple of beaten eggs. Mix. Spray a nine-inch cast-iron skillet with no-stick spray. Pour the mix into the skillet, cover, and cook over a slow heat—the lower the heat, the more nutrition your bread retains. You do need to ensure that the eggs are thoroughly cooked. Add grated cheese just before done. Vegans can omit the eggs and cheese.

Sprouted wheatberries make great casserole additions. Put them through a blender (add water) or a food mill. Add tomato paste, a vegetable, garlic, onions, olives, spices, etc. Cook very slowly so as not to destroy vitamin content. Use sprouted wheatberries in place of macaroni—they are richer in vitamins. You can also make veggie drinks in your blender and add raw sprouted wheatberries for an energizer.

Oat Milk

A great substitute for cow's milk. Use it for drinking or cooking.

> 1 cup dry oats (or more for thicker milk)
> 2 quarts cold water

Pour one cup dry oats into a pitcher. Add two quarts cold water. Refrigerate for twenty-four hours. The oats will be soft and mushy; strain them into another pitcher through a fine-mesh kitchen strainer. Use a fork as you do so and press on the oats to strain all the "juice" out.

Add:

> 2 tablespoons brown sugar
> 2 teaspoons vanilla
> 1/4 teaspoon salt

Stir sugar, vanilla, and salt into the oat milk. Keep refrigerated. Shake or stir before each use. Use as you would milk, as a drink or in cooking. Save the oat pulp for other cooking needs—as cooked cereal, in bread recipes, to thicken soups, or in oat burgers (recipe below).

Oat Burgers

Oat burgers can be made without all these ingredients by simply adding a raw egg to one cup of oat pulp, but the following recipe is a much tastier and more nutritious one.

> 1 cup strained, wet oat pulp
> 1/2 cup dry soy milk powder
> 2 beaten eggs (or egg whites)
> 2 tablespoons soy sauce
> 1 tablespoon sesame seeds
> 1 teaspoon dried sweet basil
> 1/2 teaspoon marjoram
> 1/4 teaspoon salt
> pinch celery seed

Mix ingredients together well. Shape into patties. Lightly oil a cast-iron skillet. Add patties. Cover. Covering creates steam that cooks the burgers without having to deep-fry them. Cook over medium heat for two minutes. Turn burgers and cook for two more minutes. Put on a bun with fresh tomato slices, onions, lettuce, ketchup, mustard, and mayo—wonderful!

Rice Milk

An excellent substitute for the cow's milk you usually use in your cold cereal or drink with your peanut butter and jelly sandwich. You can even add chocolate and create chocolate milk. But if you use it for cooking, remember that it is really rice water and will act as any starch will and thicken up. After making rice milk, the rice pulp left over can be cooked as a thin, creamy hot cereal, or cooked just as you would rice: use two cups of water for every cup of rice pulp.

Put two cups raw brown rice in the blender with four cups water and blend at highest speed for two minutes. Strain into a large pitcher, using a fine-mesh kitchen strainer. Some rice will stick to the inside of the blender. Add four extra cups of water to the blender container, rinsing it around to release extra rice. Pour this through the strainer. Add one tablespoon honey or sugar, two teaspoons pure vanilla extract, and a scant one-quarter teaspoon salt. Keep refrigerated.

Fried Green Tomatoes

An early American classic, fried green tomatoes have been enjoyed in the early summertime for many years. Why wait for the red ones? We'll have plenty of those later. When the big green tomatoes appear, enjoy a distinctive treat.

Slice green tomatoes and dip in a beaten egg, then into dry corn meal. Lightly oil a skillet. Over medium heat cook, covered, three to four minutes, then turn. Cover again and cook until done. Optional additions to the corn meal include garlic or onion powder and Parmesan cheese.

Food from the Rain

For this dish count on rains to bring dock, turnip, and dandelion greens! Turnips are easy to grow, and the young seedlings might not be as hot, and are great eaten raw in salads. To encourage the turnip bulb to grow pick the larger leaves off the plants. Those are quite edible once steamed.

4 cups barely sprouted wheatberries, steamed
1 large handful of a combination of fresh dock, turnip, and
    dandelion greens, steamed
2 1/2 cups cooked garbanzo beans
    Combine above ingredients. Make a sauce of:

1/4 cup olive oil
1 clove minced garlic

Heat sauce enough to impart the garlic flavor into the oil. Drench the dish with the sauce. Try adding green pepper, miso, and spices to the sauce.

For pennies, a cup of herbal tea, hot on a winter's day or iced on a summer day, not only quenches your thirst, but can be healing too. Buy herbs in bulk or grow your own tea. Try peppermint, spearmint, chamomile, strawberry leaf, raspberry leaf, rose hips, lemongrass, anise, ginger, licorice, ginseng. Go for a walk and look for these: pine needles, rose hips, strawberry leaves. Don't gather anything from an area that might have been sprayed, like under power lines and along some roads.

Corn Sprouts

When your garden produces an abundance of corn, save some ears to dry and make sprouts. You can also purchase or order dried corn from natural food stores. Make the sprouts by removing the kernels from the cob and soaking them in water for a night. Pour the water out and rinse twice a day until they sprout. Corn sprouts are a different kind of treat and are good steamed or dropped into soup. They can be lightly steamed, then ground and mixed with mayonnaise and celery for a sandwich spread, or try grinding raw corn sprouts to a paste and then adding raw vegetables or a delicious brown gravy.

Marinated Corn Sprouts

Soak one cup of dried corn kernels for twenty-four to forty-eight hours. Drain. Rinse daily until they sprout. Once sprouted, steam until tender. Add to steamed corn sprouts:

2 tablespoons veggie oil
2 tablespoons tamari

1 1/2 teaspoons vinegar

1 teaspoon basil

1/2 teaspoon curry powder

1/2 teaspoon kelp

Blend and refrigerate. Other additions could include sauteed mushrooms, green onions, garlic, parsley, chives, spinach leaves, spirolina, or chopped veggies.

Frozen Vegetables

Large bags of frozen corn, frozen peas, and other vegetables are good bargains. You can reach into the bag and grab a handful for a quick side dish or to throw into the main dish. Peas added to rice will provide the amino acids you need to make a complete protein. Corn added to beans will do the same.

Enjoy!

Suellen's book, Acorns and Eat'em, *a vegetarian cookbook and field guide to oaks, with complete directions for preparing acorns, is $13.50.* Poor Jonny's Cookbook: Healthy Eating on Next-to-Nothing, *is $14. Either or both can be ordered from her at Ocean-Hose, P.O. Box 444, Willits, CA 95490.*

LIVING OFF THE LAND

Tom "Broken Bear" Squier

I first read about Tom Squier in, of all places, the Wall Street Journal, *which quoted Tom as saying (about road-killed meat), "Food's food, whether I get it with a gun or a Goodyear." I wrote to him and read* The Wild and Free Cookbook, *which, as he will explain, has a lot less to do with road kill as sustenance than his publisher asserts. But whatever sells . . .*

I have really been living frugally and off the land all my life, and it is something that everyone can learn, but not everyone can do. The reason for this is simple: there isn't enough land for all of us to live off of anymore. There are too many people and too little turf. I really am fortunate enough to have been one of those persons who can say I grew up poor, but didn't know it. My grandfather, who practically raised me until school age, helped me learn to appreciate what the natural world has to offer in the way of food and medicine and other gifts. He was a Cherokee Indian and was something of a "root doctor," or medicine man, and though not highly educated, he was highly respected as a wise and knowledgeable man. He taught me to hunt, fish, and gather plants for food and medicines. Even among Native Americans, much of that ability and knowledge has now been lost.

In order to really "live off the land" we must also take care of it. Being a steward of nature is just as important as taking advantage of her bounty. Now, I must warn you that this bounty may come from strange places. By that I mean along the side of the road. For a total of about ten years, I taught survival classes at the Army's Special Qualification course—the "Q" course, which teaches young soldiers the skills needed to become a "Green Beret," and in the SERE school (Survival, Evasion, Resistance & Escape)—better known as the P.O.W. school on using wild plants for food, medicine, and other purposes. I also taught the class formally known as "Preparation of Fish and Game," but referred to as the "kill class" because it taught soldiers to do things they couldn't learn from books.

I would demonstrate for them how to kill a chicken and a rabbit, clean the animals, and dispose of the carcasses in a manner that wouldn't get them compromised in a combat environment. After watching me, each student would be given a chicken or rabbit of his or her own and would have to kill the animal, clean it, and eat it as part of their hands-on training. We also had one or more goats, which we used as training aids to show how to clean a larger animal. These soldiers go all over the world and may have to obtain food from the wild or even surreptitiously from domestic herds. To make the training more realistic, I often used real wild animals such as raccoons, rabbits, squirrels, and deer that I found along the road where they had been killed by automobiles.

Eventually this practice led to some celebrity. Some of my students made me a bumper sticker that read "Caution, I Brake For Road Kills!" At the time I was also writing a locally syndicated column called "Living Off the Land," which covered the gamut of outdoors and nature writing, from fishing and hunting to gathering wild mushrooms and picking the berries and fruits of the season. As such things do, eventually the story of my using road-killed animals for instruction and for my own food got out, and several television stations did stories on it. With my wife's assistance I wrote a book called *Living Off the Land* and then the *Wild Foods Cookbook*. Finally, a much larger edition of the book was bought by a publisher of military and paramilitary books who wanted to hype the road kill aspect. Well, business is business and it worked well. The revised and greatly expanded book contains over four hundred fish, game, and wild plant recipes, nature notes and anecdotes, and is a legitimate cookbook. However, at the publisher's insistence a chapter was added on eating road-killed animals. They put a banner on the cover of the new book, *The Wild and Free Cookbook*, that proclaims "Includes a Special Road Kill Section." This really got me a lot of attention, including more television appearances. I went on "The Chevy Chase Show" and together he and I cooked a rattlesnake and ate it for his audience.

More newspaper stories followed and several radio interviews from as far away as Canada and England. "Let's say, God forbid," said the English radio host, "that you happen upon a squirrel that has been run over. Do you mean to say that you could eat it?" "Absolutely!" was my response, and once again, I had to explain that we aren't talking about "road pizzas," or the ones that attract buzzards and other carrion eaters' attention, but freshly killed and, for the most part, intact carcasses.

My local radio station's morning host had me on a couple of times and still occasionally mentions the book and its author. Overall, though, I think the best publicity I got came from appearing live on the air with John Boy and Billy on "The Big Show" from the studios of WRFX in Charlotte, North Carolina, where once I cooked a rattlesnake and they had it sizzling on the microphones for the benefit of the listeners. The show is on at least twenty-six different stations across the South, and lots of people called the publisher as a result. Another time I went down there and prepared venison barbecue from a road kill, and it was delicious.

John Boy was bragging about it on the air so often that a Highway Patrolman came to the studio to try some and stayed for several sandwiches. Then when Christmas rolled around and I was on the show again, I was introduced with "I Came Upon a Road-killed Deer" set to the music and feeling of "It Came Upon a Midnight Clear." The publisher, Loompanics Unlimited (1-800-380-2230), was flooded with phone calls and orders.

Let's begin with the basics. Most people aren't fortunate enough to have grown up eating wild foods these days. In fact, many people don't even know what fresh vegetables taste like. Wild fruits and vegetables are often smaller in size than their commercially grown counterparts, and because they aren't sprayed with pesticides, they may have to be cleaned carefully. It's a good trade-off, though, for wild plants often contain more nutrients, including trace minerals, than those grown commercially in a field full of chemicals or even hydroponically in a tank of water. For the same reasons, wild game is usually better for you than farm-raised animals because it isn't full of steroids, growth hormones, and antibiotics and, with a few exceptions, game meat is higher in protein and almost cholesterol-free because game usually lacks the fat that farm animals develop. The exceptions are young pigeons or rock doves, which are known as squabs, and greasy animals like possums.

We don't eat road-killed possums unless it's a matter of life and death, if, for example, you are starving and can find nothing else. People do eat possums, though more people joke about it than actually do it. Before the white man came, you could eat wild free-roaming possums because they didn't have our dumps to feed on. Nowadays they dine in our trash cans and off the great quantities of food that ends up in our landfills each day. If you want to eat a possum, you have to keep it up in a pen for a week or more to "clean it out," feeding it fresh fruit, corn bread, and milk and vegetables. Then, when you do clean it, unless it is a very young one, you will have to boil it once to get rid of the grease and then either bake it, cut it up, and fry it, or boil it again in a stew.

Possums aside, it's obvious that I can't tell you all the ins and outs of preparing food from the wild in this short article. That has filled three books. This is just to give you an idea of what I do and what you can do to live frugally off the land.

Whether you decide to become a hunter-gatherer or a gleaner of road-killed animals, remember this: In most parts of this country there is at least one type of poisonous snake, and in some parts there are four kinds—the maximum for North America. Poisonous snakes can kill you, but more often than not they just make a healthy adult sick—if they inject venom at all. Snakes often retain their poison, which they use primarily for subduing their prey. No matter where you live, chances are that more people die from lightning strikes or allergic reactions to bee stings than from snake bites. The key is to learn to identify the four poisonous snakes in case you encounter one or if you want to use snakes as food. We have one poisonous snake in the Southeast and Southwest, called the coral snake, that is related to cobras and has a neurotoxic venom that doesn't sting as it's injected. Whereas the venom of our pit vipers—rattlesnakes, copperheads, and water moccasins—burns like fire. A trip to your local zoo or nature museum will help you learn to identify these snakes, though always remember that the best way to be safe around snakes is to leave them alone.

If you still have an appetite for snakes or other reptiles, you're in luck: they're safer than mammals and birds with regard to diseases. Being cold-blooded, they don't carry many of the illnesses we can get from warm-blooded food sources. Road-killed snakes are common in many parts of the country and can help us live frugally. With a poisonous snake, carefully remove and bury the head immediately. A dead snake can bite for some time after death, even with the head severed. Snake skins can be easily converted into hat bands, belts, and other items to sell at craft shows and flea markets or in specialty stores. The vertebrae that make up the backbone can be used to create unique and beautiful earrings and other jewelry, either bleached or painted.

Just as with poisonous snakes, it is best to learn to identify the poisonous plants in your area and avoid them. Poison sumac, poison ivy, and poison oak can be very aggravating and will easily ruin a foraging expedition. Some persons have such allergic reactions to these plants that their breathing is threatened or compromised and they are temporarily blinded by their eyes' swelling closed. Learn to identify the plants that cause irritation or rashes. The key to using wild plants for food and medicine is to avoid any plants you cannot positively identify.

I will say that again.

The key to using wild plants for food or medicine is to avoid any plants that you cannot positively identify!

You can learn about plants from visiting botanical gardens and museums, attending "plant walks" and lectures, and spending time with people who know about plants. You can also learn from books and videos, but use multiple sources. Don't overlook obvious or not so obvious experts, such as someone's granny who gathered creasy greens, wild asparagus, and poke salad in her youth or an enthusiastic Boy Scout working on a merit badge.

Back to the poke salad. It was made famous in the song "Poke Salad Annie," and a lot of books will tell you that poke is a very popular spring green in the South. What some don't tell you is that it isn't a salad at all but a "sallet"—the Old English word for *cooked* greens. Poke is easy to find and identify and is both nutritious and tasty, but it must be parboiled in three changes of water to avoid serious gastrointestinal problems. The root is used in medicine for cancer treatment and other purposes but is extremely poisonous. This is an obvious example of why it's important to get the whole story about the plants you intend to use for food or medicine.

You can save or make a lot of money gathering wild mushrooms, but this is a job for experts. There are two types of poisons in mushrooms. One works on the digestive system and you get sick quick, throw up, and wish you could die, but with fluid replacement and a little time you recover quickly, too. The really bad ones work on the nervous system and by the time you realize you have poisoned yourself, it is usually too late to help you, even with a liver transplant, which some survivors require. And there is a family of mushrooms called Coprinus that have a natural form of Antabuse in them, which, when eaten with wine—say, along with a spaghetti dinner—produces copious and violent vomiting. Some good ones to learn to identify are oyster mushrooms, chicken of the woods, and the puffballs, the morels, and the chanterelles. It is worth the effort to become expert at identifying the right mushrooms and avoiding all the rest no matter how good they look or smell.

Living off the land frugally can also mean growing some of your own food. I have always sustained and improved the soils in my garden and around the house by composting. When starting a garden I bury vegetable scraps and trimmings deeply and replow the soil frequently to keep the material from simply rotting. You can ask the produce manager at the store to save you the leaves and other parts they trim from cabbage and other vegetables and get a lot of compost material this way. Compost all your eggshells, coffee grounds, and similar materials. Bury fish bones and skins and entrails to keep the animals from digging them up and eating them.

Grow your own herbs for seasoning, even if it is in a pot or half-barrel. Herbs are among the most expensive items we buy in the grocery store and are often easily grown and preserved. Learn specifics. This is also good for stress relief and relaxation, as are other forms of gardening.

Despite eating lots of wild game and plants, my grandfather always raised corn, beans, and tomatoes. All of these can be canned, dried, or frozen, and you could grow a surplus and barter some or give it away. The good thing about eating wild game—road kills or hunting successes—is that you don't need any special recipes. Just substitute game for beef, pork, chicken, or whatever in your favorite recipes, and you are in business. After you get comfortable with it, then you can start getting fancy!

My grandfather raised some animals. The occasional calf, hog, or goat supplemented the chickens, rabbits, and pigeons that we raised and ate. The chickens were kept in a large pen at night but were allowed out to roam free during the day. You can keep just enough roosters to ensure a constant source of new chickens and enjoy eggs and chicken meat all the time.

Squabs, or pigeons, though expensive in the markets and restaurants, are quite cheap to breed. My grandfather built nesting boxes inside the barn for easy access, and the openings allowed the pigeons to come and go as they pleased, feeding themselves. Initially, to keep them from flying off, you may have to keep them in a wire enclosure and feed and water them until they nest and begin raising young. Don't be surprised if your pigeons will attract other pigeons; they will usually fill all the nest boxes you can build.

Again, learn all you can about plants and about which plants you can gather to make medicine. Sage and rosemary are herbs but can be made into a tea for headaches and tension. The best remedy for poison ivy and bee stings comes from a plant called jewel weed, which can easily be naturalized on your property. Sassafras tea is excellent for lowering blood pressure and fighting "stones." A strong diuretic, it is effective in weight loss as well. In fact, most weight loss medicines are combinations of laxatives and diuretics. Store-bought aspirin can cause bleeding ulcers, but a safe aspirin can be brewed from willow bark and twigs. Mullein flowers are good for earaches and mullein leaves can be smoked or made into tea for relieving asthma. Look to classes and books to learn about what is in your area.

We heat our house with wood. A Black Bart stove in the fireplace radiates like an oven and ceiling fans circulate the warm air to keep the house toasty. The ashes go in the garden as compost, adding potash and other nutrients. The rich people at the golf course pay as much as $200 for a load of wood, and others pay $4 for five or six sticks at K-Mart and other stores. We get ours for free. The power company cuts down the trees around electric lines, and the city has a place where they pile up this sort of refuse wood for anybody who wants it. Check with your local landfill authority or the streets and maintenance department of your town or country. An industrious man could make a good living cutting down unwanted or damaged trees for one person and selling the wood to another.

Using road-killed animals may sound gruesome, but a lot of people do it. It's actually quite easy to learn to identify freshly killed animals, but that's not enough; you must also know the laws and make friends with game wardens. You must learn to clean the animals, information that can be had from butchers, extension agents, or farmers. Try to use as much of the deer as possible. The Indians used even the hooves, boiling them to make glue or a shellac-like substance and also made containers from the stomach and other organs. Look in hunting magazines for companies or individuals who will turn the hide into leather clothes. The more hides you send, the cheaper the cost. Other places advertise to buy the tails from squirrels and other animals, as well as bird feathers, which are then used in making hand-tied fishing lures.

You can learn enough about living off the land to actually do that, quitting your job and living not only frugally but comfortably.

If you have specific questions, you can send me a SASE and I will do my best to get you an answer quickly. My address is 4925 Ashemont Road, Aberdeen, NC 28315-5437.

Tom's Wild and Free Cookbook, *published by Loompanics, is available from him at the above address for $23.95, and he'll autograph your copy if you ask him to.*

Radical Simplicity or Good-bye, Accrual World

⠿

Catherine Roberts Leach and Britt Leach

Britt and Catherine Leach, he a successful actor and she a successful media marketer, opted out of their careers and into rural California, where they started Country Connections, *which despite its name is more* Utne Reader *(thankfully without* Utne *angst) than* Mother Earth News. *This is their story of how one life change can lead to others.*

We think it's important in the telling of our tale to be honest about things. Make that *things*. Voluntary simplicity does deal with them, their surfeit, the way their accumulation distracts from what's really real. But we were never into them. So we never had to give them up. What few *things* we had have sort of fallen apart or rotted over the years or assumed a different function, from *objet* to object, from loveseat to cat pedicure aid. There was never any wholesale eschewing of *things* in our move to simplicity. Maybe we need to call ourselves *radical simplicists* to distinguish us from those *voluntary simplicists* who held a bonfire of the vanities and moved to a yurt.

Things. No, we weren't acquisitive but we could have given that impression. We lived south of Ventura Boulevard in Studio City, California, and that was considered a better neighborhood than north of Ventura Boulevard among the class-conscious in Hollywood (everybody); but we didn't know north from south when we moved in, or that an apartment's location could be called a *thing*.

Once, also, we bought some decent clothes from Brooks Brothers. And one time one of us (Britt) drove a friend's new Mercedes down I-5 from San Francisco and did not retch once from shame. He even put that sleek, black baby into cruise control, cranked up the stereo, and screamed "Eeee-hah!" And, no, he did not feel the need for penance, for the lash, when he stepped out of the car and back onto *terra indigenta*.

Once we had a dinner party catered. Once we ate chateaubriand and drank Puligny-Montrachet. Yet we still say we were not into *things*. We just weren't thinking; we were reflexively "living in L.A."

We began thinking about things (as in all of life, not materialism) when Britt was informed by that cliché, vaudeville doctor (the one who is morbidly overweight and is smoking as he lectures you about your health) that he was drinking too much booze and his triglyceride level belonged at the head table in Sybaris.

Oh, we said.

We gave up red meat. This was about 1980. It wasn't an ethical choice; it was very much an ego decision called saving one's rear. We started to prepare chicken and fish with health in mind, and somewhere around the fiftieth attempt at preparing naked chicken or fish à la bland we thought, To hell with it, we're vegetarians, this flesh stuff without the grease is hopeless; maybe we can find some veggie recipes for food that won't make us gag. (Catherine once prepared a baked fish dish that came out of the oven so desiccated that it no longer looked ichthymorphous. It looked in fact alphabetic, like the letter *U.* You had to stop it from rocking before it could be consumed.)

But this won't remain a gastronomic odyssey except as it bears on simple living. We assure you that our tale is on its way out of Los Angeles and into a tiny mountain community and a double-wide modular home and different jobs—okay, *lifestyle* if you must—and it's a tale that began when we changed our diet. Radically. We met some good people who were vegetarian and out of that something happened about the way we viewed the world.

In seeking some veggie recipes and instructions on how to prepare vegetarian dishes we had to attend meetings of vegetarian clubs and animal rights groups. We weren't intentionally seeking out vegetarians, for God's sake, we just wanted some recipes! But back then you had to go to a meeting to learn. This is still the early 1980s, remember, and there weren't many books on the subject. John Robbins of *Diet for a New America* was still scooping ice cream, and Deepak Chopra hadn't found his first publicist. We're talking the Dark Ages of Gastrointestinal Enlightenment, when you had to get out there among them to find out how in the hell to survive without flesh foods.

Those meetings opened a door for us. Now is a good time to introduce ethics. Simplicity won't be far behind.

People who become vegetarian and stay with it for a while usually have made at some point an ethical commitment even though their diet evolution often starts as a simple move toward healthy living. But when you stop eating the animal something happens: you start actively thinking about it. As opposed to the passivity of saying things like, Oh, what a nice-looking pork chop, as if it existed only as a manufactured shape and not as part of the life and death of a creature. And to think about another creature is ethics even if the creature is an "animal." (We humans are "angels," of course.) So what might start as a health matter becomes an ethical matter. And when animals are included in a moral system it opens up that moral thinking, makes it more inclusive. You allow yourself to consider *everything* ethically when you include in your moral system the beasts you once ate. It's a drumroll moment.

We seem to be making a claim here for a gastro-ethical-spiritual connection and wouldn't dream of going into its physiology or its theology in detail. It's not the subject of this odyssey, but believe us when we say that becoming vegetarian sensitized us. We did not stay mere recipe-seekers. Becoming vegetarian made us start thinking about how our choices affect others. Ethics.

Those meetings were full of activists, people who believed in getting out there on the barricades for the cause they believed in. Farm animals, animals in laboratories, a few others. We became involved in civil disobedience; we were arrested. We also became environmental activists. It was a different experience from solipsistic Hollywood. Until this time in our life we were into Britt's being an acting luminary (twenty-five years as a character actor) and Catherine's climbing the corporate PR ladder. Showbiz. A dinner party loses its significance once you've occupied a lab in an animal action or hung banners from bridges for Earth First!; activism made all the froufrou seem like froufrou.

So we're becoming radicals now, and evolving into *radical simplicists*. We'll take that definition of *radical* that says: "arising from or going to a root or source; basic." In beginning to think about animals, diet, ecology, we were beginning to think about everything: root causes, all hierarchical connections; we were questioning everything, everybody, the world.

Is making that connection a leap of faith? We don't believe it is, but if you don't agree, please bear with us while we leap about some more. We promise to address simplicity. Soon. But we can't get there unless we thoroughly explore the animal connection. It was our path.

It's our belief that by choosing to eat flesh we were choosing a paradigm of predation in our life. In other words, we were not *passive* diners; we *had* thought about those animals we were eating beyond their processed(!)-and-packaged-for-your-convenience shape and were saying by our continuing to eat them that such is the acceptable way of the world. We were perpetuating hierarchical thinking by what we were eating, because there is nothing in fact more hierarchical than our relationship to the animals we slaughter unnecessarily. We don't *require* animal flesh for nutrition; thus, to continue to eat animals with that knowledge must be at best whimsical and unthinking, and at worst an implicit acquiescence in a predatory philosophy. An animal diet provides *a way to think about our relationship with the world*. When we changed our diet we changed our relationship to the world.

Here's what happened then. We moved north of Ventura Boulevard. Oh, no! We had to move because we were making less money and couldn't afford south of Ventura. And we were making less money because we began to choose the kind of work we would (and would not) do. Sensitized. We didn't look around one day and say, We're killing ourselves for *this?!* That seems to be the pattern for many who move to a simpler life. Our move came by way of making ethical choices, out of which came work choices, which began to limit our income as we radicalized our life, integrated our beliefs, thought about root causes, and noticed effects.

We'll start with Catherine. She was offered a great-paying job with a major television network "flacking" soaps—that's placing stories in the media about daytime drama, for those of you who speak English and not Hollywoodese. Her office would have been in the basement with no windows. And she would be selling worthless television. (Let's not dwell on *that* redundancy.) She didn't take the job.

There's a constellation of motivations here of course. What do soaps sell? Other than Proctor & Gamble's lather, other stuff. None of which is necessary to a good life. What television really sells is this message: "Your life, television viewer, is worthless. We will make you whole with our products. You are ugly, sexless, and you smell bad. Right this way." Silly stuff. And Catherine was becoming serious, terminating her complicity in what she considered harmful. Eventually she started an environmental PR firm with a partner and a window.

Britt was moving in the same direction. As an actor he had made a decent living doing commercials along with other television and film work. He stopped commercial acting and started making choices about other acting jobs (away from projects with violence and sexism). His income dwindled. If we keep this honest, then Britt has still not resolved his feelings about acting. He had retired from it, but recently returned to help support *Country Connections,* the magazine we've published since 1995. His confusion and complaint about acting exist beyond the aspect of gratification. He is willing to slog it out with acting to support the magazine. His work on it is gratifying and the magazine is worthy.

But what about participating in something that might be harmful—the entertainment business—in order to support something worthy? His concern is almost simple: Why do we need all this entertainment? If our life is good, if our job is one we believe in and that contributes to a positive goal, why do we need massive distraction? Shouldn't we work on changing our lives, the *world*? The entertainment business is the biggest business in the world. It grows with the collective malaise. "Opiate of the people" comes to mind. Britt's still thinking about it as this is written, but the answer seems clear. Choice.

That choice will be made from far north of Ventura Boulevard now. We live in a small community in the Los Padres National Forest, an hour from Los Angeles. We pay seven hundred dollars a month for a three-bedroom house. We are living on Britt's pension, some income from acting, and hope for the magazine. It's never been better.

There are a few encumbrances. We live low on the tofu chain with a rather limited budget, so we have reinvented our idea of entertainment. Conversation has become very important, and we talk to friends now with great appreciation. Luxury for us is a trip to L.A. and a vegetarian meal at a restaurant. Our cars are paid for even though the Volvo is leaning on the side of the house for the winter while we raise money to fix it. Yes, we still have the dread television, but we limit our viewing. Instead of watching the news in the morning we put seed outside for the birds and then watch them gather. We have identified seventeen varieties that feed around our house.

We still go through the cycles of life, and some days we are down. But Britt has discovered what he calls Therapy by Blackbird. Brewer's blackbirds, red-winged blackbirds and bicolored blackbirds make the most beautiful racket. It's both soothing and funny. Roger Tory Peterson says of them, "Notes, a loud *check* and a high, slurred, *tee-err.* Song, a liquid, gurgling *konk-la-ree* or *o-ka-lay.*" Britt says, "The sound is goodness itself. It clears the sinuses. Brings a smile. Vodka for the soul without any of the cost."

Scrub and Steller's jays demand peanuts once a day. And the

northern flicker, a dazzlingly beautiful woodpecker, is a loner who comes around rarely; you learn how to be quiet and just observe, honored by his visit. And peevish band-tailed pigeons, flitting chickadees, and nuthatches. All so energetic in their search for sustenance. So funny and fabulous, an endless daytime drama that has nothing to do with the pollution of "Brought to you by . . ."

This might be a good time to talk a bit about our magazine, *Country Connections*. It is our connection to the bigger world. It's where we debate all the elements we believe should make up a decent life. Low consumption is one, but we also deal with social activism, progressive politics, and ecological protection. We include articles written by people who have "made the big move." Some are successful, some not. Some go back home to their former life. We want the magazine to present the reality of moving to a simpler life. Given the strong matrix of our consumer culture it can be a shock to leave it. We are honest in our presentations of what to expect. We have been here seven years and believe that we know. Ironically, though we live in the country we have never felt more connected or understood better the need for connection. The magazine's banner says, "Seeking the Good Life—For the Common Good." What's implicit here is: Yes, find your way to a simpler life. It's so rich you can't imagine it, but please don't drop out. You are needed. People who are bright and talented and sensitive and compassionate are needed in the world. There is much work to be done. In our magazine, *worldly* isn't pejorative. Even though we live in the country we don't tout it as the only place for simplicity. As a matter of fact, simplicity can be damned complex when you are cut off from supplies by icy roads. The good and simple life can be had anywhere. And if you believe as we do in the importance of "the common good" there is much work to be done in the city. As much as we love it here, we know that one day we will return.

One of the best quotes from Duane Elgin's *Voluntary Simplicity* is, "The moderation of our wants increases our capacity to be of service to others, and in our being of loving service to others, true civilization emerges."

Radical simplicity is the name we have given our path. It's been interesting. Challenging and worth it. We could have planned better, but we didn't know what we were doing, that we were becoming *simplicists*. We were just making choices, trusting that we were making them with integrity. By using this book you might be able to smooth out some of the bumps. But whatever your path, we wish you the very best and offer the following tips with our hope that you will find the true Good Life.

Ten Tips

1. Put some money aside. *Poor* is not *simple*.
2. Be patient with your friends. They won't understand at first why you can no longer join them at fancy restaurants, but true friends will come around eventually and might even join you in your journey.
3. If you move out of the city you must remember that folks in the country don't necessarily share your values unless, like you, they recently moved there. So either move to a country place where there are other urban refugees or be prepared to call the friends who have stuck with you (see #2) when you need conversation.
4. You will need conversation. We are social animals. There is a honeymoon period in the country where you will walk the hills like the happy wanderer and imagine that one day you will have simplified your life to the extent that you will only wear a loin cloth and eat only fallen fruit. That might happen, but if it does you will still want to tell somebody about it. (See #2.)
5. If you decide to simplify your life in your current city, treat it as if you were moving to a place you do not know. Because when you have simplified your life, you won't.
6. Put some money aside. *Poor* is not *simple*. (Bears repeating.)

7. Regarding bears. If you move to the country, don't domesticate the wildlife by making them dependent on you. They were wild before you arrived from the city and will need their wild skills if you leave. We put out more seed for the birds in the winter, but otherwise limit their dependency.

8. Be patient with yourself regarding creature comforts. Unless you are going for the title "Ascetic of the Century," realize that in attempting the simple life you are not required to reverse several millennia of progress. But if you decide you want to try, we can sell you a loin cloth cheap. Being warm is okay.

9. Limit your yodeling. You will want to express your joy at the peace of the country, but the natives might not understand.

10. Humor is important. A person who has taken off snow chains for the first time might get so wet and cold that he has to strip naked on the front seat of his Volvo to dry off. Humor helps.

Country Connections is $22 for a one-year (six-issue) subscription. The address is 1443 Ventura Blvd. #407, Sherman Oaks, CA 91423. For a long (#10) SASE, they will send you their free Guide to Getting Out and Getting a Decent Life.

SAVE BIG ON YOUR FOOD BILL

❂

Rhonda Barfield

Rhonda Barfield feeds her family of six on fifty dollars a week, and she has done so for years, even though she lives in suburban St. Louis and does not have a large garden. Here's how she does it. And how you can, too.

Could you use an extra $50 a week?

Several years ago, $50 a week—$200-plus a month, $2,600 a year—was a literal lifesaver for our family. Just after our third child was born, we faced a financial crisis. I lost my part-time job and all our insurance benefits; my husband was working a low-paying job. Then our neighborhood went downhill.

We figured we needed an additional $50 a week to survive. Rather than trying to earn the extra money, we decided to cut our $80- to $100-a-week grocery bill in half. It wasn't easy, on such a low budget, to learn how to buy the food our family of five needed. But the effort was well worth it. That extra $50 a week helped get us on our feet again and moved us out of a bad neighborhood into a much bigger house in a safe suburb.

Saving on food has to be part of an overall financial plan, of course. Ideally, you should be cutting costs wherever you can. In the meantime, though, *you can start saving money on groceries immediately*, the very next time you shop. And trimming the food budget may very well be the single most important move you make in improving your finances. It was for us.

In this chapter, I'll recommend ten steps to help you begin. The first four are guidelines that I believe to be essential in working with a limited food budget. The next six are options, strategies to try. If they fit your lifestyle, they will help further reduce your spending. The goal is to help you set up an individualized program to trim your grocery bill substantially so you can use that $100 or $200 (or more) a month for a nice vacation, a college savings program, a new car, or other things you really need or want.

So let's get started.

I. TAKE CHARGE OF YOUR FOOD BUYING.

Set a budget. Have you found that if you go to the supermarket with $20 in hand, you'll probably spend it? On the other hand, tell yourself in advance that you'll buy only milk and bread—and take just enough money to do so—and chances are you'll spend much less. Stick to your limit, and soon you'll find all sorts of creative ways to buy more for less.

Make a detailed shopping list. With careful planning, you can shop only once a week, or even once every two weeks. My own list starts with basics (milk, flour, eggs) and then I add other foods I also want to buy. I estimate the total cost of everything on my list. If I'm under $50 I can add more; if over, I may have to rework my menus and buying plan.

Keep a price notebook. This won't take any time if you shop at a different store each week for four weeks. Simply take along a lined notebook, with categories such as "whole wheat bread" and "2 pounds carrots" penciled in on the left-hand side. Leave a few blank spaces for items that offer choices; for example, "canned green beans" may have subcategories of "generic," "store-brand," or "Green Giant," one subcategory per horizontal line.

The first week you shop with your price notebook, write down the name of the store at the top of the page. Underneath, jot down the cost of items as you buy them there. The next week, go to a different store and fill in another column. By the end of the month, you'll have a record of everyday prices on foods you buy at four supermarkets.

2. FIND THE CHEAPEST FOOD SOURCES IN YOUR AREA.

Choose the store with the best deals as your base store, and do most of your shopping there.

Also consider a second stop. You can decide where to go by consulting the supermarket flyers, price notebook in hand. If ground beef, fresh produce, and other items on your list are going for bargain prices at IGA, then make a fast run-in there after shopping your base store. Have you collected a number of coupons, and A&P's offering triple-coupon values this week? Choose A&P as your second-stop store.

Keep your eyes open for alternatives to supermarkets. You may be surprised at what's in your area: day-old baked-goods outlets, cheese and dairy outlets, warehouse stores, meat markets, health food stores, produce stands, farmers' markets, wholesale grocers who sell to the public, salvage stores (that offer cans with no labels, for example, for next to nothing), and more.

How do you find these places? Start by talking to someone you know to be a very frugal kind of person, one with a reputation for being a bargain hunter. Ask where he or she finds the best buys on food. You can also come up with plenty of prospects by browsing the Yellow Pages under "Grocers" and "Food." Then, the next time you're in the area, drop in, price notebook in hand, and check out this new "find."

It's not worth it to drive twenty minutes to save a quarter on fresh produce. But you can plan your outings around the bargain places, and save some of your grocery money for when you know you'll be going. For example, I've found a store that carries the best beef (in my opinion) in town, and they are also very reasonable. I do part of my grocery shopping there about once a month because to me it's worth driving four extra miles to save ten dollars on top-quality meat. I buy fresh half-price spices now and then from a little spice shop in a nearby historic district on my way to the post office. An outdoor produce stand is also a regular stop en route to another store.

3. PLAN YOUR MENUS AROUND STORE SALES AND CHEAP, NUTRITIOUS FOOD.

If you're serious about saving money on groceries, take a close look at both your purchases and your menus. Then ask yourself these questions:

* *What foods offer the best nutritional value and the best price?* Many healthy foods are bargains year-round: carrots, potatoes, whole chickens, rice, pasta, etc. Serve meals that feature these basics, and you'll automatically reduce your food bill.
* *How many name brands am I buying?* Store brand and name brand products are usually identical. Purchase the store brand and you'll still get top quality as well as a substantial savings. Also try generic versions. If you find the taste of any product to be inferior, return it for a refund.
* *How much meat am I buying?* Nutritionists now recognize that our bodies need less meat, especially red meat, than we once thought. Buy lean cuts—like chicken—and eat small portions. Think of meat more as a side dish than the main course. Serve more vegetarian meals, like vegetable soup and homemade muffins.
* *How many convenience foods am I buying?* Prepackaged dinners, bakery breads, frozen vegetables in sauce, and ready-made desserts are all expensive. You'll save a fortune if you prepare more foods from scratch.

4. LET STORE PERSONNEL HELP YOU SHOP.

Supermarkets are anxious to have your business, and will go out of the way to make your shopping a pleasant experience. Your challenge, though, is to avoid the high-ticket temptations and learn where the real bargains are. The key word to remember here is *ask*.

Ask the produce manager which fruits and vegetables are in season, as they'll be cheapest and most flavorful. Ask if he's willing to sell slightly damaged or very ripe produce, like bananas (you can make fruit shakes and frozen fruit pops and banana bread). The first time I did this at a store, the produce manager explained, a little condescendingly, that they didn't do that sort of thing at their store. So the next week, I asked the assistant manager, who also said no. The third time I visited that supermarket, I happened to see the store manager and asked him. Lo and behold, this store now sells big bags of spotted bananas and all sorts of slightly damaged fruits and veggies. Apparently word got around that several customers wanted to buy them!

Ask the store meat manager to recommend good, inexpensive cuts and also ways of tenderizing and cooking meat. One Christmas, I asked a butcher's opinion on the best brand of whole hams. He recommended the *cheaper* variety. When several were sliced for customers, he said, this brand was consistently leaner. Even better, the store offered a two-dollars-off coupon and the company offered a five-dollar rebate on the ham, and I took advantage of both. That Mickelberry ham cost about a dollar a pound.

Wherever you shop, ask about good buys. Explain that you're on a limited budget and you need to get the most for your money. What do they have on sale this week? Some people may brush you off; if so, ask somebody else, or go elsewhere next time. But do be persistent. By asking, I've found a half-price meat bin (perfectly good cuts and packages, usually overbuys nearing their expiration dates), generics, damaged boxes, food service–sized cans, bargain produce (like grapes detached from their stems, for 75 percent off) and all sorts of half-price foods, marked down for one reason or another. You don't have to spend any time looking for these bargains; just ask.

Once you've mastered these four basic guidelines for saving on groceries, you may want to tackle some specific strategies, and save even more money. (I've purposely left out several, like couponing, that are covered elsewhere in this book.) Try these strategies and see what works for you.

5. BUY IN BULK.

Warehouse clubs can really help a budget if you're disciplined, but be careful! The last time we bought the jumbo size of tortilla chips at Sam's Warehouse Club, we ate them all in two sittings. I'll bet this has happened to you, too. I'd recommend that you do what we didn't: Package all the tortilla chips in that big sack into little bags—for school lunches, for example—and guard them with your life. Or buy foods you know you can't overindulge on, like vanilla or flour.

Consider buying a half side of beef from a butcher or, better still, directly from a farmer. Most people don't have the freezer space for this, but if you can split the beef (and the cost) with two or three friends, you'll get top-quality meat for, generally, half the going rate. Pick-your-own produce places are often a real bargain. We buy about sixty pounds of apples, usually for thirty-five cents a pound, every year from a nearby orchard. (Our four children really look forward to a wagon ride behind the tractor and a romp in the hay castle.) Stored in a cool place, the apples we pick usually last until January and provide delicious snack food. Check to see what's available in your area: strawberries, raspberries, apples, pumpkins, peaches, apples. While you're at it, find out if you can go in and pick at season's end. Sometimes an orchard will discount its produce rather than let it go to waste.

6. CHECK OUT COOPERATIVES.

If eating natural foods is important to you, a cooperative can help you save, especially if you're currently buying from a health food store. I'm not a member of a co-op, but I buy bulk yeast, canola oil, and brown rice from a friend who is a member.

Cooperatives are set up to function as sort of grass-roots retail outlets. A group of people organize, go through a wholesaler's catalog, make their selections, and order a large quantity of food, usually once a month. Several days later, their order arrives by truck. Members meet again to package individual orders.

If you'd like to locate a cooperative near you, call the National Cooperative Business Association at 202-638-6222 and request a free information kit.

Or perhaps you'd like to organize your own informal co-op. I once met a group of five women who use their combined buying power to purchase discount produce. Once a week, one woman from the group travels to a large, downtown farmers' market. There, she buys enough produce for all five families. Because of the quantity bought, prices are wholesale, from 50 percent to 75 percent below regular supermarket rates. She divides the total produce and delivers equal shares to the other four families as well as her own. Next week, it's another woman's turn.

7. CONSIDER SHARE.

This unusual organization can be a real help to family food budgets. It's a nonprofit national program whose primary goal is "to build community by helping people work together to stretch their food budget."

Here's how it works: a community organization—a church, tenants' group, or club, for example—fills out an application to become a host organization. This host provides a place where members and people in the neighborhood can register for discounted food packages. Standard packages are a $30 to $35 value for $13 and include six to ten pounds of meat; four to seven fresh vegetables; two to four fresh fruits; pasta, rice, or cereal; and a few specialty items. Packages also come in different varieties: some SHARE groups offer vegetarian, all-meat, holiday, and/or mini-packages.

At registration, participants pledge two hours of community service for every package to be purchased. Pledges can be fulfilled through normal church and volunteer activities, or even through helping to sort bulk foods at the SHARE warehouse. So if you teach Sunday School and help with Boy Scouts every week (two hours total), you can request one package a week. The host organization tallies the number requested, places an order with local SHARE headquarters, and sends a team of volunteers to pick up and bring back the food.

SHARE is rapidly expanding and may be in your area. For information, call 1-888-742-7372 toll free.

8. BE ON THE LOOKOUT FOR FREE OR NEARLY FREE FOOD.

If you know where to look, you may be able to pick up the best bargain there is: free. Consider this personal example. When my boys were very young, we used to walk around the neighborhood, and one October day we discovered an apple tree with hundreds of apples. No one was picking the fruit, and some of it was rotting on the ground. I asked the owner's permission to take the apples in exchange for cleaning his yard. He agreed, gladly.

The boys and I spent three afternoons there. Christian sat strapped in the stroller, munching apples, and little Eric helped me rake up bad apples and pile them into trash cans. We collected hundreds of good apples—for free—and thoroughly enjoyed ourselves as well. Pass the word around your neighborhood and to relatives that you'll be glad to take any excess food. We've done this, and have been given fresh carp, venison, and moose meat (from a hunter), all sorts of vegetables (from neighbors' gardens), pears (from an unharvested tree), food from a friend's pantry (on moving day), and even sandwiches and juice (when our church had leftovers after a reception).

My sister-in-law, Joan, once worked out a deal with a local supermarket. The produce department boxed up damaged produce and called Joan, who picked it up for free. Not bad, right? It may be worth your while to call nearby produce managers and at least ask. I remember a time when Joan visited us and brought along three crates of cucumbers and a huge box of all sorts of fruit, including strawberries. And she still had plenty left over for her own family.

Sometimes orchards or farmers will let you pick "seconds" at no cost. A large vegetable company owns fields near my hometown and, after harvest, allows anyone interested to glean leftover potatoes or green beans. A family friend, Eunice Welker, used to pick a year's worth of free beans; she canned one hundred quarts or more each summer. Eunice says she has salvaged free vegetables from other fields as well, even when on vacation. She checks at local grain elevators to learn harvest days, or simply stops to ask a farmer's permission to glean.

9. USE A COOKING SYSTEM.

Perhaps you've heard of once-a-month cooking, in which you prepare thirty dinner entrees all in one day. Food is carefully packaged and frozen; then, homemade "convenience food" is ready whenever needed.

This cooking system can save a great deal of money if economical recipes are used. When cooking large quantities at a time, bulk-buy groceries are cheaper. Butchers often offer big discounts on "family-size" packs of meat, for example, and you can buy the cheaper, industrial-size cans of food and produce by the crate.

To tell the truth, though, I have my own cooking system that saves just as much money (or more) and works better for us. I call it fifteen-minute cooking.

Fifteen-minute cooking is my term for fast, low-cost dinner preparation. The concept is simple: assemble a home-cooked meal in two fifteen-minute sessions, one in the morning and one right before dinner. Or choose instead to cook, say, Tuesday night, then finish a second session just before Wednesday's dinner. In other words, divide your cooking time into two segments, either morning/evening (the same day) or night before/evening sessions.

I've written a book called *15-Minute Cooking* that explains exactly how to prepare a month's worth of dinners—each with an entree, bread or pasta, veggies, and dessert—in only half an hour total per day. The system features very basic, cheap ingredients, uses leftovers efficiently, and saves a great deal of both time and money.

10. REMEMBER WHY YOU WANT TO SAVE MONEY ON FOOD.

Are you a victim, forced to survive on a measly budget because you have no other options? Or are you a competent manager, determined to slash your food bill, thus freeing up money for other things you need or want?

If you see yourself as a victim, thrifty living will be a dreary chore. If you see yourself as a competent manager, trimming the grocery budget can be a challenge and a pleasure.

Why are you trying to save money? Write it down. Think about it when you're waiting in line at the supermarket, tempted to fill your cart with a lot of glitzily packaged, overprocessed foods. Remember your budget and your goals.

The first time I went to the grocery store on my "$50-a-week budget," I walked out with three skinny bags of groceries. Believe me, that wasn't enough to feed all of us for seven days! I had to do some research before my next shopping trip, and it helped. Each week, I bought a little more food for my money.

Don't feel overwhelmed if you can't do it all. Do what you can to cut your food bill, perhaps just one small step at a time. The savings will quickly add up.

Rhonda's book, 15-Minute Cooking, *is available through Lilac Publishing (the Barfields' home business), P.O. Box 665, Dept. LR, St. Charles, MO 63302. To order, send $12.95 or write to the Barfields for more information. Rhonda is also the author of* Eat Healthy for $50 a Week *(Kensington Publishing), which is available at or may be ordered through most bookstores nationwide.*

MAKING FROZEN ASSETS

■

Patti Anderson

Patti Anderson's interesting approach to plan-ahead food preparation can conserve both time and money. And it's not as complicated as you'd think, as you will soon see.

Do you work a "second shift?" In this busy era of working parents, most women finish their "real" job and go home to put in another tiring shift. As much as you love your family, it is still stressful and exhausting to return home to fix dinner, do laundry, supervise homework, etc. The list can go on all night!

How would you like to come home each night to the welcoming smells of a warm dinner? A real meal, not expensive, fat-laden fast food you hustled to pick up on the way home. Imagine! No more whiny kids in the kitchen while you are rushing to throw something together! No more last-minute trips to the grocery store or the deli! You can save money, time, energy, and most of all your sanity!

Does this sound too good to be true?

I can't tell you how to eliminate that "second shift," but I can show you how to simplify your life with freeze-ahead meals.

Learn to freeze your meals in advance and you will always have a meal waiting in your freezer to be heated for dinner. You can freeze a week, two weeks, or even thirty days or more in advance! If your refrigerator has a freezer, you probably have enough space to freeze dinners for a family of four for a week. Freeze your meals in advance and you will save lots of energy. Do you have a food processor? How often do you really use that marvelous appliance to chop and slice and save you time? If you are like me, I hate to drag it out to chop veggies for one meal. But if you cook and freeze once a month, you'll pull it out of the cupboard only once! How many times in the last thirty days have you browned ground beef? Cook and freeze in advance and you will only have to dirty that pot to brown ground beef once this month. Plan your meals in advance and you can take advantage of bulk buying. You'll save 50 percent to 90 percent on your food bill!

It sounds like a lot of work to get started, but after you have tried this method, you'll wonder why you didn't start sooner.

First, go to the bookstore or library and find a book that contains a chart on frozen food storage. Some foods can be frozen for as long as a year and others for just a few short weeks! Of course, you need to know which is which. For instance, most casseroles can be frozen for up to a month.

Make sure that everything you freeze is airtight! You don't want freezer burn to ruin the taste of your meals. Freeze in plastic freezer bags. They lay flat in the freezer and you can stack several bags on top of each other to save space. Or try disposable aluminum pans. They can be found in most grocery stores and with washing can be used over and over. Or hunt for extra pans or muffin tins at garage sales. Line your own casserole dish with foil, fill with your casserole, freeze until firm, and pop out. Wrap airtight with more foil and return to the freezer. You can just put it back in the original pan to thaw and cook, and you won't have to buy—or dirty—more pans!

Whatever you use to freeze your meals in, remember to label the package. You don't want to end up with "mystery meals." Label each package with contents and expiration date. If you freeze a dish today, don't label it with today's date. You'll be standing at the freezer, mumbling, "Okay, I froze this pot roast on January third and this dish can be frozen for six weeks so it is good until . . ." You'll get frostbite trying to figure out if the meat is still good! Always label your dishes with the date that they expire.

Find a calendar and decide if you will be freezing for one, two, or four weeks. Make a list of how many days for which you will plan meals. Remember to note special occasions. Do you need a special meal for a birthday or a holiday or, gulp, because your in-laws are coming? Note which days the kids have a soccer game or you have a meeting that will affect your mealtime.

Go through the local grocery ads and write down what is on sale. No—honest!—I don't expect you to run all over town to save a few pennies. Call your favorite store and ask if they will honor their competitors' prices. Many stores will give you the same price if they have the same product because they want your business. You can make one trip to one store and get all the sales prices, saving time and money. Remember to take the competitors' ads with you to prove the sale price.

Go through your freezer, fridge, and kitchen cupboards to ascertain what ingredients you have on hand. Write a menu using sale items and on-hand ingredients as much as possible. Then go through your menu, listing the ingredients you will need to pick up. Remember also to list what kind of containers you'll need to store the finished meals. Nothing is more frustrating than cooking a few weeks' worth of meals and having no way to store them! Add up how many pounds of chicken you'll need or how many cups of chopped onions. You'll soon see which items you'll be able to buy in bulk. Check your telephone book for warehouse markets such as Sam's or Costco. These markets are scattered across the country and can save you a bundle. Most require an annual fee, but they will often let you try out their store for a day without a membership card. Call ahead and check with their customer service department.

Before you go shopping in bulk, clean out the freezer and the fridge. You'll need room for all those groceries! And move heaven and earth to go shopping without your kids. (I know . . . dream on!) But it will lower your stress. Besides, you will need room in your cart and your car for all those groceries. Even if you have to hire a sitter the savings on your food bill will be worth it. Or trade with a neighbor and watch her kids when she goes shopping. How many times have you gotten to the checkout stand and had the checker ring up items you never saw before? Kids have a way of filling your cart with goodies that weren't on your list or in your budget.

When you return home, put away the perishable foods. Don't try to put the staples away. There isn't enough room. But don't despair—when you are done cooking, almost all of that food will hopefully be tucked away in the freezer.

The ideal way to cook for four weeks is to spend a weekend day cooking and storing those meals assembly-line style. Believe me, that one day cooking is effort well-spent. Think of all the evenings that will be less stressful because you cooked that day. But sometimes it is impossible to set aside one day for cooking. Here are two solutions that might fit your schedule. The first is to break up the cooking chores into two evenings. When my children were little, I would put them to bed and work while they slept. In the hours between nine and midnight, I would get the work done without their help. (With their "help," it would have probably taken an hour longer!) The first night, I would do preparation work. I would cook chicken, chop celery and onions, or brown hamburger. I would store it in the fridge. The next night, I would combine the dishes, label, and freeze. It was worth a few hours' lost sleep to come home to dinner, ready to be heated, for weeks to come! The second method is really easy. Each night, just cook double the amount you need. Half goes on the dinner table and half goes in the freezer. In a few weeks, your freezer will be filled! It will cut the number of times you prepare meals in half.

One day spent preparing for the next few weeks is worth the effort.

Before you begin, empty the trash and put in a new bag. Line up the spices and staples you will need. I put containers in one area, cover the kitchen table with canned goods, and try to organize as much as possible. Write down a list of what needs to be done. When you put it in writing, it is easier to see how much beef needs to be browned or how much celery needs to be chopped. You'll save steps. Chop or clean vegetables that you will need and set aside. Start cooking, trying to conserve your time and steps. As you fill containers, make sure that they are labeled well. I write out all my labels in advance. Do not leave food out at room temperature as you prepare. Use precautions and handle food with care. You don't want food poisoning!

Bulk buying will save you time and money but there are a few tricks to learn. Most recipes are written for a family of four. They usually list smaller-size cans among the ingredients. For example, an eight-ounce can of tomato sauce is the most common size. So if you just brought home a giant, gallon-size can of tomato sauce, what do you do? Use this handy chart to adapt your recipes:

tomato sauce	8-ounce can = about 3/4 cup
most cream soups	10.75-ounce can = 1 1/4 cup
	12-ounce can = 1 1/2 cup
most vegetables	14–16-ounce can = 1 3/4 cup
	17–18-ounce can = 2 cups
	20-ounce can = 2 1/2 cups
	29-ounce can = 3 1/2 cups
most juices	46-ounce can = 5 3/4 cups

If your recipe calls for a size not on this chart, buy the smaller can the first time you freeze the recipe. Empty the contents of the can and measure. Mark this amount on your recipe card for next time.

What do you do if you have a gallon-size can and don't use all of the contents? You might try to persuade a neighbor or friend to join you in your efforts, and then you can split the cost and contents with them. I used to split costs and cooking chores with my sister-in-law. Somehow, it didn't seem like a chore when we were giggling and catching up on all the family news. Both of us filled our freezers and enjoyed the few weeks of leisure that followed. You can also divide these gallon-size cans into smaller containers and freeze what you don't use for a later date. Here's a tip: Applesauce is very inexpensive in the gallon size. Freeze in half-cup or full-cup containers. Defrost and use in your baked goods such as quick breads, muffins, brownies, and cakes. Use applesauce in place of half the fat (butter or oil) called for in the recipe. You won't taste the difference, and you will cut the fat and calories in your baked goodies. But don't try to substitute applesauce for the fat in your cookie recipes. It just doesn't work. I know!

How many times have you come home from work and frantically tried to cook dinner only to find out you don't have the one ingredient you *have to* have? I used to turn off all the burners, throw the kids in the car, and run to the store to get the item I needed to finish the meal. When you freeze in advance, you won't have that last-minute dash! You'll know on cooking day if you forgot something. If you did, just put that dish in the fridge until you get the item the next day, then finish preparing it. I used to spend a fortune on impulse shopping. If I ran into the store for "just one thing," I probably came back out with a whole bag!

Each night when you finish the dishes, check your freezer for tomorrow night's dinner. Place the frozen dish in your fridge to thaw. *Do not* thaw on the kitchen counter! You don't want to run the risk of food poisoning. When you come home from work, pop the dish into the oven or microwave. Sit down and relax while it heats. You have given yourself a precious gift! A few minutes to calm down at the end of the day can make a big difference in how the rest of the evening is going to be. Share that gift! When a friend has a new baby, bring her a frozen meal to pop in the freezer. She'll be very thankful some night when the baby has colic and she has no time to spare.

Ten Tips to Make Planning and Freezing Meals Easier

1. Look in your phone book for stores that supply restaurants. Call and ask if they will sell to the general public. A lot of them do but don't advertise the fact. You can find great buys and great food. Often, I will bring home "restaurant"-type dishes such as chicken cordon bleu or veal Parmesan ready for the freezer! You can give your family and guests the same restaurant-quality dishes at a fraction of the cost. I keep trying to convince my husband to tip me as well as he tips waiters.

2. Undercook pasta or macaroni before freezing. You also need to slightly undercook rice. Use "real" rice—not the converted or

"instant" type of rice. It takes longer to cook, but it freezes well. "Instant" rice turns mushy when frozen. Brown rice freezes well!

3. If you buy chicken or other meat products in large bulk bags, such as ten or twenty pounds, you save a lot of money. But you need to repackage that bag. Spread individual pieces of chicken out on a cookie sheet and freeze until firm. That usually takes about forty-five minutes. Pop off the pieces and place in a freezer bag. Now that your chicken is "loose packed," you can take out as many or as few pieces as you need. This method works well with pork chops, hamburger patties, and even bacon slices.

4. Meatballs are great to keep in your freezer because they can be used in so many ways. Add to canned spaghetti sauce for a quick meal. Use for appetizers or make a hot meatball sandwich. Add one-half teaspoon baking soda to each pound of ground beef when making meatballs. This addition will help keep your meatballs firm when cooking after freezing. After shaping your meatballs, freeze them on a cookie sheet as described in #3.

5. For a really quick nonfat "cream" soup, try this method: Thaw a package of frozen vegetables such as broccoli. Whirl in a blender or food processor until smooth. Add enough skim milk to make a soup consistency. Heat until warm. Do not boil! This recipe is great with frozen peas, carrots, or cauliflower too. For a main dish soup, try using frozen hash browns. You can add corn and ham chunks for a quick meal or minced clams for clam chowder.

6. Fill a frozen pie shell with grated cheese, cubed pieces of meat, and cut-up vegetables. Freeze until needed for a quick quiche for dinner or brunch. Remove from freezer but do not thaw. Just add your favorite egg and milk mixture and bake until done.

7. Make your own pizza dough and shape it on a pizza pan. Freeze up to one month ahead of time. Add sauce and cheese when you're ready to make pizza. That frozen dough is fragile, like frozen pie shells, so be careful!

8. Slow cookers and Crockpots are great. You can come home to a hot meal waiting for you! Instead of spending an hour in the evening cooking, you may have spent time in the morning getting

food ready to go in the pot. Or, better, adapt your recipes to the freezer: Do everything ahead of time and freeze in a freezer bag. Thaw the bag overnight, pour into the pot in the morning, and add any last-minute touches! Don't forget to turn your cooker on!

9. Mornings are crazy at my house with five kids to get ready for various activities. I started freezing muffins to simplify the morning rush. Prepare your favorite muffins—but don't bake them—and freeze in foil muffin liners. They'll keep this way in the freezer up to one month. Make sure you use the foil-type liners because sometimes the paper ones get soggy. Remove the muffins from your freezer and drop them into the tins. Do not thaw them! Just bake in the oven, adding a little additional time, until they test done. It's so great to get out of the shower and find hot blueberry muffins waiting! It puts a smile on my face and gets the day off to a good start.

10. Okay, I admit I'm more like Roseanne than June Cleaver but every day I greet my kids after school with fresh home-baked cookies. You thought that only happened in TV-land, right? It can happen at your house too if you freeze your cookie dough! Just drop cookie dough on the baking sheets and freeze until firm. Pop off and place in a freezer bag. You can keep them in the freezer up to three months. When you want fresh cookies, just put the dough on the baking sheet. Do not thaw! Just add additional baking time until done.

That second shift is probably going to be part of your life for a long time. But life will be simpler and less stressful with freeze-ahead meals!

For a sample issue of Patti's newsletter, Frozen Assets, *send your name, address, and $1 to Frozen Assets, 6005 North 116th Plaza, Omaha, NE 68164. For a subscription, please send $12 by check or money order to the same address. For information on a two-hour Freeze-Ahead Meal Workshop, please send a SASE (same address)!*

CONFESSIONS OF A
MIDDLE-CLASS COUPONER

Lori Perkins

Coupons? Most people either love 'em or hate 'em. I live in a very competitive city grocery-wise, so I love 'em. I especially love using double coupons on sale items—that's the only way I'll buy my favorite brand of peanut butter. Here Lori Perkins tells you everything you need to know about saving tax-free dollars sensibly with coupons.

Like most people, my husband thinks of coupons as twenty-five cents off some zany food product you would never buy anyway. When he does the food shopping, he's always too embarrassed to use them. But coupons are not just for grocery shopping, and they can make a big difference in any household, giving you a lot more money for extras you would never dream about.

I'm always telling my husband how much we save each year with coupons, but he never pays attention to me. We live in New York City, and one day recently we were driving downtown to go ice skating at Rockefeller Center. As we sat in traffic on the West Side Highway, I mentioned that I had a $3-off coupon for parking, and a two-for-one coupon for a meal at a downtown restaurant. We were planning to rent some movies from Blockbuster on the way home, and I also had a two-for-one coupon and a $1.50-off a children's movie coupon. He turned to me and said, "You've got coupons for everything," and I replied, "Yeah, a dollar here and a dollar there saves us something like five thousand tax-free dollars every year." He looked at me with something approaching awe, and for the first time I knew my couponing had registered with him.

I consider myself a middle-class couponer, and I look on couponing as a hobby that stretches the family budget. I didn't always see it that way; I first got into serious couponing when I was certain that I was about to be really poor. I had just quit my job to start my own business, and I had promised my husband that I would not use any of the household monies to support it.

The last time things had been this tight was when I was newly married and both my husband and I had lost our jobs. We were out of work for seven weeks and had something like $200 in our savings account. I remembered that I had managed to buy food for the week for $22 (including meat) using every coupon I could get my hands on. So, just before I quit my job, I sent off $2.99 for one of those coupon organizers you see advertised in the Sunday supplement, and I was amazed when it arrived with an entire magazine dedicated to couponing and refunding. I never knew such a world existed, or that people took it so seriously, and that there was so much money to be saved.

It turned out that my business (I'm a literary agent) was successful from the start (one of the first books I sold was by Michelle Easter, the woman who wrote the couponing and refunding magazine). I was lucky that I never needed to seriously supplement my income with coupons and refunds. Instead it became a hobby and a passion.

I've been a serious couponer for seven years, which has given me enough time to come up with my own personal dos and don'ts, as well as a couponer philosophy.

I. ORGANIZATION

You have got to get some kind of coupon holder that fits conveniently into a purse (anything bigger than that will be left at home more often than not). You need to do this so you can categorize your coupons and go through them periodically (I do this once a month) to throw out the expired ones. There's nothing as frustrating as thinking you're saving money only to discover that the coupon you planned to use expired two days before and you're now paying full price.

Mail-order coupon holders come with categories, but I found that my categories were not covered by the labels that come with most coupon holders, so I made my own labels and used index cards to divide the sections.

2. LISTS

Make a master shopping list, so you know the types of products you use, and then clip only the coupons you know you will use. After you've been clipping for a while, you'll see that there are certain categories and manufacturers that often give coupons, and you'll change your categories. For instance, when I first started couponing, I made up my categories only by what I wanted to save money on, but I quickly learned that what I wanted to save on didn't jibe with the coupons that were available. So I had a big file for toiletries, which for me included everything from shampoo to makeup to pharmaceuticals (which actually meant bathroom stuff), and a very thin file for meat and dairy products (although you do find these occasionally).

3. IMPULSE COUPONS

When I first started using coupons I clipped everything, and when I was no longer destitute (pure poverty keeps you very close to the shopping list with no extras), I found myself buying everything because it was "on sale" and overdoing my budget big-time. I soon realized that for every fifty cents I was saving, I was spending two dollars, so I learned not to clip what I call "the impulse coupons."

4. MORE ON IMPULSE COUPONS

Now that I'm a mother of a four-year-old, whom I take shopping with me, I have a big file of kid impulse coupons. These are coupons for things I know my son has seen advertised on TV, and that he'd like to try, but which we don't need. These include everything from disgustingly sugary breakfast cereals (my husband is the one who really eats these) to Pop-tarts and Trix yogurt. It's hard for a four-year-old to sit still through a two-hour grocery shopping session with my mom and me (we shop every ten days), so I let him pick one special thing during the shopping trip. I let him know what we have coupons for, and he's always pleased as punch with his purchase, and so am I, because we never pay full price for these things, and he knows they're a one-shot deal in our house.

5. EVEN MORE ON IMPULSE COUPONS

I also keep a fairly large file of "Mommy impulse coupons" which include coupons for makeup, fancy candy, magazines, etc. If I see something on sale (especially the makeup) and I have a coupon for it, it's always great to get a double dip. Occasionally, I save more than usual on a shopping trip, and I want to get myself a little something extra—and that's where the Mommy impulse coupons come in.

6. MISCELLANEOUS

I have a large miscellaneous file, which includes a lot of non-supermarket stuff, like coupons for Kentucky Fried Chicken, Blockbuster Video, parking lots, or toy stores. I carry these with me in my wallet just in case we decide to use them on the spur of the moment. I can't tell you how much we've saved doing this.

Because we don't live near a single fast-food restaurant chain, I never used to clip these coupons, and I would always kick myself when we'd go to one of these restaurants and I didn't have any. I've learned. When you have a four-year-old, the fast-food restaurant world is a magnet, and it pays to be ready. I also always bring these coupons when we go on vacation because we end up eating this stuff quite a lot when we're on the road.

7. MEMBERS ONLY

More and more supermarkets have these "membership" cards,

where you have to show the card to get the store's specials. I have cards at all three of the supermarkets I shop in, and I keep them all in my wallet, with my credit cards, so I'm never caught without them.

Most of these supermarkets have specials two or three times a year that let you get a free turkey (Thanksgiving) or a ham (Easter) or a picnic lunch (Fourth of July) if you buy a certain amount of groceries in a certain period of time. Since I shop with my mom, we use one membership card during these "food drives," so we always get the free food. You don't have to use this free food yourself—you can donate your bounty to a local food drive or shelter and give someone else the benefit of your frugality for the holidays.

One of our regular supermarkets has a big two-for-one sale at the beginning of each month, so my mother and I often buy the items that are on sale and split the purchase. If you have the same deal at your local supermarket, it's a good idea to shop with a relative or friend to take advantage of these sales (because otherwise you won't buy the two pounds of turkey breast for $5.99, which is really an excellent deal).

8. FREE AIRLINE TICKETS

It took me a while to realize that coupons extended outside the Sunday supplement. One day I realized that I was spending a ton on my phone bill and my American Express card and that I could tie them together to get quite a few free airline tickets a year.

With family throughout the country, we need three airline tickets almost every time we travel. By getting two-for-one tickets from my phone bill and cashing in my "credit card miles," we have not paid for three airline tickets once in the last two years. We also rent a car every year for a trip to Maine, and manage to get a free one-week rental from the credit card miles.

The thing about these free airline and car coupons is you have to plan ahead. I try to figure out where we're going at the beginning of the year, and guesstimate how many credit card miles we'll have by the time we take that trip. I budget those miles, so we know what we're paying for and what we're getting free. You have to put in for the free tickets about six weeks before your trip (otherwise half of what you save is eaten up with Federal Express and speedy processing fees), but it's worth it.

The other thing about these free airline tickets is the cost of the ticket itself. If I'm planning trips to both Miami and California in the near future, and only have credit card miles for free tickets for one trip, I'll use the free tickets on the California trip because the cost of a round-trip to California from New York is always greater than that of a round-trip to Miami.

9. OTHER NONFOOD DEALS

Once I started cashing in the frequent flyer miles, I found there were coupons all over. Once or twice a year, Blockbuster offers a booklet of twelve $1.50-off kids' movies coupons if you buy the big kid hit from them (*Toy Story* last year). We knew we were going to buy it, so it paid to purchase it there, especially since it was at the same price as all the other discount stores.

I also started reading the local paper and the local coupon flyer I got in the mail. There were tons of coupons for the local dry cleaner, car wash, pizza delivery, etc.

Don't overlook big store flyers either because many department stores now include 10 percent or 15 percent off coupons with their holiday catalogs. All the big department stores seem to offer 10 percent off if you sign up for their credit card, so if you're planning a big purchase and don't have one of these cards, it might be worth it to sign up and use one of the 15 percent off coupons on an item they already have on super sale (we bought dishes for eight and flatware for twelve for less than $100 this way).

Credit cards can also be a way of receiving coupons. I recently signed up for a Toys R Us credit card. They send me $10 in coupons for every $1,000 I spend (it builds up faster if you buy stuff at Toys R Us or Kids R Us). The card had a low interest rate, it was right before Christmas, and I've found that I've already saved more in coupons than the interest on the card, especially if you pay it off right away (this particular card has no grace period). They also send additional coupons all year long, so I'm way ahead of the game. When you have a kid, you're always buying toys, if only for the endless birthday parties your child is invited to.

I also get coupons just before Christmas from my Bloomingdale's card, which I take with me mall shopping, and use them all. It's the only time I use the Bloomingdale's card, and I pay it right away, so the 15 percent off is always worth it.

A number of stores and restaurants offer birthday discounts, which I always take advantage of. My favorite discount fashion store, Loehman's, gives you an additional 15 percent off if you buy clothes during the week of your birthday, so my mom and I always spend a day shopping on each of our birthdays (which happen to fall at the end of two fashion seasons, so we end up getting unbelievable discounts—we each bought full-length, full-skirt winter coats last year for about $35).

10. REBATES

I don't have a lot of time to clip box tops, file forms, and circle register receipts, but I do keep my eye open for these. Once or twice a month, I sort through an envelope where I've stashed these and mail them in. Most are for two or three dollars. I keep a register of when I've sent them in (it takes three to six weeks for the checks to arrive), and then I deposit them in a savings account for my son. When I have $25, I buy him a savings bond.

You have to collect the forms ahead of time, so I clip them from the Sunday paper, or look for them at the supermarket. Occasionally, they're on the box of the product you buy.

11. BOX TOPS AND FREE STUFF

I work from home, and sometimes the babysitter calls in sick. When this happens, it's almost impossible to get my four-year-old to come to the mailbox with me (and I need to get the mail every day for my business). What I've done to bribe my son to the mailbox is mail in the box tops from his cereal boxes, or the UPC symbols from his snack foods, so he knows we're waiting for his Johnny Quest comic or his free Smud. I've also signed him up for every free kids' club membership there is, so he gets magazines and free stuff around his birthday (I get coupons too). Besides, he loves getting his own mail.

Once in a while, there's great free stuff for me too. I mailed in for some free pantyhose and a travel razor, which were quite nice.

My son's school also collects box tops. They get supplies by sending in massive amounts of these box tops. So I clip these and donate them to the school.

I once read that an entire town saved up labels to get a free baseball pitching machine for the local Little League team, so there's a lot to be said for helping out one box top at a time.

Often there are more coupons for the product you just purchased on the inside of the box or on the back of the label, so always look.

12. MAILING FOR MORE COUPONS

Occasionally, the inside of a box or the back of a label has a form to mail in for free coupons for other products by this manufacturer. If I know it's something I use often, and the coupons promise to be worth more than the postage, I usually send them in.

Double couponing doesn't work for me because the local stores that allow double couponing only do so if the coupon is worth less than fifty cents. Most of the stuff I clip is worth more, and the time it takes to go to an out-of-the-way supermarket is not worth it for me, but I know many people swear by this.

I will, however, visit different supermarkets and drugstores to take advantage of a sale, especially if I have a coupon for the product advertised.

I always price an item on sale before I buy it. More often than not, another brand is cheaper to begin with, so the coupon and the sale don't make a difference. On some items (such as sponges, paper towels, and plastic bags), the store brand or the cheapest brand is always the best buy for us, because we use so many of them.

There are some brands I'm really loyal to, such as my detergent, toothpaste, and hair color, so I'm always looking for those coupons.

When the Sunday supplement has a coupon for these items, I often ask my mom to clip them for me, so I can have a few on hand at all times. I do the same for her with her cat food and contact lens solution coupons.

Each year I get better and better at couponing, and each year I seem to come up with additional ways to save money. This hobby has given me more satisfaction and payback than anything I ever did to "get rich quick." And, at times, it's made me feel really good about myself, because I can afford to share this "wealth" with others without taking anything away from my family (I often pass out coupons that are going to expire soon if I see someone has an item I'm not going to use, or I may let someone who doesn't have a membership card use mine; I recently gave my brother one of my two-for-one airfare coupons that was about to expire, and he saved $550—of course, he thinks my hobby is great).

Frugal Fun

Shel Horowitz

*I often get asked by media folks, "But what do you do for fun?" The implication is usu-
ally that one must spend a lot of money for entertainment; therefore, since I don't like
to spend a lot of money, I can't be having any fun. Shel Horowitz has researched and
enjoyed cheap entertainment more than anyone I know. Here is advice from an expert
on having fun—on the cheap.*

For much of my life, I've had very little money—but that's never pre-
vented me from enjoying a good time.

In 1979, I became a VISTA volunteer in New York City, at $82
per week. This was a big increase in my earning power; for the previous
several months, I'd been working as a clerk in a fruit store, one day a
week, and bringing home a princely $15. My total monthly income
from all sources had been $160 a month plus $60 in food stamps, so
the VISTA stipend felt like a king's ransom.

Even during this period, I never lacked for pleasures—yet I lived
within my means. In fact, I managed, after a year and a half as a VISTA
volunteer, to put away enough to live on for the next six months that

followed my tenure there. I had long since developed some internal guidelines that allowed me to live both cheaply and well, and from these guidelines eventually came *The Penny-pinching Hedonist: How to Live like Royalty with a Peasant's Pocketbook*, my 280-page guidebook on how to save money on travel, entertainment, eating out, gourmet cooking, kids' activities, sports and recreation—even romance.

In this brief chapter, of course, I cannot cover all of these. So we'll concentrate for now on entertainment, but we'll also touch on dining and shopping. Since much cost-slashing in these areas begins with good preparation, the first three guidelines elaborate on that idea.

1. RESEARCH WHAT IS FREE OR CHEAP TO START WITH.

For travel, entertainment, and new purchases, the more you learn, the better position you will be in to snap up a bargain.

Here are some of the bargains we've been able to take advantage of—first in travel, and then in entertainment.

I subscribe to an e-mail bulletin from a low-airfare travel agency. Most of the time, their rather shrill messages are annoying, but I put up with them because thanks to these bulletins, we're going to Puerto Rico for about 40 percent less than the going rate. Through other research, I've kept track of airline fare wars and taken advantage of several really great deals. My wife and daughter and I all flew to London a few years ago, on a regular flight of a scheduled airline, for the unbelievable price of $198 per person, round-trip. We've often taken advantage of sales on domestic fares to fly across the country for $99.

As far as entertainment, you'll be amazed by who plays free concerts if you keep your eyes open. I have seen free performances by well-known stars in every genre: Arlo Guthrie, Leonard Bernstein, Stevie Wonder, Marion McPartland, Bonnie Raitt, Cris Williamson, John and Yoko Lennon, Pete Seeger, and countless others.

Local newspapers, bulletin boards, college, library, and museum calendars of events, membership mailings from sponsoring organizations, radio announcements, even postings on the Internet can keep you informed of events and opportunities. If you're lucky, prices will be listed. If not, follow up with a phone call. It's amazing how many free and cheap events are out there! While researching for *Hedonist*, I counted twenty-one free cultural events, and another nine events between $3 and $6 in one issue of our local weekly newspaper. Several of these were staged by very well known performers. That's just in one issue, in a rural college area.

As for shopping: knowing what items usually cost lets you recognize real bargains—and avoid being taken by a "sale" on low-quality, overpriced merchandise. Patience is definitely a virtue here, particularly in technology purchases such as computers and stereos (where the longer you wait, the more the price drops and performance increases). By moving quickly when the right price comes along—and by taking last year's top model after a newer and more powerful one is introduced—I've been able to get deals like a $2,100 computer for $1,300, a great-sounding CD player for $69, and an $850 color monitor for less than $400.

Research helps in another way: if you prefer to buy locally, but you have a catalog or advertisement from a competing store or mail order company, many stores will honor the competitor's price. Thus, you get local convenience and mail-order prices.

2. USE EVERY AVAILABLE LEGITIMATE DISCOUNT AND FREEBIE.

Many stores and attractions offer reduced prices for students, elders, disabled people, members of their own and other organizations—or reduced prices during certain slow days and times. If you have an AAA, AARP, or college ID, be sure to ask if you qualify for a reduced price. You may be able to get a lower price as an alumnus of your college, a member of a union or professional trade association, a visitor from a foreign country. . . . Be as creative as you can; the worst that can happen is that they will say no.

And if you're shopping for any kind of noncontroversial charitable cause or organization, be sure to discuss the cause or organization with a store manager, if possible at least two weeks ahead of when you need the items (a month is better)—particularly in a large corporate store with deep pockets.

Here's a real-life example: I was in the supermarket (part of a large regional chain) just after an article had come out locally about *Hedonist*. An acquaintance stopped me and asked if I had any ideas about lowering the cost of supplies for a school theater production organized by the Parent-Teacher Association. I suggested she approach the manager and ask for a discount. Because the request had to go through channels, she didn't get a better price that day—but the store agreed to donate all the supplies for the next event.

For more controversial causes, find sympathetic local business owners who don't answer to a big corporate bureaucracy. Reward their generosity by publicizing their donations.

If you're going to an event or attraction with a group of friends, ask ahead of time about group rates. Often, even ten people qualify for a group discount.

3. CONSIDER PRICE AS A FACTOR WHEN CHOOSING AMONG ACTIVITIES.

On a recent trip to New York, my wife and I discovered a bounty of entertainment options. There seemed to be at least a dozen interesting plays, or unusual concerts. When we started doing some phone shopping, we found most of the events we were considering ranged from $25 to $75 a ticket—and our interest in going out that night began to wane. But then we found an African dance and drumming event with bottom-rate $15 tickets still available.

The concert was five hours long, and included over twenty different acts. The quality of the performers was outstanding. We were exhausted and exhilarated by the end of the evening, and we felt as if we'd gotten much more than our money's worth.

On another weekend in New York, we chose (for a warm summer evening) from among five different free performances of Shakespeare at various parks around the city. Once again, we got a lot more than our money's worth (which, in this case, was only subway fare). And again, we enjoyed ourselves just as much as if we'd paid $60 per ticket—more, in fact, since we didn't have to worry about getting a good value for our hard-earned dollar.

This principle holds true anywhere, not just in New York. Often, performances in outlying areas or by lesser-known artists can be electrifying, as well as inexpensive. In Granada, Spain, we traveled to the far end of the city in order to spend an unforgettable (and amazingly reasonable) New Year's Eve in a Gypsy cave, watching live flamenco from inches away (and chatting with the dancers before the performance started). In Key West, Florida, we experienced the grand spectacle of the promenade at sunset: an unending carnival of (mostly very talented) fire-eaters, jugglers, musicians, breakdancers . . . all playing for voluntary donations from passers-by. In college towns, we've often gone on campus, where many events are subsidized for the college community but open to the general public. In our own town, we've learned which community theater and music groups consistently deliver excellent performances, and we seek them out. Of course, we also keep our eyes open for free and cheap performances by well-known stars. In all of these situations, there were much more expensive alternatives than the ones we chose. And yes, every once in a while we hit an event that we wished we had skipped. But we've also been in situations where an expensive event wasn't worth it—even some big names have an off night once in a while. Fortunately for us, we weren't paying for many of these events because we had used the following strategy.

4. BENEFIT AN EVENT THROUGH YOUR SKILLS OR LABOR—IN EXCHANGE FOR FREE ADMISSION OR EVEN A PAYCHECK.

Either direct or indirect work exchanges can open up a world of entertainment and recreation opportunities, while leaving your wallet securely in your pocket. Many events or organizations could not exist without volunteers, including prestigious concert halls, music festivals, theater series, and so forth. Often, the commitment is minimal. Ushering, for instance, generally means you have to put on fancy clothes, show up an hour or so before the performance, learn the theater layout, and escort patrons to their seats. (It also means you may be sitting on the steps during the performance if the show is sold out.) In other situations, you may need to put in more time. For twelve years, I've volunteered at a nearby folk festival. Volunteers buy a T-shirt and receive all their meals plus free camping privileges on the grounds. What a deal! The typical shift for their fifteen hundred(!) volunteers is two hours working, two hours off, all day long for two days. But, even then, there are many jobs that can only be done before or after the festival—or jobs that require close proximity to the various stages—so it's possible to see and hear quite a bit of music. Tasks include, among others: driving performers; assisting disabled patrons; staffing retail sales booths for the sponsoring organization; set construction and teardown; litter-picking and recycling; cooking for the volunteers and performers; stage managing; sign-language interpreting; and security.

How would you like to get paid to go to a show? If you have good analytical and writing skills as well as some degree of knowledge about the art, you can cover performances for a local community newspaper or radio station. I've been a freelance concert and theater reviewer since the mid-1970s, getting paid anywhere from nothing to $50. Typically, it takes me about an hour to write my story after the show—and I do have to pay careful attention and take good notes during the performance. Even if a particular paper doesn't pay, I think it's worth it for the hundreds of dollars a year in free tickets. Reviewing (or previewing) has some extra benefits, too. You may get to interview your favorite stars, or take home their latest recorded works.

Of course, any kind of paid or volunteer position within the performance hall—selling tickets, designing costumes, waiting tables, building sets, running the sound and light boards—generally includes free admission to the events you're working on, and sometimes other events in the same facility. Also, make friends with the box office staff. Early in a production run (before the reviews come out) they may be looking for people to "paper the house"—to make the hall look crowded, even though many tickets haven't been sold. Let them know you're available for this kind of "work."

5. SEEK OUT NONTRADITIONAL ENTERTAINMENT.

A century ago, entertainment was usually created, not just consumed. Live public performances were rare in most places, and movies and sound recordings were in their infancy. So families made their own music, put on their own theater productions, and found many alternate entertainments. All these choices, and many more, are even more accessible today. You can easily develop and explore an interest—perhaps something that will grow into a lifelong hobby—in dozens of areas: local history, ethnic genealogy, gardening, birding, tree and flower identification . . . the list is limited only by your own creativity.

Where can you explore these cheaply? Once again, there are myriad possibilities. To name just a few: libraries, museums, parks and forests, art galleries, specialty stores (for browsing and window shopping), trade shows, even surfing the Internet.

6. EAT CHEAPLY AND WELL: NINE WAYS TO ENJOY GREAT RESTAURANT MEALS.

Come for lunch: Save 30 percent to 50 percent of the dinner cost, enjoying the same food at the same table. Look for business lunch specials and save even more. Or buy your take-out dinner at lunch time and reheat it for dinner.

Come early: Check around for restaurants that offer an "early bird" dinner special, typically served from around 4:30 to 6:00 P.M.

Order carefully: There may be some excellent $8 or $15 entrees in a $25 per plate restaurant—or $5 choices in a $12 restaurant. Vegetarian dishes are often much less expensive, or there may be a low-priced seasonal special. Mixed appetizer plates, pasta- or rice-based dishes, salads, and stuffed potatoes all lend themselves to saving money. We just took six people to one of the most expensive restaurants in our town, and we only spent $31.75. We shared one entree and five side dishes; all of us were sated and happy, and we even took home leftovers.

Compare à la carte and full dinners: What extras come with a full meal? Do you really want them? If the answer is yes, eat the salad, bread, and side dishes to your heart's content, but as your belly fills, pack up the rest of your main dish—and get two meals for the price of one. If you don't need these, order your entree alone and save 20 percent to 40 percent.

Share: Whether or not you're in a Chinese restaurant, a Chinese-style dinner with lots of people passing dishes back and forth can result in a much richer experience. Come with a group of four to eight people and order three to six dishes. You'll all get to sample a delightful array, and save the cost of a meal for every fourth person.

Coupons and dining clubs: To increase their market share, many restaurants offer discounts or two-for-one meals through newspaper ads, coupon books, or dining club memberships. Both the coupon books and the clubs work pretty much the same way: you pay a fee (typically $10 to $30) and present either your coupon or your membership card when you order.

Skip the drink: Eat-in alcoholic beverages have a huge profit margin. The three-dollar single bottle of beer you order in a restaurant is identical to the brew in a five-dollar six-pack. But at your table, each ounce costs twenty-five cents instead of seven cents. At a liquor store, a whole bottle of the same wine the restaurant serves may cost only slightly more than the glass on your dinner table. So have your meal out, and then, if you want a drink, go home afterward (or find a B.Y.O.B. restaurant). I drink seltzer at home, water in restaurants. If you do buy a drink, get your money's worth. Request it without ice, or consider sharing a pitcher rather than buying individual glasses.

Go just for dessert: If what you really want is the experience of being served amidst elegant wood paneling, far from the hoi polloi, have your dinner elsewhere, walk off the food, and then go to the best restaurant you know for dessert. Enjoy fabulous coffees and pastries on a silver tray, placed gently before you on a lace doily over a white linen tablecloth while you relax in a comfortable chair and enjoy the view—or at least the people-watching. It won't be cheap, but it will give you much of the ambience of a restaurant meal, at perhaps a quarter of the cost. (Go well after peak dining times; otherwise you might be resented.)

Go on your birthday: Many restaurants offer a free meal on your birthday. You might even have lunch in one restaurant, dinner in another, dessert in a third, and a drink in a fourth—all free.

7. BARTER.

Everybody wins on a good trade deal. If you're trading your own products and services, you're getting the deal for your wholesale cost. Better still, if you can barter something you bought but don't need anymore, you're trading your junk for someone else's treasure.

Here are three of the great barters I've been part of:

* We had a friend in massage school who couldn't practice in his own apartment. He gave all his practice massages in our conference room and traded us one free session for every two he did on other people.
* In my poverty-stricken post-college days, I joined the collective of a student-run coffeehouse, which allowed me free food and entertainment. I wasn't a student and was upset when the rest of the collective wanted to close for the summer, so I kept it open as a volunteer manager and talent booker and got to fill up the place all summer long with entertainers I wanted to hear. Managing a coffeehouse also looked great on my resume.
* I traded a series of newsletters, flyers, and marketing strategy sessions for an Oriental rug I could never afford to buy.

Shel's book, The Penny-pinching Hedonist: How to Live like Royalty with a Peasant's Pocketbook, *is $20 book rate (or $22 first-class postage) within the U.S. and Canada. Massachusetts residents please add 85¢ tax. (All prices in U.S. dollars.) All major credit cards accepted.* Phone: *800-683-WORD or 413-586-2388.* E-mail: *orders@frugalfun.com.* Mail order: *P.O. Box 1164, Northampton, MA 01061. Preview the book at http://www.frugalfun.com.*

THE FRUGAL ENTREPRENEUR

Terri Lonier

Many years ago a friend of mine invented a luggage tag. After an airline expressed an interest in his tag, he made plans. Big plans. A corporate jet. A Mercedes for a company car. And so on. His venture failed, however, because he did not put his money where it would do any good. Terri Lonier was not there when my friend needed her advice (not that he would have listened, anyway), but she's been serving new entrepreneurs for several years now. In today's business environment, small businesses must follow the "lean and mean" lead of large businesses. And there's no one I know of who can help keep you leaner than Terri Lonier can. But you'll have to work on the mean yourself.

The recent era of corporate downsizing, rightsizing, and—some have said—capsizing has led a growing number of individuals to start their own small businesses. They realize that there is no such thing as "job security" anymore. There's only what I call "skills security." Instead of turning to others for financial independence, they look inward and discover ways that their skills, talents, and abilities can become a business that brings them personal as well as professional rewards.

Starting a business can be both thrilling and terrifying. There are a lot of things to manage—including the finances. In this chapter, I'd like to share with you tips and techniques I've gathered during my twenty years as a solo professional, as well as insights shared with me by the thousands of entrepreneurs I've encountered along the way. Whether you're a business newcomer or an experienced pro, you'll find ideas to help you maximize your resources.

THE FRUGAL MINDSET

Meet the frugal entrepreneur—dedicated to using creativity instead of cash to generate business success. These savvy individuals know the value of their time, energy, and money, and they spend each in the manner that will best benefit their businesses.

The best practitioners of frugal entrepreneurship are not tight-wads, bent on saving every cent. They know that while a penny saved is a penny earned, business success comes from more than adding up pennies. For example, you won't find these business owners spending time cutting up brown paper bags to create economical mailing envelopes. You will, however, find them recycling packing materials to save money and the environment. That's the style of a frugal entrepreneur: practical and useful without being outrageously penny-pinching. In other words, frugal with a view of the big picture.

When it comes to being masters of frugality, entrepreneurs know three important rules of success:

* *Cheap can be expensive.* Savvy frugalists don't buy based on price, they invest based on value. They know that a quick, cheap solution may cost them more in the long run—when they'll be forced to make a replacement purchase or redo an action. The best frugal investments pay off over time.
* *Time is more valuable than money.* The most experienced frugal entrepreneurs know that time is their most valuable asset. They understand the limited nature of this resource: you can't make more, buy more, or even steal more. Entrepreneurs who manage

their days, weeks, and months best are the ones who get twice as much done in the time allotted.

* *Little things add up.* While most frugal entrepreneurs aren't obsessed with micromanaging every penny of their business, they do sweat the details. They realize that a few dollars saved or wasted here and there can make a big difference in a company's bottom line at the end of the year. They understand the positive impact of time, energy, and money focused on the right target.

Frugal entrepreneurs also recognize the value a single idea can contribute to their business success. As you read the following sections, see how many ideas might save you time, energy, and money in your business.

MARKETING

Savvy entrepreneurs understand that one of the most powerful marketing tools costs nothing at all: it's your attitude. When you think of *every aspect* of your business in terms of its marketing impact, then even simple things take on new importance. This ranges from the design of your letterhead to the way you answer the phone. Give yourself a mental checkup and see how fine-tuned your marketing mindset is.

The six magic words you can say to your customers are: "How did you hear about us?" Their answers can tell you volumes about how well your marketing is working, and where you should invest your future marketing dollars.

When you're introduced, the first words out of your mouth can send a powerful message about you and your company. Take time to develop a *"60-second brag"* about yourself and your business. It's not meant to turn you into an egotistical bore. Instead, it's designed to give you the self-confidence and the foundation to speak spontaneously about yourself for several minutes. Armed with a well-prepared "60-second brag," you can turn any impromptu encounter into a big win for you and your business.

Voice mail can do more than just capture incoming messages. Consider including a brief "sound bite" of *marketing news on your voice mail announcement.* For example, you can mention a new product or service—or a recent award. It's a great way to keep customers informed on news of your company, and it can be a conversation starter when you call them back. Just remember to keep it to a few seconds and weave it into your general announcement.

If you're looking for a relatively inexpensive way to make your marketing materials stand out, explore the possibilities of using *colored paper.* Color and texture add visual interest, and give the impression of a classier piece—often for just a few pennies more.

The greatest expense of any printing project is getting the press rolling. Frugal entrepreneurs can save money by shopping around to locate printers who will do *"gang" printing.* These printers will combine like jobs (such as printing postcards or brochures) and print the work of several clients at once. The economies of scale are then shared by each of the clients. This approach works best if you have a flexible time schedule and your printed piece doesn't require any special preparation, ink colors, or trimming.

TIME MANAGEMENT

Successful entrepreneurs guard their time like hawks and devote their energies to specific long- and short-term goals. They understand *the difference between activity and achievement.* When deciding how to spend your time, choose with intent. Focus on actions that will advance your goals, not merely fill up your days.

The telephone can be a big time-waster if you don't monitor its usage. Four unplanned fifteen-minute calls *rob you* of an hour of your work day. *Use a script when making outgoing calls* so you can be sure to cover all the important points of your discussion. Jotting down a few notes on paper before you call can save you the hassle of calling back later to cover one forgotten point.

Save time, energy, and gasoline by planning a daily *circuit of errands* to places such as the post office, bank, office-supply store, or copy shop. Visit each in geographic order—with a list in hand, if necessary. By eliminating backtracking on your route, you'll be finished in half the time.

Remember the carpenters' maxim: *measure twice, cut once.* Taking the time to plan and do things right is always cheaper and quicker than doing things in a hurry now and having to redo them later.

FINANCES

Once a year, take time to *review the fees* your bank and other financial institutions charge you. Often these fees are negotiable—but you have to ask.

Savvy frugal entrepreneurs with several credit cards know the monthly closing dates of each credit card billing period, and pay off their bills in full each month. They also *choose cards with a grace period*—ones that accrue interest starting at the end of the billing period instead of on the date of purchase. By making charges early in the card's monthly cycle, they get "free" rental of money for several weeks before the bill becomes due.

You don't need to spend extra money to get a "corporate" credit card. Just *designate one of the credit cards you currently own for business use* only. When it is used only for business purposes, the credit card's annual fees are tax-deductible as a business-related expense.

Ordering checks by mail can save you up to 50 percent off the prices that banks charge for checks. Mail-order check firms offer a wide variety of designs from which to choose, ranging from cute illustrations to more sedate business styles. You'll need to send a voided check with the appropriate bank routing numbers for your initial order. Many firms accept reorders by phone or fax.

OFFICE OPERATIONS

When designed well, your office can become your *invisible assistant.*

Take time to analyze your office layout so it helps you focus your time and energy—which will translate into dollars.

If you're looking to move your business to another site and you're short on funds, consider *bartering for space.* Companies that have extra space may be willing to swap in exchange for a product or service you can provide.

Be creative with the unused space in your office, including such surfaces as walls and ceilings, and even under furniture. A tablecloth can create instant storage, while hanging things on walls or from the ceiling can *stretch your office space.*

When it's time to outfit your office with furniture, avoid the temptation to buy new desks, chairs, computer stations, filing cabinets, or wall dividers. Instead, check out *used furniture* options such as auctions or companies going out of business. Check the real estate or business sections in your newspaper, or the Yellow Pages for listings. Remember, even if you buy a brand-new desk, it will become a used desk one day after you start working behind it.

Office supplies can be a lot cheaper when purchased in *bulk quantities.* Consider joining a warehouse club or creating your own group of like-minded frugal entrepreneurs. By pooling your purchases, you can enjoy bigger discounts and reduce your individual costs of mail-order shipping and handling fees. Some simple networking can bring you big savings.

Is your office filled with stuff that you just can't seem to toss out? Here's a clutter liberation tip from professional organizer Sheila Delson. If you know the materials are going to end up at the dump or recycling center someday, ask yourself what's going to increase their value between now and then. The only thing they're doing is causing you guilt or a knot in your stomach each time you see them. They're going to be tossed out sooner or later. Why not make it sooner? The sense of freedom is a sweet reward.

TECHNOLOGY

Investing in technology is a lot like jumping onto a moving train. At some point, you just have to make the leap—knowing full well that the equipment is likely to become cheaper, faster, or better as soon as you make your purchase. Here's my *ninety-day rule for making technology purchases:* If you can put the piece of equipment to use in your business to generate income within the next ninety days, go ahead and buy it. If your plans are further out, wait. Make your technology dollars work for you.

If you think *telephone headsets* are only for secretaries or telemarketers, you're missing out on a great productivity tool. Studies show that using a headset can improve your productivity up to 43 percent. With both hands free, you can be a whiz at doing multiple activities while you're on the phone. You'll also be doing your body a favor, since you won't be crunching your neck into uncomfortable poses.

If you're just starting a home-based business, you may want to consider *piggybacking a telephone line* instead of installing expensive wiring or adding a call waiting feature. By subscribing to "distinctive ringing" service from your local telephone company, you can establish an independent telephone number that rings in a different pattern. It lets you know before you pick up if the caller has dialed your home or business line, without the annoying beeps or interruptions found in call waiting.

If you have a home-based business and want to install a business telephone line, you'll find the installation charges can be outrageous. Frugal entrepreneurs know that it costs much less to *change a residential line to a business line.* Be kind to your budget: When setting up or expanding your home-based business, install an additional residential line first. A few months later, call the phone company to change one of the lines over to an "official" business line. You'll find the changeover fees to be substantially less than new business line installation charges.

When making a technology investment, be sure to calculate all the costs, including *post-purchase expenses.* This includes things like toner, cartridges, batteries, tune-ups, potential repairs, insurance, and more. Also consider the ease of finding the supplies or repair personnel. The unit may have the lowest purchase price, but it may not be the best value for your business in the long run.

POSTAGE AND SHIPPING

Many post offices now accept *credit card payment for postage.* If postage is one of your company's big expenses, consider charging it to a credit card that gives airline miles. All those stamps and meter fill-ups can actually add up to a free flight.

Priority Mail from the post office can be a great deal if you're sending materials that will fit in its standard two-pound Priority Mail envelope. The post office charges a *flat-rate Priority Mail fee* for the envelope, and whatever you can stuff into it will go for the two-pound charge. For small, heavy items such as books, you can save money over the other shipping options. There's also a flat-fee Global Priority service, for international shipments, that offers significant savings over other international mailing options.

Dropping off overnight letters and packages at authorized shipping sites can save you several dollars off the standard rates for pickup service. Make the trip toward the end of the day, in conjunction with other errands, to make the most efficient use of your time.

Try popcorn as an *inexpensive, light packing material.* It's cheap, lightweight, and easy to make as much as you need. The recipient can scatter it on the lawn and give the local birds a treat.

When packages arrive at your business, consider how you might *recycle the shipping cartons.* Once empty, give them a letter or a number grade as to their value and scribble it on a corner of the box. Containers in good shape should get a high grade, meaning they can be used again. Those in poor shape will get a low mark and end up being flattened and taken to the recycling center. As boxes accumulate, the grading allows you to determine easily which ones to keep or toss.

When you're making travel plans, learn to use the *power of silence*. If the agent on the telephone comes back with a price that's too high, pause and ask, "Is that the best there is?" Then comes an important step: Stop talking. Let the request hang in the air and become the agent's concern. Most likely, the agent will continue to hunt and somehow turn up a fare or rate that's lower than the first one quoted to you.

If your flight gets canceled, *let your fingers leapfrog the lines*. Avoid the long lines of frantic people scrambling to get rerouted. Instead, head for the nearest bank of pay phones and call the airline. The agents on the other end of the phone will be accessing the same computer as those behind the counter, and they can give you your options without your having to contend with an environment filled with dozens of irate passengers. It's a good reason to keep the toll-free numbers of your regular airlines in a handy spot.

Looking for a way to *get a printout from your laptop in a hotel,* and the business services center is closed for the night? Hook your computer up to your in-room telephone line and send your document to the hotel's fax number. Voilà, a hard copy of your file will be waiting for you at the hotel desk just a few moments later, often at no charge.

The next time you're facing a bulging suitcase at the end of a trip, remember the humorous truism that dirty clothes always end up requiring more space than clean ones. It's the reason seasoned travelers suggest that you *tuck a lightweight collapsible nylon suitcase into your original bag* before you depart. In addition to being a handy way to save time during homeward-bound packing, the spare bag can be filled with new purchases or bulky items such as sweaters.

Have these ideas jump-started your thinking about ways you can save time, energy, and money in your business? If so, you're on your way to becoming a frugal entrepreneur! May you reap the rewards of being part of this community—using creativity instead of cash to build your business. I wish you much success!

Terri Lonier is a nationally recognized expert on solo entrepreneurship. She is the author of The Frugal Entrepreneur and the creator of the "Working Solo" series of business resources, including books, audiotapes, Web site (http://www.working solo.com), newsletters, and seminars. Ms. Lonier is president of Working Solo, Inc., a marketing consulting firm based in New Paltz, New York, that works with Fortune 500 and high-tech firms that offer products and services targeted to the rapidly growing small business market. For details on Working Solo resources, call (800) 222-SOLO (7656) or send an e-mail to: info@workingsolo.com. Terri Lonier can be contacted via e-mail at terri@workingsolo.com, or at (914) 255-7165.

The Frugal Entrepreneur and "Working Solo" are registered trademarks of Terri Lonier.

FRUGALITY GOES TO COLLEGE

✴

Brian R. Boyer

Brian Boyer is the youngest of the contributors to this book. Though there seems to be a media thing about Boomers and Generation Xers supposedly not getting along, my observations of Gen-Xers are overwhelmingly positive. I see many of them in my frugality class. They are already shopping thrift stores, and many of them have already decided (probably based on their parents' experiences) that, while they may need a job, they want a life as well. In my opinion, this new generation has its act together far better than we Boomers did at their age. Those things we considered our due—a good job, a higher standard of living than our parents had, etc.—they know they will have to earn. But they are, so far at least, determined to earn these things on their terms, and they seem a lot less prone to whining about their situations than we were (and are). In short—dare I say it?—Generation Xers strike me in many ways as being more mature than their parents. Read Brian's story and see if you don't agree.

After a series of major life setbacks in the late 1980s, I decided to return to college as a full-time student. Before this I had taken many community college courses, but I had never been a serious student. I chose a state university with the lowest tuition and living expenses: Southern

Illinois University at Carbondale (SIUC). I was worse than poor. I was in debt and had to live a suburbanite's worst nightmare: my home was mobile, but I was not. I had found a flimsy, drafty, $165-per-month trailer, while working a minimum-wage part-time job and commuting by foot. About all I had brought with me was clothing, basic school supplies, and a strong desire to start adult life all over again.

Out of necessity I begged, borrowed, liberated, scrounged, made do, reused, adapted, and innovated to make every dollar and every hour do more. Always keeping my eyes and ears open for recommendations and opportunities, I would exchange anecdotes and advice with others similarly situated. At a Red Cross blood drive one evening (always the source of a free meal and a reassuring blood test) I exchanged ideas with a graduate student who had just come from the University of Illinois at Champaign-Urbana. He was amazed that there were no local frugality guides for Carbondale as there were in Champaign, and he suggested that we could write such a book together. The conversation inspired me to draft an outline and make a few notes. This outline grew daily until I had enough material for a booklet. Created at the campus computer lab, the first edition of *Whatever It Takes to Get By: A Financial Survival Guide for SIUC Students* was around twenty-five pages long. Knowing nearly nothing about marketing or publishing, I just printed a few flyers and posted them around campus. Sales were abysmal. Undaunted, I kept up with revisions and updates (including a national edition). I learned more and my writing improved. With a version I thought more marketable I went to the local college bookstore and asked if they would carry the book on consignment. Surprisingly, they agreed. The following week I called the campus newspaper (*The Daily Egyptian*) and suggested they do a piece on the book, which I had retitled *The Slacker Handbook: A Financial Survival Guide for College Students* (Carbondale edition). They also surprised me by accepting. Two days after the *Daily Egyptian* article, I received a call from the local ABC affiliate (WSIL-TV). They wanted to do a story on me! Between the newspaper article, the television appearance, and some promotion on SIUC's SPC-TV, sales were great. I was printing and stapling a new shipment nearly every week. People who knew or recognized me congratulated me on the idea.

It's now a perennial favorite in Carbondale, sold in all the college book-stores. Freshmen and transfer students love it.

Expanding on a good idea, I drafted a national edition for college students and those planning to attend college. Submissions to national publications resulted in a few favorable reviews and much-appreciated sales. The national edition is now promoted on the Internet (http://www.wcnet.com/slacker/index.html) and has been favorably reviewed by many publications including *Bottom Line/Personal; Living Cheap News; Quick, Easy, Cheap and Simple . . . The Newsletter,* and *Factsheet Five.* New and updated information and hot links make it a popular Web site for high school and college students.

My increasing ability to live cheap and simple allowed me to work minimum hours and do the real work of college: studying. Frugality also sharpened my mind. My first year at SIUC I took a calculus class with no previous exposure to the material. I thought I had studied adequately, but I failed the first test. I was shocked. I hadn't failed a test since my pot-smoking years in high school. I subsequently spent forty hours a week doing homework and studying for this class alone, ultimately receiving an *A* for the final grade. This is my proudest academic achievement. If I had to work extensive hours, would I have been able to devote the necessary time to this task? And the problem-solving skills developed through calculus study stayed with me, more so than the meager funds I would have earned McJobbing.

I graduated *magna cum laude* in May 1995 with degrees in civil engineering technology with surveying option and paralegal studies for legal assistants (I unintentionally chose the two degrees with the longest names). Looking forward to traditional financial success, I took a job as an engineering technician in Decatur, Illinois. Decatur is an awful place with poisoned air and water and a shrinking gene pool. The town and its people exhibit the worst of both urban and rural environments. Laid off a year later, I was glad for the opportunity to seek employment elsewhere. I now do Web page development for Web Consulting, an Internet company that caters to small businesses that desire a Web presence.

*   *   *

THE SIMPLE LIFE

I believe that a slacker is someone who makes the most of the college experience by being intelligent and innovative enough to avoid wage-slave McJobs. I find it ironic that the most important thing I did in college was to write a book on how I barely made it through because of financial difficulties.

Slackers always consider how to acquire a good used item before they will pay full retail for new merchandise. Good used products can be acquired from friends, relatives, yard sales, pawn shops, resale shops, repair shops, auctions, junk yards, recycling centers, classified advertisements, trade papers, community bulletin boards, and elsewhere. Any idiot can pay retail. But it takes creative thought, research, initiative, and patience to make the most of your money. It also helps to refer to the ratings in *Consumer Reports* and/or *Consumer Digest* to ascertain the best products. This quick research will also help you to determine when buying new is the best option (recommended for such items as shoes, tires, nondurable electronics, etc.). Remember, it's not a bargain if you're going to have to replace it in a few months, or spend the equivalent of the retail value on repairs.

The alternative is to work harder or longer as a wage slave to enjoy the same standard of living as someone who follows this cash-conserving philosophy. A true slacker gets the most benefit from every minute that was spent "at work." (That includes getting the most from every dollar earned there.)

Even though I no longer need to be frugal, I continue my simple ways. It has advantages. I'm always able to save money—a habit that kept me financially stable when I was unemployed—my student loans will be paid off early, and other than that, I'm not only debt-free, but investing. Money is security. It should be budgeted first for necessities, then put aside for savings and investing, and only last spent on nonessentials. The mix of necessary spending, investment capital, and disposable income is a personal decision, based primarily on how confident you are about the future. By deciding to do without, I avoid clutter in my life and in my cabinets. I have less stuff to store, so I live in a smaller, less expensive apartment, saving for a house or condominium of my own.

My most concise and possibly most profound bit of advice: reduce waste. Time, money, and material resources are all wasted in the modern American consumer's lifestyle. Tract suburban houses are less efficient structures than apartment buildings or rural homesteads. Driving an automobile is less efficient than bicycling or walking for most local outings. The textile industry is one of the world's most polluting and is apt to use the labor of children and political prisoners. But because of fad and fashion Americans buy far more clothes than they will ever need or use up and rarely donate them for reuse. Wise consumers will build their wardrobe around well-made versatile pieces instead.

As members of the university recycling team I and others found and recovered an unconscionable amount of waste at the university level. The student computer labs used tractor-fed printers that wasted a sheet of paper for every one printed (if they were working correctly!). A university mainframe computer lab would spit out box after box of paper, only to throw it away. Chemistry departments would order unnecessary chemicals so as to avoid a budget cut in the following fiscal year. These chemicals would be stored in the subbasement until their labels fell off. Unidentifiable chemicals have to be disposed of as hazardous waste in a very expensive manner. If it weren't for these and other forms of waste (college presidents with four secretaries who spend most of their time playing computer games on state-of-the-art systems, for example), higher education would not be so expensive. My efforts to reduce waste include printing all drafts of this chapter and *The Slacker Handbook* on law office scrap paper, and then recycling that.

Try not to consume too much as a consumer. Be more demanding: look for higher quality and lower prices. The authors don't expect everyone to live as we do, just simplify their lives even a little to live *more*. But if a few million or tens of millions more lived like us, we would all have a higher standard of living with fewer cars on the road, better product design, lower prices, less pollution, less stress, lower taxes, and less waste. With simpler lives we would also have less of the biggest threat to our lives and liberties and the biggest waster of resources: government.

All the Internet addresses below can be accessed from the Slacker Handbook Web page.

1. When the Universal Price Code (UPC) system first appeared in supermarkets and discount stores, there was a strong consumer distrust that the scanners would register incorrect prices. Especially since stores no longer priced merchandise individually, to save on labor costs. To assuage consumer fears, most stores adopted a policy that if the scanned price differed from the shelf or advertised price, you would get the item free. That policy is still in effect in most stores. Take note of the shelf prices of your purchases. If they do not scan alike, enforce the policy in your favor by pointing out the discrepancy to the cashier or manager.

2. The Financial Aid Information page (http://www.cs.cmu.edu/afs/cs.cmu.edu/user/mkant/Public/FinAid/finaid.html) links to a wide variety of other sites about financial aid, scholarships, fellowships, loans, etc. The ScamAlert site provides advice on how to identify and avoid scholarship scams. You'll also find links to free database searches for scholarships and free documents such as "The Student Guide" from the U.S. Department of Education (http://www.ed.gov.prog_info/SFA/StudentGuide/), which provides instructions on how to fill out the federal financial aid forms, articles on financial aid, and worksheets that show what schools expect a family to contribute to the annual college tab.

3. An excellent GPA is often not enough (or not even a factor) in receiving scholarships or awards. Most commercial scholarship searches are based on overgeneralized and outdated information. The best is the Cashe system, freely or inexpensively available at many high school guidance offices, public libraries, or the financial aid office of a local college or university. More than 150,000 grants, scholarships, loans, and work-study programs are catalogued in Cashe. If you'd like to conduct a free database search

for scholarships, check out http://www.studentservices.com/fastweb/.

4. If you plan on staying in town for at least three years and have a small down payment, it might make sense to buy a trailer, pay the mortgage and lot fees for the duration, and then sell the property at graduation. If relatives have the resources, the same project can be accomplished with a house or an apartment building.

5. Several university departments (usually in the colleges of agriculture or science) offer free housing (rent, local telephone calls, electricity, water and sewer, and heating) in exchange for work done on or near the property, or performing or checking on experiments. The work can be as simple as watering plants in greenhouses, but more often involves tending livestock or coming in at odd hours to check progress on a running experiment. It helps to be majoring in agriculture or science. Of course, experience and references also work in one's favor. Ask the chairmen and tenured professors in the college.

6. Waterbeds are common fixtures in the lives and bedrooms of college students. Used beds are for sale in ample supply. You should pay no more than fifty dollars for a used queen- or king-sized waterbed in good condition. This would include the frame, pedestal, hardware, mattress, heater, thermostat, and maybe some sheets and blankets. The liner should be replaced. Ironically, bookcase headboards are a pain if you read in bed. And the waterbed is an energy hog. To reduce associated energy costs by more than fifty percent, place inch-thick rigid insulation (available at hardware and lumber stores) under the mattress and around the sides during setup. *Do not* place the insulation between the mattress and the heater.

7. For a mere $14.95 postpaid, the Rocky Mountain Institute's *Homemade Money: How to Save Energy and Dollars in Your Home* by Richard Heede is probably the most useful energy-efficiency publication available. For one dollar, you should order *Water Efficiency in Your Home* as well. Seven "Home Energy Briefs" are currently available: "Lighting," "Windows," "Refrigerators & Freezers," "Water Heating," "Cooking Appliances & Dishwashers," "Washers,

Dryers & Miscellaneous Appliances," and "Computers & Peripherals." Each brief is two dollars postpaid, or can be accessed through the Internet. RMI (1739 Snowmass Creek Road, Snowmass, CO 81654-9199; 303-927-3851) is a cutting- edge source for information on resource efficiency. Their newsletter is highly recommended reading. Save trees and petroleum by viewing it online at http://www.rmi.org.

8. Several companies will give you free use of a car. These "driveaway" businesses are paid to move a single vehicle from one location to another, usually cross-country. Arrangements (deposit, payment, allowable passengers, delivery date, fuel costs, etc.) vary, but you must have a valid driver's license and a clean driving record. Contact Anthony's Driveaway Company, Inc. (P.O. Box 502, Rutherford, NJ 07073; 201-935-8030 [NJ]; 312-226-6616 [IL]), A Across America Auto Driveaway (800-800-0809), and Auto Driveaway (310 South Michigan Ave., Chicago, IL 60604; 312-939-3600 or 800-346-2277). See also "Motor Homes," "Rental Cars," and "Recreational Vehicles" in your local Yellow Pages.

9. It's never too early to develop the habits of success. If you haven't already, college is an ideal time to start. All successful people make and refer to lists. The lucky ones keep their lists mentally. The rest of us must use pen and paper, calendars, and organizers. Develop a system and use it to make the best use of a nonrenewable resource: your time.

10. Refrigerators are most efficient when they are three-quarters full. If yours does not remain that full, fill bottles (such as gallon milk jugs) full of water to act as thermal flywheels and reduce the number of start/stop cycles on the compressor, extending its life and saving electricity. The water also serves a purpose for disaster preparedness.

11. Attending a community college for your first two years and then transferring to a larger, more prestigious university can save you thousands of dollars in expenses. If you satisfy the minimum hours requirement (usually three or four semesters) your diploma will have the name of the university for all it's worth. Also, stud-

ies have shown that transfer students generally do better academically than four-year residents.

12. For every degree a house thermostat is raised in the summer, air conditioning costs are reduced 7 percent to 10 percent. Since an air-circulation fan (ceiling, paddle, or portable) allows a thermostat increase of about four degrees with no decrease in human comfort, it can provide up to 40 percent savings in cooling costs.

13. Free firewood is available from broken pallets, scrap pieces in the woodshop, national forests (Firewood, Publication #559, Forest Service, P.O. Box 2417, Washington, D.C. 20013), and construction or industrial site trash.

Shameless plug: Self-advertising can work wonders. Don't be afraid to promote your product or service at every opportunity. No one else can be as motivated to do it as you are. This is also important in job-hunting. You never know if the person to whom you're speaking has a friend or relative who's hiring.

Since 1980, inflation has averaged 4 percent but college expenses increased an average of 9 percent, higher than the increases for all other goods and services. With the average overall four-year cost of public and private institutions at over $40,000 and $85,000, respectively, most students discover that this is the time of their life when their budget is at its tightest, paying such mortgage-sized expenses. The purchase of *The Slacker Handbook: An Insider's Guide to Collegiate Success in the Nineties* (the title of the latest edition) will be the best value of your college career. Used properly, it will save you several hundred times its cover price every year. For the fiscally challenged or even those more financially fortunate, *The Slacker Handbook* contains many great ideas to create and conserve capital. You might want to carry it with you during your first few weeks on campus.

I've read many simple-living, money-saving, and investment publications and found the majority to be 10 percent information and 90 percent fluff. That format is a waste of paper and ink, as well as the reader's time. I wrote *The Slacker Handbook* to be information-packed and fluff- free. It's now a multimedia publication, frequently revised and updated in print and electronically. Because I'm self-published in a flexible format I retain creative control. To keep abreast with developments in financial aid and other aspects of the college fiscal and social life, I take interesting classes at community colleges, read voraciously, and have friends who are still in college. I'm also an avid Net-surfer and e-mail correspondent. I struggled and learned, but the reader doesn't have to retrace my steps. Just read the book and refer to it as needed. The habits, skills, and knowledge you gain from following the advice in the book will help you at all stages of life.

And finally: Get a worthwhile degree at college! If you are attending college to increase your employability, choose a major whose graduates get hired: engineering—yes, sociology—no.

To order a copy of the latest revision of The Slacker Handbook *(currently forty-four 8½-by-11-inch information-packed pages) send $7.95 (shipping included) in cash, check, or money order to: The Slacker Handbook, c/o Brian Boyer, P.O. Box 636, Arlington Heights, IL 60006-0636. It's an ideal gift for those who left the nest yet still call home for money. Sample pages are also available for a dollar and a SASE.*

Visit the Slacker Handbook Web page at http://www.wcnet.com/slacker/index.html for updates, reviews, excerpts (including important hot links), sale merchandise, and more information. Contact the author via e-mail at brianb@wcnet.com. For advertising rates, bulk orders, and distributor information call (847) 202-2852.

How Much Will My Funeral Cost?

Lisa Carlson

Few if any of us have been confronted with a situation as abrupt and violent as Lisa Carlson's when she found her first husband dead of a self-inflicted gunshot wound. She had no money at all—let alone money for a funeral. Imagine the courage it took, in her shock and her grief, for her to stand up to the local funeral industry and announce that she was going to handle the funeral herself, which she did, with the help of friends and family. Helping people avoid high funeral costs became, for her, a calling. She wrote Caring for Your Own Dead: The Final Act of Love, *which tells her story as well as the stories of others who elected for financial or personal reasons to prepare and bury their loved ones themselves. The book also examines the obstacles the funeral industry has put in the way of those who choose this option as well as how to save on funeral costs even if you have professionals do the job for you. Her book has just been reissued with updates. Last year, Lisa became the executive director of the Funeral and Memorial Societies of America. She is the* expert *on combating high funeral costs, and she is self-taught. Here are her tips for controlling the costs of your funeral.*

As parents we try to help our children learn how to handle money; we talk about our political, religious, and probably even sexual values. But one of the great and mostly unacknowledged lessons of life teaches one to be prepared for the death of a close family member or friend. How are we doing? Not very well. Barely 25 percent of the people who arrange for a funeral get their information from family members and friends, according to a 1995 funeral industry survey. More than half get their information from morticians.

Unfortunately, the funeral industry has committed such widespread, documented abuse that the federal government was forced to pass consumer protection regulations that—among other things—told funeral directors they could no longer lie to the public. Enforcement of these regulations is weak and far from ideal. Once you are gone, it is your survivors who are vulnerable to manipulative sales tactics at a time of grief. With most states having far too many funeral homes (see the chart at the end of this chapter), it is a situation that invites abuse.

When your survivors arrive at a funeral home, the car they drive and how they're dressed will be quickly assessed. If your family is already known in that area, the funeral director probably has already calculated your financial worth. But that's part of the funeral director's job—to give customers what they want. After all, a car dealer won't try to sell you a Hyundai if it appears you can afford a Cadillac, and a sensitive funeral director isn't going to insult an affluent client by showing bottom-of-the-line merchandise. In fact, no one wants the image of a down-and-outer, so your survivors, too, will probably be on their best behavior in this fancy establishment.

While the formal aura of a funeral establishment is set to honor the dead, it inherently intimidates the average person. How will your survivors respond? And what can you do now to ensure that your death is not an occasion for unreasonable expense?

"GIVEN YOUR FATHER'S POSITION IN THE COMMUNITY, I'M
SURE YOU'LL WANT TO . . ."

An expensive funeral is a memorable one . . . or is it? Unless they flaunt the funeral bill, it's more likely to be the personal and unusual touches that friends and neighbors remember about a particular funeral.

Oprah Winfrey did a show questioning high-cost weddings, another occasion for overspending. Interviews with those who attended showed that the expensive, fancy flowers and fancy dresses were *not* the things people remembered. A fancy casket probably won't be remembered either. And in some families, it will become a "loaded" issue when one member who would have honored your preference for inexpensive arrangements is expected to share the cost of a more elaborate one or watch your estate diminish, simply because a more dominant family member got swept up in the emotions of the moment.

> "YOUR MOTHER HAD EXCELLENT TASTE. WHEN SHE MADE ARRANGEMENTS FOR UNCLE GEORGE, THIS IS WHAT SHE CHOSE."

Is there a good reason to have the same kind of funeral again this time? Were the prices the same when Uncle George died? Or will the funeral director slip in something "extra" or a little higher-priced if your family members simply say, "I want one just like Uncle George's. That was nice"?

> "I'M SURE YOU WANT THE BEST FOR YOUR MOTHER."

Who doesn't? What is best for your family, however, may not have anything to do with how much they spend.

Most of these sample quotes fall into the category of "controlling with guilt." Death often brings out the "if only" emotions, and some will rush to spend, eager for atonement. It also may seem easier to go along with the offered suggestions (and high prices) than to try to justify your frugality. If your family *knows* you want a simple, low-cost funeral, however, they are far less likely to be the willing victims of such ploys.

1. TALK WITH YOUR FAMILY.

What if your family doesn't want to talk about death and funerals? Insist. Try a little humor while it's still easy to smile. We are all "terminal"—we just don't always know when. Don't take "no" for an answer.

Those who have the most difficulty talking about funerals are probably the ones who need your help the most. It will be the most loving thing you can do. Help them to look at the funeral rituals that cost money and those that can be personalized with little or no expense. Find out what rituals are important to them and let them know what your preferences are.

According to *Cremation Concerns* by W. E. Phipps, Franklin Roosevelt left detailed instructions for his funeral, but he deposited them in his safe without informing anyone. Only after his funeral did his family realize that he explicitly rejected much of what had been done—the embalming, the use of an expensive casket, and the grave liner or vault. He desired a rapid return of his crippled body to the elements.

2. PRICE SHOP BY PHONE OR IN PERSON.

According to the Wirthlin study, which was commissioned by the funeral industry, 88 percent of the population does *not* shop for a funeral: 45 percent use a funeral home that served someone else in the family at a prior time, 33 percent call the nearest funeral home, and 10 percent call a funeral home based on a perceived religious affiliation. The industry knows this and counts on it. Is there much difference from one funeral home to the next? Yes! Price shopping can save you thousands of dollars. During the eighties and nineties, there has been a phenomenal growth of corporate-owned funeral home chains, positioning themselves for the deaths of the baby boomers. They have picked prime locations and jacked up the prices. In some parts of the country, they own 50 percent to 75 percent of the market. The economies of scale are passed along—not to the consumer but to the stockholders. The mom-and-pop funeral home in town may still have the same name it always had and some of the same employees, but it now may be owned by a funeral chain.

The Federal Trade Commission (FTC) requires that mortuaries give prices over the telephone. By stopping in person, however, to pick up a "general price list" (GPL), you may learn a great deal more. Does the price list use disparaging language such as "basic disposal" or "incineration container" for cremation? Is a low-cost casket displayed with the same dignity as the higher-priced ones?

The first price to check, regardless of what kind of funeral you and your family might want, is the fee for "basic services of staff and overhead." Although the national average for this fee is $1,025 (1996), you need to remember that it is little more than a funeral-planning charge (and a guaranteed unemployment benefit for the undertaker)—everything else will be extra. At a chain-owned mortuary—or even some of the more avaricious independent firms—this fee will be 50 percent to 90 percent higher than the already-inflated average.

What should this fee be, you might ask? Well, if your travel agent doesn't charge for planning your vacation, and the car salesman fills out all paperwork as part of the sale, what are you willing to pay to have someone else plan your funeral? The level at which this fee is set *may* be a quick indicator of the pricing ethics at a particular establishment, which is why it's worth your time to take a look at several and compare.

Get familiar with the parts and pieces of a funeral so that you have a sense of how much each will cost. A viewing, for example, might seem important to your survivors when you first start discussing funerals, but may be much less important when everyone finds out how much it will cost after all the "extras," such as embalming, are added in. (In the case of an unexpected death—before the family has had a chance to say their good-byes—you may want to ask for a private family viewing. It is rarely listed on the price list so there may be no charge.)

To see if you'd be getting a reasonable deal, estimate the actual time you think each funeral option takes. Then add an hour or two for behind-the-scenes work for each one. (Remember, too, that funeral homes have large property-tax bills, twenty-four-hour phone coverage, and expensive Yellow Pages ads.) Carefully total the cost for everything and then ask, "Will there be any other charges?" If you will be paying more than $100 per hour, you've got a high-priced mortuary.

If the cost for services seems reasonable, be sure to check the cost for caskets (see #6 below). Many mortuaries depend on a high markup on these for their profit.

3. PLAN A MEMORIAL SERVICE WITHOUT THE BODY PRESENT.

In that case, there would be no need for embalming, a fancy casket, or expensive transporting of the body back and forth. Private family visitation and "good-byes" can occur in the hospital or home, before you call a funeral director. Use a church, park, community center, or your home for the memorial service without any attending funeral home staff. The memorial service can be planned at a time that is convenient for the family, too—perhaps at a favorite summer retreat a month or two later—without creating hardship in work schedules.

The FTC requires that funeral homes offer a package price for "immediate burial" and "direct cremation." If the local prices seem too high, you should consider using a low-cost funeral director from another community to transport the body directly to a crematory or cemetery. Because family and friends won't be going to the funeral home, it won't matter that the mortuary is in another town.

Many people find that, without a casket present, a memorial service shifts the focus to the more spiritual and personalized aspects of a life well lived. In *From Beginning to End*, Robert Fulghum gives the entertaining details of Martha Carter's last rites, including the George Burns joke she wanted told. After reading about Mrs. Carter's exit, I felt pleasantly challenged to come up with some new ideas of my own. I'm almost looking forward to the big event.

4. CONSIDER BODY DONATION TO A MEDICAL SCHOOL.

In some areas, there may be no cost to the family whatsoever. In other circumstances, the cost of transporting the body may be the only cost. Often—if you ask—cremated remains will be returned to the family after scientific study, usually within a year or two.

One elderly gentleman decided to change his plans when a daughter was unhappy with the idea of body donation. This is a perfect example of why it's so important to talk about your wishes ahead of time. Cremated remains can usually be returned to the family, making body donation more of a "loan." Does this make it easier for someone to accept? If you make the arrangements ahead of time, will that help with any reluctance? Most medical schools prefer that you sign up while you're still alive, but others will accept a body from the next of kin.

If you travel a great deal, make sure any body donor card you carry is marked with "or nearest medical school." Otherwise, your family will have to pay the expense of shipping your body back to the original medical school you chose. (Of course, some people really want to get into a place like Harvard—even if only through the back door—and they don't care how much the final trip will cost.) There is an urgent need for body donation in most foreign countries.

Even if body donation is your choice, be sure that your family knows what your backup wishes are. If you were to die on the operating table during by-pass surgery, for example, your body would not be accepted for medical study. Obesity is another common reason that schools reject a body donor. So, if you're spending too much time sitting in front of a computer and your figure is beginning to look like a Bartlett pear, your family will definitely need an alternative.

5. CONSIDER CREMATION.

Immediate cremation is almost always the least expensive offering on a mortuary price list if body donation is not chosen. But be sure to ask if the price includes the actual cremation process. I know that sounds like a stupid suggestion; after all, how can you have an "immediate cremation" without the cremation? Basically, the FTC permits the funeral home to leave that charge out and bill it later as a "cash advance" item if it doesn't own the crematory. Some include it anyway, but many don't.

Prices for immediate, or "direct," cremation vary widely around the country. In Florida and on the West Coast, a commercial cremation company might charge only $450 (1996) to pick up the body, supply a cardboard casket, cremate the body, do all the paperwork, and return the cremated remains to the family. In Connecticut or Wisconsin, you might have a hard time finding the same services for less than $2,000—unless you really shop around. Even then, it's likely to be higher, especially in the states where there are too many funeral homes. With an immediate cremation, the family would then be free to plan the memorial service without the need for mortuary staff. This is not the only option, however. One could certainly have a viewing and funeral service with the casket present, and choose cremation after that.

The crematory is not likely to accept a body unless everyone agrees. Hard feelings may erupt among surviving siblings, for example, if there is no unanimity on the final method of disposition—another reason it is so important to talk about funeral choices now while you can. If you sign a cremation permit ahead of time, would that make it easier for others to honor your wishes? Only a few states have laws giving priority to the wishes of the deceased, although case law may support your wishes over those of the survivors in other states.

It costs a great deal less to ship cremated remains from one state to another. Cemetery space will cost less than the space needed for body burial, and cremains can be buried or scattered wherever you choose. Well, sort of. In California, the scattering of cremains is forbidden—except on the ocean—but you may keep them in your home. The state has no "cremains police" to see if they're still on your mantel.

The funeral home is likely to try to sell you an expensive urn for the cremains. Pier I has brass vases at a fraction of the prices charged by most funeral homes. Or perhaps you know a potter. Then again, the simple cardboard container in which the cremains are shipped from the crematory is perfectly acceptable for most purposes. Few cemeteries require an "urn vault." The ones that do tend to be the high-priced commercial ones looking for a way to cash in on the rising popularity of cremation, now that their income from fancy funerals is shrinking.

6. HAVE A FAMILY MEMBER MAKE A SIMPLE WOOD CASKET OR BUY ONE FROM A LOCAL ARTISAN IF YOU PREFER BODY BURIAL.

If a funeral home charges more than $400 for a modest casket, it's a good bet those folks are taking a 300 percent to 500 percent markup. Some of the older morticians still seek most of their profit from the casket—a holdover from the days when the only prices posted were for the "casket, including all services" (whether you wanted them or not).

Their nondeclinable fee may have been modest then, but the casket prices now will seem outrageous.

A cloth-covered wood casket wholesales for about $150. A non-sealing, twenty-gauge metal casket wholesales for about $350. If you'd like to see what other wholesale costs are, check the Web site run by a Catholic priest in Arizona (www.xroads.com/~funerals).

Morticians often tout the "protective" qualities of some caskets, preying on the public's fears of the unknown. "Protective of what?" one should ask. Nothing the industry sells can deter the ultimate course of nature forever, and it can create a lot of mischief. What happens to the body in a sealed casket? It putrefies when the anaerobic bacteria take over, instead of the natural dehydration that would otherwise occur. (Gravediggers much prefer working in the older part of a cemetery where everything has turned to rich loam.) By the way, the rubber gasket used on "sealer" caskets costs the mortician only $8 or so—but it usually adds $800 or more to the price of the casket.

With that thought, perhaps you'll decide on a simple but dignified plain pine box. The widow of a well-respected Vermont judge was told the funeral home didn't have the plain pine box her husband had wanted. Trying to find one was just too overwhelming in her moment of grief, so she ended up with a $2,000 casket instead. If a plain pine box is what you want, however, you should insist that they find one—for indeed they can; the conscientious funeral homes will happily oblige.

In Georgia and North Carolina, only a mortician can sell a casket. I've suggested to artisans and woodworkers in those states that they sell "hope chests." There's certainly no law against burying someone in a hope chest in any state. In fact, I think that sounds rather nice. Plans for building a casket can be found in Ernest Morgan's book, *Dealing Creatively with Death,* if you'd like to try one on your own.

While you may like the idea of going out in a hope chest, let's say you're arranging for the death of a parent in the meantime. You may feel obligated to consider something a little more ornate because you're concerned about what a particularly difficult relative, Aunt Nellie, might think of a plain pine box for Mom. In that case, check the list of casket retailers on the FAMSA Web site (www.funerals.org/famsa).

Most ship anywhere in the country, overnight. Just as you did with funeral homes, shop among these retailers as well; some charge only $200 or so over wholesale plus shipping; others are higher. And if the funeral director makes a nasty crack to your Aunt Nellie that you didn't order a "sealer," you can tell her you wanted to make sure Mom could get out if she ever woke up. (Some of the Victorian caskets had a periscope-type tube with a bell at the top that protruded above ground—just for this purpose.) It is illegal for a mortuary to charge a handling fee for using a casket obtained elsewhere. One woman, however, reported, "My husband made his dad's casket. When the funeral director found out, he was unbelievably rude to us the whole time after that." So you should, indeed, be prepared for a hugely disappointed undertaker.

One last idea: You might choose a minimum container from the mortuary. These are usually unfinished wood or cardboard, but you can drape it with attractive material of your own taste if the casket will be present at the time of the service.

7. SKIP THE EMBALMING.

This is the only country where embalming is widespread, and to no good end. According to the Centers for Disease Control and Prevention it serves *no* public health purpose whatsoever. Funereal-type embalming may delay decomposition for a few days, but that's it. And if people knew what was involved in the process, I strongly suspect they wouldn't choose it. Jean DeSapio—a long-time industry researcher and writer—opted for an immediate cremation with no embalming. So did Jessica Mitford, author of *The American Way of Death.*

Why do the undertakers push embalming? Because once the body is prettied up, they can probably sell a more expensive casket. Some are genuinely convinced that the viewing process is a necessary, therapeutic ingredient in the bereavement process. If Gram has been failing for some time, however, most family members have said their good-byes— perhaps in the process of caring for her—and there is little further need to see her body to accept her death.

In the case of an unexpected death, there may be a much greater need to spend time with the body before being ready to let go. For me—losing my first husband when I was thirty-one—it was much easier to let go, seeing that he was really dead.

8. ASK FOR A GRAVE LINER—RATHER THAN A COFFIN VAULT—AT A MUCH LOWER PRICE.

Some—but not all—cemeteries require purchase of a grave liner: five or six slabs of concrete (four sides to line the grave, a top, and sometimes a bottom). By carting away the displaced dirt, they can put the lid on, roll the sod out, and go back to mowing tomorrow. It reduces maintenance for the cemetery. But the "outer burial container," or coffin vault, is quickly becoming a new way for morticians to increase their income and can be an added burden on your funeral finances. Priced as high or higher than a casket, remember that it is just a box-for-the-box, and it quickly disappears beneath the cemetery lawn.

The marketing of these is astonishing, however—copper lining, marble lining, just about anything you want. Of course, the mortician is likely to suggest a "sealer" vault. These are the kind that popped out of the ground and floated away during the Midwest flood of '93. It was a real problem to figure out where everyone belonged. If you want to stay buried, get the cheapest thing you can, something with a hole in the bottom.

9. CONSIDER HANDLING ALL ARRANGEMENTS WITHOUT USING A MORTUARY.

Years ago, Grandma was laid out in the front parlor. Families knew what to do at a time of death. But in just three or four generations we have lost touch with that tradition.

A pediatric oncology nurse in California told me that the emotional recovery for parents who have lost a child is dramatically improved when the family handles all funeral arrangements. It's probably the only aspect of their situation that they have any control over.

By handling all funeral arrangements, a family can personalize the funeral rites, too. That was what I chose to do when my husband died. In fact, if I'd had money, I would have overlooked a meaningful experience. Now that I've been through it, I'd never choose any other way than to handle things myself. What did we do? A friend and I drove John's body to the crematory. We held an open house in his memory two days later. We played his favorite music from *Oliver*, the Children's Theater production he'd produced at school the year before. There were lots of flowers—John had been an avid flower gardener. We talked, we laughed, and we cried. Hundreds came, or so it seemed, each sharing memories that had touched their lives, then leaving on their own schedule. John's mother said later, "I never knew so many people loved him." But she wasn't counting how many showed up; she was moved by the kind of personal sharing that spontaneously erupted in that homey, close-to-nature, country setting. That was John, and that was "right" for him.

Caring for your own dead is permitted in forty-two states, the District of Columbia, and all Canadian provinces; the eight restrictive ones are Connecticut, Illinois, Louisiana, Michigan, Nebraska, New Hampshire, New Jersey, and New York. As of this writing, there is a current effort in New Hampshire to change those laws. (If it doesn't succeed, perhaps the state motto should be changed to "Live Free or Die in Hock to the Funeral Director.")

My book, *Caring for Your Own Dead*, tells what permits are required in each state, where and when to file them, plus a great deal of other practical information for anyone choosing this meaningful way to say good-bye.

10. JOIN A MEMORIAL SOCIETY.

Memorial societies were started in the late 1930s as a result of the rising cost of funerals due to embalming and manufactured caskets. Spurred by an angry minister who thought that expensive funerals were a terrible waste of our resources, a group in Seattle got together and found a cooperating mortician. He agreed not to push fancy funerals on the group's member and offered a discount in exchange for their advertising his services to others.

There are now 150 memorial societies across the United States and Canada. They are nonprofit, nondenominational, educational organizations, most of which are run by volunteers. Many of these memorial societies do an annual price survey of area mortuaries. Families who feel overwhelmed by tackling such a task themselves will appreciate the convenience of this one-stop price shopping.

Some societies have negotiated a contract with local mortuaries for discount services. All societies have funeral-planning literature that should make family discussion of death a little easier. The membership fee is modest, and there are reciprocal benefits if you move to or die in another state.

In the early sixties, the societies banded together and formed a federation to fight for better funeral consumer protection nationwide. That group was influential in getting the FTC to pass the original Funeral Rule, the regulation that makes it possible for consumers to pick and choose only those funeral goods and services they want and to get prices over the telephone. That right to choose, however, has been eroded by the industry's abuse of the nondeclinable fee. Until this nondeclinable fee is abolished, the cost of funerals will be insulated from any market forces that would benefit informed consumers. FAMSA is seeking new changes in the Funeral Rule. By joining a local memorial society, your membership supports this effort.

To find a memorial society near you, call 1-800-765-0107.

Why The Cost of Dying May Be Much Higher In Your Community

A 1994 loophole in the FTC's Funeral Rule now allows mortuaries to add all overhead to a nondeclinable basic charge for planning the funeral, a fee that at $100 per hour, should be less than $400.

However, the absence of limits on this fee has given rise to a situation that invites abuse of consumers, especially in areas where there are far more funeral homes than can be supported by the death rate. With funeral directors treating this fee as guaranteed income, it has risen $1,000 to $2,000 or more in just one year, with all other costs such as the casket and funeral service being added on top of that.

Using a simple death-rate formula and assuming that most mortuaries can only handle one funeral a day, the following chart compares the demand for funerals with the supply offered by the funeral homes.

While taking into account that there are undoubtedly some funeral homes that can handle more than one funeral a day, which reduces the needed number accordingly and probably explains the figures for California, Hawaii, and Nevada, and assuming that in rural areas with sparse population, a funeral home does not expect the dying business to be a full-time one and more establishments will be needed to cover the geographic area than the number generated by a simple death-rate formula that still leaves us with a glut of mortuaries. In Kansas, Pennsylvania, and Vermont, there are almost four times the needed mortuaries; in Iowa and Nebraska, there are five times too many! Where that is the situation, a funeral bill is likely to be inflated, especially the nondeclinable fee, in order to support the underutilized staff and facilities. Furthermore, there is no need for competition when all can stay in business by charging high fees that people continue to pay.

State	Needed	Existing
Alabama	157	327
Alaska	9	19
Arizona	124	133
Arkansas	100	278
California	863	757
Colorado	90	155
Connecticut	113	326
Delaware	24	77
District of Columbia	28	40
Florida	559	794
Georgia	212	603
Hawaii	28	21
Idaho	32	76
Illinois	408	1,385
Indiana	200	700
Iowa	106	582
Kansas	89	332
Kentucky	140	495
Louisiana	151	333

State	Needed	Existing
Maine	45	158
Maryland	156	263
Massachusetts	216	719
Michigan	316	805
Minnesota	140	498
Mississippi	101	306
Missouri	204	707
Montana	28	87
Nebraska	59	290
Nevada	41	29
New Hampshire	34	103
New Jersey	283	790
New Mexico	45	66
New York	666	1,904
North Carolina	238	686
North Dakota	23	109
Ohio	396	1,271
Oklahoma	122	350
Oregon	103	161
Pennsylvania	494	1,845
Rhode Island	38	127
South Carolina	123	310
South Dakota	27	135
Tennessee	186	436
Texas	516	1,064
Utah	39	97
Vermont	19	80
Virginia	197	474
Washington	153	195
West Virginia	79	289
Wisconsin	169	590
Wyoming	13	35

Compiled from 1992 Mortality Statistics supplied by U.S. Dept. of Health &
Human Services and a report of established funeral homes per American Funeral
Director, 1993. When quoting from this chart, please credit FAMSA.

Lisa Carlson's Caring for Your Own Dead: The Final Act of Love is a
state-by-state manual that covers all laws and procedures for handling a death without
the use of a mortician—a logical and welcome extension of the Hospice ideal. Lisa is
a nationally recognized consumer advocate on funeral issues, and has included such chap-
ters as "Understanding the Tricks of the Funeral Trade: Self-defense for Consumers"
and "FTC: Boon and Boondoggle." But the single chapter that may do the most to change
the American way of death is "How to Start a Funeral Committee in Your Congre-
gation: Free Funerals for Your Members." To order the $16.95 book, call 1-800-
310-8320.

Remembering Joe Dominguez

Vicki Robin

On January 11, 1997, Joe Dominguez died. The coauthor of *Your Money or Your Life* was a visionary thinker, and his work lives on through the hundreds of thousands of people who have used his simple methodology to liberate themselves from slavery to money.

Helen Keller said, "Life is either a daring adventure or it's nothing." Knowing and working with Joe these past twenty-six years has been a daring adventure: not a foolhardy adventure, but the adventure of seeing reality clearly, and then responding to it with passion.

Joe had an engineer's mind. His genius was that he saw exactly what was there—without adding or subtracting anything—and then acted on that knowledge. He asked, What is it? How does it work? How can it be improved? He was always willing to see and say that the emperor had no clothes.

Joe was grounded and practical almost from day one. When he was a kid, he requested tools, not toys, for birthdays and Christmas. He tinkered with all his mother's appliances—with varying results. He was even kicked out of kindergarten for reading the *New York Times*. His father had already taught him the basics of reading, and Joe built vocabulary by studying the *Times* and underlining words he didn't know. Getting caught doing that during nap time is what got him into trouble—and into the first grade.

Growing up in Spanish Harlem, Joe worked to supplement his family's income from the time he was nine, and early on he sensed that there had to be more to life than "making a living." By attending Bronx High School of Science, then training as a mechanical engineer at City College of New York he earned a ticket out of the ghetto. In 1960, broke and in debt, he set out to learn all he could about money and personal finances, choosing Wall Street as his laboratory.

Moving up through the ranks of the financial world, he examined attitudes, fears, and misconceptions about money, learning from the successes and failures of those around him. By 1965 he was out of debt, and well on his way to learning the basic attitudes and principles of a successful relationship with money. Using only his modest salary, by 1969 he had established a safe, steady source of income from U.S. Treasury Bonds that was adequate for his needs for the rest of his life. At the age of thirty-one he resigned from his paid employment and never again accepted money for anything he did.

I met Joe in 1970 shortly after he retired, while he was exploring how to live outside the cultural box that said the "good life" means "getting and having more." He soon discovered that life was far richer when he donated his time and talents to the service of others.

In the process of this spiritual expedition, we spent three years in northern Wisconsin helping to set up a rural retreat center for street kids from Chicago. The "land" was fourteen acres of cranberry bog. It was our task to turn that into a road, buildings, and a one-acre garden. The perfect playground for an engineer's mind! Here's one story: Joe discovered that peat moss came from the very sphagnum moss that covered our land. What if we pulled up the moss to help the land dry up? And what if we had our own peat-moss factory? He hooked up an old rototiller engine to our food mill and turned an acre of sphagnum into beautiful, dry peat. That's the kind of genius you'd never find in books.

For many years he traveled, seeking ways to be of service. It soon became clear that what people most wanted was to learn how he'd become financially independent. Joe's first seminar—which later evolved into *Transforming Your Relationship with Money and Achieving Financial Independence*—was done for friends in the living room. Then, noting that many of the nonprofit groups he volunteered with needed money, Joe began presenting his seminar to the public, with the income going directly to the host organization. Between 1980 and 1985 his audiences grew from groups of twenty to crowds of four hundred. Meeting the demand became grueling. Joe's popularity was creating the kind of notoriety and intense work schedule he'd left behind on Wall Street. So he produced the seminar as an audiotape course to allow it to go out around the world. And, to reach an even broader audience, Joe and I wrote *Your Money or Your Life*, which was published in 1992. We saw it not only as a tool to help individuals achieve financial sanity, but also as a strategy whereby humanity could moderate the destructive patterns of consumption that threaten the health of our biosphere.

Joe brought his engineer's mind to everything he did. To personal financial independence. To reclaiming a swamp. To helping people solve their financial problems. To making the world work for all of life. His solutions were always extraordinary in their simplicity and directness. He often said, "If the truth were complex, we'd have figured it out long ago. The fact that it's simple is what has us stumped." His gift was a single-minded focus on service, a service that led him to preach what he'd already learned so well to practice.

CLOSING THOUGHTS

Several of the contributors to this anthology asked that I address a couple of issues. The first issue is the "movement" issue. As in, "Is there a movement?"

Admittedly it is difficult to assert, in view of the fact that both credit card debt and personal bankruptcy filings are at all-time record levels, that Americans are, en masse, embracing frugality and simplicity. Various statistics reported in the *Wall Street Journal* in the space of a month in 1996 demonstrate that we Americans are indeed a conflicted people financially. Fifty-eight percent of Americans are dissatisfied with the amount they are saving. A whopping eighty-two percent say that most of us buy and consume far more than we need, and eighty percent say we should use our possessions longer instead of buying new things. But only *thirty percent* actually save for the future, and of those who do, the median amount saved is $1000. Half of all Americans in their late fifties have less than $10,000 saved. These data show that, although we *know* what we need to do, as a nation we're not doing it. At the same time, it is a fact that many people *are* taking control of their lives and their finances. Enough people are "just saying no" to a lifestyle of consumption, debt, and bondage to increasingly insecure jobs that it is attracting the attention of nearly every newspaper, magazine, and television network in this country. But does this make frugality and simplicity a "movement"?

Several years ago I was interviewed on a southern radio station. One of the suggestions I made during that interview was that, if a person is in the market for an item such as a major appliance, that person should ask the salesperson if the item will be on sale in the near future. The interviewer was slightly taken aback.

"Wouldn't you be afraid the salesperson might think you're a bit, well, er, uh, *cheap?*" I had unwittingly blundered, with my midwestern "put your cards on the table" approach, into a part of the country where manners and appearances are still very important. But the radio interviewer was also somewhat off-base by mistaking a business transaction for a social event.

For a few seconds I tried to think of a diplomatic answer, but I failed. "Who cares?" was all I could come up with. And that's my response to the question, "Is there a simplicity or frugality movement?" Who cares?

When we were children, our parents often told us, "Even if ten thousand people do a foolish thing, it's still a foolish thing." That's advice that was, is, and always will be true.

In this country's Declaration of Independence, Thomas Jefferson wrote that certain truths were self-evident. I can't help but believe that not only are the advantages of frugality and simplicity self-evident, but that frugality and simplicity are a way for each of us to issue our own individual declarations of independence. Independence from consumption, from paying retail, and, if we wish, from employers and employment.

The key word here is *individual.* Whether enough people are embracing frugality and simplicity to constitute a movement is not important. You are important. And whether you incorporate frugality and simplicity into your own life is important only to you. And the choice is yours and yours alone.

The second issue I'd like to discuss is one that caught me by surprise. When I went into this project, I had considered "voluntary simplicity" and "new frugality" to be pretty much synonymous. But several of the contributors to this book assert that the terms have different meanings. And it seems that, in certain parts of the country, that is true. This seems to be primarily a West Coast issue, though one of the contributors who first raised the issue lives on the East Coast. At any rate, I'll take this opportunity to explain, as I understand it, the differences in philosophy.

Those in the simplicity movement, as I see it, are perhaps more likely to be concerned with environmental, political, population, and social concerns as *overriding* issues. Simplicity, to some, is a subset of frugality. Those who consider themselves inclined toward frugality, while certainly concerned with environmental, political, population, and social issues, tend to see things more in terms of costs and savings—stretching a dollar to the breaking point, in other words. One example of where the two viewpoints might diverge could be whether to buy at a garage sale clothing made by sweatshop labor. Those in the simplicity movement would be inclined not to buy because of the ethics involved in the items' manufacture. Those practicing frugality would buy the clothes (if they could use them) because they would see this as a way to get a good deal on something that would otherwise go to the local landfill. Those following simplicity, in other words, are more likely to let their purchases be determined by ethical considerations. Those following frugality try to avoid letting anything (and especially their money) be wasted.

Each group has a valid viewpoint. Neither is "better" or "worse" than the other. There is also a good amount of overlap. Again we find ourselves back to the important word, *individual*. The decision as to which, if either, philosophy you want to follow (and how far you want to follow it) is an individual one. You'll have to make up your own mind.

Well, now that I've (1) cleared that up or (2) mucked it up beyond belief (choose one), I want to leave you with what I consider the three most important things you will ever learn about your finances.

The first is: Get started saving now. The sooner you start, the sooner the "magic of compound interest" will start working for you. Consider this: Gail Sheehy, in her book, *New Passages* (Random House, 1995), says that a couple without an additional pension would need $660,070 to retire. Ms. Sheehy comments, "nobody can really save this much." Baloney! If you're twenty-five years old, you and your partner can save this much by the time you're sixty-five if each of you puts a whopping $3.49 a day into an investment that earns 8 percent interest! But get started now. If you wait until you're thirty-five, you'll each need to put $7.98 in the same investment. At forty-five the figure is $19.76. At fifty-five it may well be too late: the daily savings each of you will need is $62.42. Put time on your side. Get started now.

Second: Do what makes sense to *you*. Listen to the advice of your family and your friends. They may have some good ideas. But when it comes to how to spend or invest your own money, that is your call. And you don't owe anyone an explanation or a defense of your decisions. When I began looking for homes in the 1970s, friends advised that I buy the biggest and most expensive home I could afford. I couldn't see paying to heat and cool space I didn't need, so I generally bought homes that were smaller than I could have "afforded." I have been very happy with this decision (I was especially happy during the oil embargo years). When I first moved to Kansas City in 1978 (or, more correctly, the first time I moved to Kansas City), friends recommended that I buy a home in the Kansas suburbs because of the school system. I had no children, so paying high property taxes to support a school system I wouldn't be using didn't make sense to me (and Kansas discriminates against single taxpayers by charging them a higher income tax rate). I bought a home in a Kansas City neighborhood that appealed to me and was less expensive than the 'burbs. Of course you never know what the future will bring. A U.S. Supreme Court decision in 1990 doubled Kansas City's property taxes overnight. And my neighborhood has been "discovered" by hordes of roving yuppies who have raised housing prices, property taxes, insurance costs, etc. I may have to take my profits and move to a cheaper neighborhood.

Getting back, though, to your friends and family. Remember that, although they undoubtedly have your best interests in mind, if you follow their advice and lose money, they're not going to give you back the money you lost. Again, it's *your* money.

Third: If you're not going to take the advice of friends and family (who know you and who have your best interests in mind) when it doesn't make sense to you, then you certainly don't need to pay too much attention to the conventional wisdom of our times. Listen and read. But *think* before you follow any advice from the financial gurus du jour. For every financial seer gazing into his or her crystal ball today and advising that, for example, stock mutual funds are best for everyone, there was a counterpart in 1929 who advised that this country had reached a "permement plateau of prosperity" and one in the 1980s who assured "no money down" suckers that real estate had not declined in value for fifty years running and would always go up in value because "they're not making any more of it."

My own financial strategy is one that is embraced by no financial advisor that I know of. And yet I left my corporate job in my midforties because it worked so well for me. My strategy is this simple: Run your life as if it were a business. Cut costs, live cheaply, pay off your debts, invest, and when you can, live off your interest. This is my KISS (keep it simple, stupid) financial strategy. And yet, you would not believe how many financial advisors have advised me to complicate my strategy. When I encounter one of these experts, I'm reminded of a cartoon I once saw, depicting a potential customer saying to a financial advisor, "If you'll explain to me why you're still working at a job for a living, maybe I'll listen to you." My KISS financial strategy may or may not be for you (and I'm *not* a financial advisor). Whatever you do, though, develop your own approach and ignore the advice of "experts" when it doesn't make sense to you.

Think for yourself. Remember that if something has happened before, be it a stock market crash, a real estate debacle, or, yes, a depression, it can and probably will happen again. Beware of conventional wisdom; it is merely the conventional wisdom of the day.

Most of all, ignore the conventional wisdom that says or implies that your future or your finances are beyond your control. As one of the millions of people in the San Francisco Bay Area who rode the bucking earth for a few terrifying seconds in 1989, I can assure you that some things are, indeed, beyond your control. That does not, however, mean that you should cast your financial fate to the wind. Control what you can and prepare for those things you cannot control. You could get run over by a truck tomorrow. But the odds are you're going to live to a ripe old age. Whether you will spend that old age comfortably or whether you will spend it learning the human nutritional value of cat food depends on what you do now. You can take control of your tomorrows by controlling your spending today.

The final question I'd like to address for those of you who are now hooked on frugality and simplicity is: Where do you go from here?

In the next section you will find many resources you may want to check out. I suggest you do just that: when possible, check them out—of your library. It doesn't, after all, make sense to spend a lot of money to learn how to save money. And you're paying for your local library with your tax dollars, anyway, so get your money's worth. In the case of the newsletters listed (and many libraries will subscribe to newsletters if they get enough requests), as I said many pages ago, be kind to the newsletter editors. Send them a dollar and a self-addressed, stamped envelope (SASE), and you're almost certain to get a sample issue.

I hope you've enjoyed reading this book half as much as I enjoyed being its editor. I am truly honored to have had the opportunity to work with such a wide variety of people who not only have great minds but who are also really nice people.

I thank them and I thank you. Keep cheap—and simple.

Resources

The following are resources I have found helpful or enjoyable. I *do not* recommend that you buy all of the books, newsletters, etc. listed below. As I said in the previous chapter, I recommend that you get the books that sound interesting to you at your library. If your library does not have what you want, they can almost certainly order it through the interlibrary loan program. Sometimes there is a charge of 50¢ or $1 for this service. Even if you are charged for this service, it will cost you less than buying the book (unless you buy the book at a garage sale). In the event you cannot find the book at your library, and you want to buy it, look it up in *Books in Print*, which lists books by subject, author, and title. One volume of *Books in Print* is a list of publishers. Many of these publishers have toll-free numbers, and you can order the book directly from them. Many of these books may be out of print. In that case, and if your library does not have them, look for a good used bookstore (in fact, even if the book is in print, check for it in used bookstores).

In the case of all newsletters, I suggest you "try before you buy," since tastes and interests vary. What I might find excellent, someone else might find underwhelming. So please send $1 and a self-addressed, stamped envelope and get a sample copy. And then decide. And, once again, please don't ask the newsletter editors to send you a free sample at their expense. Let's go over this one more time. Don't ask the newsletter editors to send you a free sample at their expense. Repeat after me: Don't ask the newsletter editors to send you a free sample at their expense.

You can often get your library to order self-published books. *Liv-*

ing Cheap, which I self-published in 1990, is available at or through nearly every library in the country. It got there because people asked their local libraries to order it. If you see a book listed below that you'd like to see in your library, ask the librarian to order it, and ask your friends to make the same request.

HISTORY AND PHILOSOPHY

Voluntary Simplicity, by Duane Elgin (Quill, 1993)

The Simple Life, by David E. Shi (Oxford University Press, 1985)

Plain (P.O. Box 100, Chesterhill, OH 43728)

The American Transcendentalists, by Perry Miller (Anchor Books, 1957)

American Transcendentalism, by Paul F. Boller, Jr. (G. P. Putnam's Sons, 1974)

Transcendentalism in New England, by Octavius Brooks Frothingham (University of Pennsylvania Press, 1959)

The Spirituality of the American Transcendentalists, edited by Catherine L. Albanese (Mercer University Press, 1988)

INTENTIONAL COMMUNITIES AND CO-HOUSING

Communities Directory: A Guide to Cooperative Living (Fellowship for Intentional Community, 1995)

Communities (Fellowship for Intentional Community, Rt. 1, Box 155, Rutledge, MO 63563)

CoHousing (The CoHousing Network, P.O. Box 2584, Berkeley, CA 94702)

"BACK TO THE LAND"

Back Home (P.O. Box 70, Hendersonville, NC 28793)

The Mother Earth News (P.O. Box 56302, Boulder, CO 80322-6302)

Homesteading, by Gene Logsdon (Rodale, 1973)

The Modern Homestead Manual, by Skip Thomsen and Cat Freshwater (Oregon Woodworks, 1995)

The Owner-Built Homestead, by Barbara and Ken Kern (Scribner's, 1977)

Country Bound!™ Trade Your Business Suit Blues for Blue Jean Dreams, by Tom and Marilyn Ross (Communication Creativity, 1992)

One Acre and Security, by Bradford Angier (Vintage, 1972)

Bummers & Gummers (P.O. Box 91, Lorane, OR 97451)

Backwoods Home Magazine (1257 Siskiyou Blvd., #213, Ashland, OR 97520)

Living Free (Jim Stumm, Box 29, Hiller Branch, Buffalo, NY 14223)

Dwelling Portably (P.O. Box 190, Philomath, OR 97370)

Eureka Resource Catalog (Box 2356, Martinez, CA 94553)

Lehman's Non-Electric Catalog (Box 41, 4779 Kidron Rd., Kidron OH 44636)

Campmor Catalog (Box 997, Paramus, NJ 07653)

The Vermont Country Store Catalog (Box 3000, Manchester Center, VT 05255)

Rural Property Bulletin, a monthly listing of rural properties for sale primarily by owners (814 Candice St., Valentine, NE 69201)

United National Real Estate is a large company that lists rural properties for sale nearly everywhere in the country (1600 N. Corrington Ave., Kansas City, MO 64120)

EMPLOYMENT

Through the Brick Wall, by Kate Wendleton (Villard, 1992)

Surviving Unemployment, by Cathy Beyer, Doris Pike, and Loretta McGovern (Henry Holt & Co., 1993)

Make Your Connections Count, by Melissa Giovagnoli (Dearborn Financial, 1993)

The Employee Strikes Back, by John D. Rapoport and Brian L. P. Zevnik (Collier Books, 1990)

RETIREMENT, EARLY RETIREMENT, AND ALTERNATIVE EMPLOYMENT

Cashing In on the American Dream: How to Retire at 35, by Paul Terhorst (Bantam, 1988)

80+ Great Ideas for Making Money at Home, by Erica Barkemeyer (Walker, 1992)

Making a Living Without a Job, by Barbara J. Winter (Bantam, 1993)

How to Survive Without a Salary, by Charles Long (Firefly, 1993)

Kiss the Rat Race Goodbye, by Elizabeth Lewin (Pharos, 1992; Walker, 1994)

Retirement on a Shoestring, by John Howells (Gateway Books, 1992)

Retiring to Your Own Business, by Gustav Berle (Puma Publishing, 1993)

Retirement Income of the House, by Ken Scholen (NCHEC, 1993)

Shadow Merchants: Successful Retailing Without a Storefront, by Jordan L. Cooper (Loompanics, 1993)

Second-Hand Success: How to Turn Discards into Dollars, by Jordan L. Cooper (Loompanics, 1994)

Bringing It Home, by Wendy Priesnitz (Natural Life, 1992)

Escaping the Current Retirement Crisis, by R. Theodore Benna (Pinon Press, 1995)

Financial Freedom on $5 a Day, by Chuck Chakrapani (Self-Counsel Press, 1995)

30 Reasons Not to Buy or Start a Business, by David O'Brian (New Century, 1995)

Six Months Off, by Hope Dlugozima, James Scott, and David Sharp (Henry Holt & Co., 1996)

Work Less and Play More, by Steven Catlin (Kimberlite, 1997)

Getting a Life, by Jacqualine Blix and David Herimiller (Viking, 1997)

GENDER

Women Pay More (and How to Put a Stop to It), by Frances Cerra Whittelsey and Marcia Carroll (New Press, 1995)

DEBT

Downsize Your Debt, by Andrew Feinberg (Penguin, 1993)

How to Get Out of Debt, Stay Out of Debt & Live Prosperously, by Jerrold Mundis (Bantam, 1988)

Wealth Addiction, by Philip Slater (Dutton, 1980)

MARRIAGE

1001 Ways to Save Money—and Still Have a Dazzling Wedding (Contemporary Books, 1994)

Two Incomes and Still Broke? by Linda Kelley (Times Books, 1996)

Your Home

Home Ownership: The American Myth, by Mitchell Levy (Myth Breakers, 1993)

The Banker's Secret, by Marc Eisenson (Villard, 1990) reveals the true cost of a mortgage and shows you how to save money on yours.

Not One Dollar More, by Joseph Eamon Cummins (Kells Media Group, 1995)

Find It Buy It Fix It, by Robert Irwin (Dearborn Financial, 1996)

Your Car

Nutz & Boltz (P.O. Box 123, Butler, MD 21023)

General Cheap

Wealth on Minimal Wage, by Jim Steamer (Dearborn Financial, 1997)

Living Cheaply with Style, by Ernest Callenbach (Ronin, 1993)

Penny Pinching, by Lee and Barbara Simmons (Bantam, 1995)

2 Minutes a Day to Supersavings, by Marjorie Lamb (HarperCollins, 1991)

How to Live on Nothing, by Joan Ranson Shortney (Doubleday, 1961)

Miserly Moms, by Jonni McCoy (Full Quart Press, 1996)

How to Live Cheap But Good, by Martin Poriss (Dell, 1971)

How to Get 20 to 90 % Off on Everything You Buy, by Jean and Cle Kinney (Parker, 1966)

Downshifting

Simplify Your Life: 100 Ways to Slow Down Your Life and Enjoy the Things That Really Matter, by Elaine St. James (Hyperion, 1994)

Inner Simplicity: 100 Ways to Regain Peace and to Nourish Your Soul, by Elaine St. James (Hyperion, 1995)

Downscaling: Simplify and Enrich Your Lifestyle, by Dave and Kathy Babbitt (Moody, 1993)

Downshifting: Reinventing Success on a Slower Track, by Amy Saltzman (HarperCollins, 1991)

Take Your Life off Hold, by Ted Dreier (Fulcrum, 1987)

Simple Living, by Frank Levering and Wanda Urbanska (Penguin, 1992)

How I Found Freedom in an Unfree World, by Harry Browne (Macmillan, 1973) reminds us there is nothing we cannot have if we are willing to pay the price.

EXCELLENT NEWSLETTERS

The Pocket Change Investor (Box 78, Elizaville, New York 12523)

Out of the Rat Race (Box 95341, Seattle, WA 98145)

Newsletter Times (P.O. Box 92051, Santa Barbara, CA 93190)

Home Business Communique (P.O. Box 3644, Lakewood, CA 90711-3644)

Common Sense Investing (P.O. Box 784, Warsaw, MO 65355)

ThriftSCORE (P.O. Box 90282, Pittsburgh, PA 15224)

A Penny Saved (P.O. Box 3471, Omaha, NE 68103-0471)

Thriving on Thrift (P.O. Box 2036, Cornelius, NC 28031)

GARDENING

Le Jardin du Gourmet, St. Johnsbury Center, VT 05863, is a good place to get seeds for your garden; they offer 25¢ seed "samples" that will be more than adequate for an urban garden.

Native Seeds/SEARCH, 2509 N. Campbell, #325, Tucson, AZ 85719

Seed Exchangers, P.O. Box 10, Burnips, MI 49314-0010

Edible Landscaping, P.O. Box 77, Afton, VA 22920

Oikos Tree Crops, P.O. Box 19425, Kalamazoo, MI 49019

St. Lawrence Nurseries, 325 State Highway 345, Potsdam, NY 13676

Bear Creek Nursery, P.O. Box 411, Northport, WA 99157

Raintree Nursery, 391 Butts Rd., Morton, WA 98356

CREATIVE ALTERNATIVES

Another Use for 101 Common Household Items, by Vicky Lansky (Book Peddlers, 1991)

Baking Soda: Over 500 Fabulous, Fun and Frugal Uses You've Probably Never Thought Of, by Vicki Lansky (Book Peddlers, 1994)

How to Build Almost Anything Starting With Practically Nothing, by Mike and Carolyn Russell (Camden House, 1993)

Non-Money: That "Other Money" You Didn't Know You Had, by Olaf Egeberg
(McGee Street Foundation, 1993)

GARAGE SALES

Garage Sale Magic, by Michael and Pam Williams (Freedom, 1994)
Hooked on Garage Sales, by Daniel A. Sands and available from him for
$11.45 (P.O. Box 3901, San Clemente, CA 92672)

ENVIRONMENTAL CONCERNS

The Green Commuter, by Joel Makower (Tilden Press, 1992)
101 Ways to Save Money and Our Planet, by the Green Group (Paper Chase,
1992)
Recycle Using Everyday Items, by Elrena Parton from her for $8 (1183
Pleasant View Rd., Woodbury, TN 37190)
How Much Is Enough?: The Consumer Society and the Future of the Earth, by Alan
Durning (Norton, 1992)
How to Live Green, Cheap, and Happy, by Randi Hacker (Stackpole Books,
1994)
HEIRS, Box 580, Chimayo, NM 87522
Needs Catalog, 527 Charles Ave., #12-A, Syracuse, NY 13209
Clear Light Catalog, Box 551, Placitas, NM 87043

FOOD

Lean Bean Cuisine, by Jay Soloman (Prima, 1995)
The $5 Chef, by Marcie Rothman (Five-Spot Press, 1991)
The Thirty Dollar a Week Grocery Budget, Volumes I and II, by Donna
McKenna and available for $10 from her at P.O. Box 391, Brook-
let, GA 30415
The Use-It-Up Cookbook, by Lois Carlson Willand and available from her
for $12.95 (1245 Malcolm Ave. SE, Minneapolis, MN 55414)
250 Wonderful Ways to Serve Ground Beef, by Georgia Ryan and available
from her for $12 (6424 E. Barker Pl., Denver, CO 80222)
This for That, by Meryl Nelson (R & E Publishers, 1992)
Sloppy Joe and the Whole Gang, by Barbara Nosek and available from her for
$4 (P.O. Box 81645, Spring Valley, NV 89180)

Make Your Own Breakfast Cereal, by Stephen Jewitt (Armstead, 1995)

Co-Op Directory Services will help you locate the nearest wholesaler for co-op food buying if you will send a long SASE to them at 919 S. 21st Ave. S., Minneapolis, MN 55404.

TAXES

How to Settle with the IRS for Pennies on the Dollar, by Arnold Goldstein (Garret, 1995)

DEATH

The Truth About Living Trusts, by Nan L. Goodart (Dearborn Financial, 1995)

Everything Your Heirs Need to Know, by David S. McGee (Dearborn Financial, 1991)

CREDIT AND BANKRUPTCY

National Center for Financial Education, P.O. Box 34070, San Diego, CA 92163

Personal Bankruptcy: What You Should Know, by Alice Griffin, Esq. (Cakewalk Press, 1994)

Credit Card and Debt Management, by Scott Bilker (Press One, 1996)

YOUR FINANCES

Money Magic: Discover Your Hidden Wealth, by K. D. Shanahan (Alpha, 1993)

How to Save a Million Dollars, by Scott Humphrey (Screen Communications, 1994)

It's Never Too Late to Get Rich, by James Jorgensen (Dearborn Financial, 1994)

Scrooge Investing, by Mark Skousen (Dearborn Financial, 1992)

How to Build a Fortune Investing in Your Spare Time, by Stephen Littauer (Dearborn Financial, 1994)

Investment Clubs, by Kathryn Shaw (Dearborn Financial, 1995)

The Only Investment Guide You'll Ever Need, by Andrew Tobias (Harvest Books, 1996)

TRAVEL AND ENTERTAINMENT

How to Save Money on Travel, Clothing and Entertainment, by Linda Slater and available from her for $5 (6135 Utica St., Arvada, CO 80003)

Travel Unlimited, Box 1058, Allston, Massachusetts 02134

Budget Lodging Guide (B & J Publications, 1995)

Travel Free, by Lynie Ardeen (TWN Publications, 1993)

If you're traveling somewhere on a budget, look for the appropriate Lonely Planet Guide. They are the best, and their "On a Shoe-string" series is especially good for those who like to travel but hate to spend money.

The Entertainment and Gold C coupon books offer 50 percent off and two-for deals; look for them in your area around the end of October each year, or for more information, write to 2125 Butterfield Rd., Troy, MI 48084.

MISCELLANEOUS

A place to buy books cheap: Edward R. Hamilton, Falls Village, CT 06031-5000

A good mailing list to be on: Career Press, P.O. Box 34, Hawthorne, NJ 07507

Places to get good deals on magazine subscriptions:

> American Educational Services, 419 Lentz Court, Lansing, MI 48917 (if you or a member of your family is a student or a teacher)

> Publishers Marketing Service (3 Oak Leaf Dr., Waretown, NJ 08758)

> Below Wholesale Magazines (1909 Prosperity, Reno, NV 89502)

When you need a part to repair an appliance: Culinary Parts Unlimited (800) 543-7549

To find an outlet store for Converse sneakers near you: (800) 428-2667 or (800) 648-5620

Great Buys for People Over 50, by Sue Goldstein (Penguin, 1991)

Good Advice Press, Box 78, Elizaville, NY 12523 offers several publications including an excellent one on stopping junk mail. Send them $1 for a current list.

Your tax dollars support the Consumer Information Center. Your local library probably has their *Consumer Information Catalog*. If not, send $1 for the catalog to them at P.O. Box 100, Pueblo, CO 81002. Information on cars, children, employment, federal programs, etc., is available through this catalog.

Geri Cook's Best Bargains in L.A. and Orange Counties (P.O. Box 67989, Los Angeles, CA 90067)

For twenty-five things to do for free in San Diego, send a long SASE to Free List, 2726 Shelter Island Dr., Suite 94, San Diego, CA 92106.

52 Ways to Make This Your Best Year Yet, by Todd Temple (Melton, 1994)

Clutterers Anonymous (a self-help group), P.O. Box 25884, Santa Ana, CA 97299-5884

World of Bulk, for those who aren't quite sure how to cook bulk bin bargains; send $1 to *LaRue*, Wild Oats, 5075 N. Academy Blvd., Colorado Springs, CO 80918.